Lecture Notes in Computer Science 13587

More information about this series at https://link.springer.com/bookseries/558

Nandinee Haq · Patricia Johnson ·
Andreas Maier · Chen Qin · Tobias Würfl ·
Jaejun Yoo (Eds.)

Machine Learning for Medical Image Reconstruction

5th International Workshop, MLMIR 2022
Held in Conjunction with MICCAI 2022
Singapore, September 22, 2022
Proceedings

 Springer

Editors
Nandinee Haq ⓘ
Hitachi
Montreal, Canada

Patricia Johnson ⓘ
NYU Grossman School of Medicine
New York, NY, USA

Andreas Maier ⓘ
Friedrich-Alexander-Universität
Erlangen, Bayern, Germany

Chen Qin
University of Edinburgh
Edinburgh, UK

Tobias Würfl ⓘ
Siemens Healthineers
Erlangen, Germany

Jaejun Yoo ⓘ
Ulsan National Institute of Science
and Technology
Ulsan, Korea (Republic of)

ISSN 0302-9743   ISSN 1611-3349 (electronic)
Lecture Notes in Computer Science
ISBN 978-3-031-17246-5   ISBN 978-3-031-17247-2 (eBook)
https://doi.org/10.1007/978-3-031-17247-2

This Springer imprint is published by the registered company Springer Nature Switzerland AG
The registered company address is: Gewerbestrasse 11, 6330 Cham, Switzerland

Preface

We are proud to present the proceedings for the Fifth Workshop on Machine Learning for Medical Image Reconstruction (MLMIR 2022) which was held on September 22, 2022, at the Resorts World Convention Centre in Singapore, as part of the 25th Medical Image Computing and Computer Assisted Intervention (MICCAI 2022) conference.

Image reconstruction commonly refers to solving an inverse problem, recovering a latent image of some physical parameter from a set of noisy measurements assuming a physical model of the generating process between the image and the measurements. In medical imaging two particular widespread applications are computed tomography (CT) and magnetic resonance imaging (MRI). Using those two modalities as examples, conditions have been established under which the associated reconstruction problems can be solved uniquely. However, in many cases there is a need to recover solutions from fewer measurements to reduce the dose applied to patients or to reduce the measurement time. The theory of compressed sensing showed how to pursue this while still enabling accurate reconstruction by using prior knowledge about the imaged objects. A critical question is the construction of suitable models of prior knowledge about images. Research has departed from constructing explicit priors for images and moved towards learning suitable priors from large datasets using machine learning (ML).

After four previous successful workshops, we found that ML approaches have found their way into multiple products for different modalities. Its cross-modality approach brings together researchers from various modalities ranging from CT and MRI to microscopy and X-ray fluoroscopy. We believe joint discussion fosters the translation of algorithms between modalities.

We were fortunate that Shanshan Wang (Paul C. Lauterbur Research Center, Chinese Academy of Sciences, China) and Jong Chul Ye (Kim Jaechul Graduate School of AI, KAIST, South Korea) accepted our invitation as keynote speakers and presented fascinating keynote lectures about the state of the art in this field. For this first in-person iteration of the workshop after the start of the COVID-19 pandemic, we received 19 submissions and accepted 15 papers for inclusion in the workshop. The topics of the accepted papers are still dominated by MRI reconstruction but cover a broad range of applications over CT, PET, ultrasound, fluoroscopy, and magnetic particle imaging.

August 2022

Nandinee Haq
Patricia Johnson
Andreas Maier
Chen Qin
Tobias Würfl
Jaejun Yoo

Organization

Workshop Organizers

Nandinee Haq	Hitachi, Canada
Patricia Johnson	New York University, USA
Andreas Maier	Friedrich-Alexander-University Erlangen-Nuremberg, Germany
Chen Qin	University of Edinburgh, UK
Tobias Würfl	Siemens Healthineers, Germany
Jaejun Yoo	Ulsan National Institute of Science and Technology, South Korea

Scientific Program Committee

Delaram Behnami	University of British Columbia, Canada
Tolga Cukur	Bilkent University, Turkey
Kerstin Hammernik	Imperial College London, UK
Essam Rashed	University of Hyogo, Japan
Andrew Reader	King's College London, UK
Zhengguo Tan	Friedrich-Alexander-University Erlangen-Nuremberg, Germany
Ge Wang	Rensselaer Polytechnic Institute, USA
Shanshan Wang	Paul C. Lauterbur Research Center, Chinese Academy of Sciences, China
Pengwei Wu	GE Global Research, USA
Guang Yang	Imperial College London, UK
Jong Chul Ye	Kim Jaechul Graduate School of AI, KAIST, South Korea
Can Zhao	NVIDIA, USA

Contents

Deep Learning for Magnetic Resonance Imaging

Rethinking the Optimization Process for Self-supervised Model-Driven MRI Reconstruction

Weijian Huang[1,2,3], Cheng Li[2], Wenxin Fan[1,2], Ziyao Zhang[1,3], Tong Zhang[3], Yongjin Zhou[4], Qiegen Liu[5], and Shanshan Wang[2,3,6,7(✉)]

[1] University of Chinese Academy of Sciences, Beijing, China
[2] Paul C. Lauterbur Research Center for Biomedical Imaging, Shenzhen Institutes of Advanced Technology, Chinese Academy of Sciences, Shenzhen, Guangdong, China
Sophiasswang@hotmail.com, ss.wang@siat.ac.cn
[3] Pengcheng Laboratory, Shenzhen, Guangdong, China
[4] Shenzhen University, Shenzhen, Guangdong, China
[5] Nanchang University, Nanchang, Jiangxi, China
[6] Guangdong Provincial Key Laboratory of Artificial Intelligence in Medical Image Analysis and Application, Shenzhen, Guangdong, China
[7] National Center for Applied Mathematics Shenzhen(NCAMS), Shenzhen, Guangdong, China

Abstract. Recovering high-quality images from undersampled measurements is critical for accelerated MRI reconstruction. Recently, various supervised deep learning-based MRI reconstruction methods have been developed. Despite the achieved promising performances, these methods require fully sampled reference data, the acquisition of which is resource-intensive and time-consuming. Self-supervised learning has emerged as a promising solution to alleviate the reliance on fully sampled datasets. However, existing self-supervised methods suffer from reconstruction errors due to the insufficient constraint enforced on the non-sampled data points and the error accumulation happened alongside the iterative image reconstruction process for model-driven deep learning reconstructions. To address these challenges, we propose K2Calibrate, a K-space adaptation strategy for self-supervised model-driven MR reconstruction optimization. By iteratively calibrating the learned measurements, K2Calibrate can reduce the network's reconstruction deterioration caused by statistically dependent noise. Extensive experiments have been conducted on the open-source dataset FastMRI, and K2Calibrate achieves better results than five state-of-the-art methods. The proposed K2Calibrate is plug-and-play and can be easily integrated with different model-driven deep learning reconstruction methods.

Keywords: Self-supervised learning · Image reconstruction

N. Haq et al. (Eds.): MLMIR 2022, LNCS 13587, pp. 3–13, 2022.
https://doi.org/10.1007/978-3-031-17247-2_1

1   Introduction

Magnetic resonance imaging (MRI) is an important tool in the clinic for the detection of various diseases. One bottleneck issue of MRI is its time-consuming data acquisition process. Much effort has been devoted to alleviating this problem, among which compressed sensing (CS) based MR reconstruction has been acknowledged as a very effective approach. It exploits incoherent undersampling and image sparsity [1–3] to accelerate MR imaging. Unfortunately, despite the promising performances reached with CS-MRI, it has several limitations such as the time-consuming iterative reconstruction process and the difficulty for the determination of its sparsity weight hyper-parameters [4,5].

To address these issues, deep learning (DL) has been introduced to accelerate MR imaging. One major group of methods are based on the data-driven approach. These methods directly learn a mapping between undersampled k-space data/aliased-image and fully sampled k-space data/artifact-free image in an end-to-end manner [6–10]. Data-driven methods are straightforward and easy-to-implement, but they fail to exploit the physics of MRI. Model-driven methods, on the other hand, incorporate MRI physics into DL-based MRI reconstruction [11–15]. These methods unroll the iterative reconstruction steps of solving physical models into the different layers of a to-be-trained neural network [11,12,16,17]. In this way, model-driven methods can integrate the strength of both DL and physical models. They have gradually become the prevalent solution for DL-based MRI reconstruction tasks.

Both data-driven and model-driven DL MRI reconstruction methods have made great progress in accelerating MR imaging. However, their performances rely on fully sampled and high quality reference datasets, the acquisition of which is not always feasible. One major reason is that fully sampled data acquisition is very time-consuming. For moving objects (such as the heart), high quality fully sampled dataset is hard to obtain without image artifacts. For the same reason, fully sampled data are difficult to obtain when serious signal attenuation happens in some applications. For example, when conducting diffusion MRI scanning with echo planar (EPI), the T2 signal decays quickly. Thus, it is hard to adopt fully sampled data acquisition protocols. Another reason is acquiring a large number of fully sampled data to train a DL model is both resource- and labor-intensive.

Recently, Yaman et al. [18–20] proposed a series of MRI reconstruction methods based on model-driven self-supervised learning (self-supervised learning via data undersampling, SSDU), which does not require fully sampled reference data for model training. The core idea of SSDU is to split the obtained undersampled k-space data into two disjoint sets. One set is used as the input to the unrolled network, and the other set is used to supervise the training of the network. Later, Hu et al. [21] proposed an improved method based on SSDU to constrain the reconstruction results on non-sampled data points via a parallel network framework. Cole et al. [22] employed Generative Adversarial Networks (GAN) to guide the optimization of the reconstruction network via discriminating simulated and observed measurements. The above methods have achieved promising results using self-supervised MRI reconstruction methods. However, since the reconstruction problem is ill-posed due to sub-Nyquist sampling, imposing precise constraints on the non-sampled K-space data points is difficult. In addition, error propagation might happen alongside the iterative reconstruction process, especially at the initial iterations.

Here, we propose K2Calibrate, a convolutional neural network (CNN) based K-space adaptation method for self-supervised unrolled networks. By sampling k-space measurements from a Bernoulli distribution in each iteration step, the model-driven reconstruction process is optimized, so as to suppress the noise ratio caused by unsatisfied constraints of self-supervised models. The proposed method has high flexibility and can be formulated in a "plug-and-play" way, which can be easily applied to existing self-supervised model-driven methods without any complex operations.

2   Theory

Let x denote the recovered image and y represent the acquired k-space measurements. MRI image recovery using model-driven methods can be formed as the following optimization scheme:

$$\arg\min_{x} \| Ax - y \|^2 + \lambda R(x) \tag{1}$$

where $A = SFC$ is the encoding matrix including coil sensitivities C, 2-D discrete Fourier transform F, and sampling matrix S. The first term represents data consistency (DC) with acquired measurements. $R(\cdot)$ represents a regularization term. λ denotes the weighting parameter.

2.1   Model Based Deep Learning Network

Model based deep learning networks [12–14] have received extensive attention due to the enhanced physical interpretability. One typical example is MoDL [12]. Let D_w represent a learned CNN estimator of noise depending on the parameters w. $x - D_w(x)$ can be treated as a denoiser to remove alias artifacts and noise. Then, Eq. 1 can be rewritten as:

$$\arg\min_{x} \| Ax - y \|^2 + \lambda \| (x - D_w(x)) \|^2 \tag{2}$$

Since the non-linear mapping $D_w(x_k + \triangle x)$ can be approximated using Taylor series [12] in the unrolled networks, the reconstructed optimization problem can be approximated as:

$$x^{k+1} = \arg\min_{x} \| Ax - y \|^2 + \lambda \| (x - z^k(x)) \|^2$$
$$z^k = D_w(x^k) \tag{3}$$

Here, index $n \in [0, ..., K]$ denotes the iteration number. Once K is fixed, the optimization process can be intuitively viewed as an unrolled linear CNN. In MoDL [12], the authors used the same denoising operator D_w and trainable regularization parameters at each iteration to reduce the network parameters. Since MoDL is a highly effective method, we adopt it as the baseline for our proposed method.

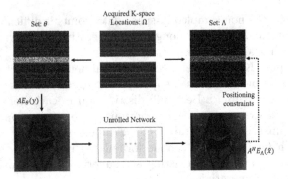

Fig. 1. The self-supervised MRI reconstruction workflow. The acquired k-space is split into sets Θ and Λ, while one is used for input and the other is used for supervision.

2.2   Self-supervised MRI Reconstruction

Due to the difficulty of acquiring fully sampled reference data, Yaman et al. [18] proposed a self-supervised approach called SSDU achieving promising reconstruction performance (Fig. 1).

Let Ω denote the undersampled K-space measurements of fully sampled measurements Γ. For each data, Ω is divided into two random subsets, Θ and Λ, and the relationship between them is $\Omega = \Theta \cup \Lambda$.

To train the self-supervised model-driven network, the set of Θ is used as the input to the network as well as the DC units, while the set Λ is used to define the similarity self-supervised loss function:

$$\arg \min_{\omega} \boldsymbol{L}(\mathbf{E}_\Lambda(y_\Omega), \mathbf{E}_\Lambda(\boldsymbol{f}(\mathbf{E}_\Theta(y); \omega))) \tag{4}$$

where $\boldsymbol{L}(\cdot)$ is an arbitrary similarity function such as 1-norm or 2-norm and $\boldsymbol{f}(; \omega)$ denotes the output of the unrolled network with parameters ω. $\mathbf{E}_\Lambda(\cdot)$ represents a K-space transform operator that sampling the measurements in Λ region, and so as to $\mathbf{E}_\Theta(\cdot)$. For clarification, let y mentioned in Eqs. (1, 2, 3) be y_Ω in this section. In this way, a self-supervised strategy is implemented. This method updates the iterative network in an efficient end-to-end training manner.

However, since the data are simulated by sub-Nyquist sampling, it inherently cannot constrain the reconstruction on the non-sampled data points $\Gamma \backslash \Omega$ precisely. This means once the reconstruction errors occur, they will accumulate alongside the unrolled iterative reconstruction process.

2.3   Derivation of K-Space Calibration

To analyze the possible impact of reconstruction errors, we now consider the output of a certain step of the unrolled networks $\tilde{x}^k = n^k + x^{*k}$. For simplicity, we omit the superscript k and draw the joint distribution as follows:

$$p(x^*, n) = p(x^*)p(n \,|\, x^*) \tag{5}$$

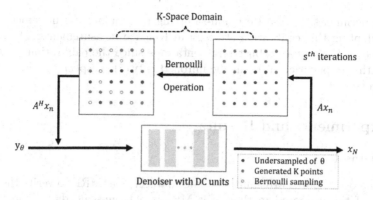

Fig. 2. The proposed K2Calibrate method. In each iteration, the sampled K-space measurements of θ are kept while the generated measurements from the network are sampled from Bernoulli distribution.

Here, n denotes the noise randomly generated from the unrolled network while x^* is the goal of the network in each specific iteration step. Due to the imaging physics of MRI, we assume that x^* is statistically dependent that $p(x_i^* | x_j^*) \neq p(x_i^*)$.

Then, we turn to consider the characteristics of the noise n. Since the task is based on self-supervised learning as mentioned in Sect. 2.2, n becomes more diverse and should be considered more carefully. [23,24] assume that n of natural image is conditional independent such that $p(n | x^*) = \prod p(n_i | x_i^*)$. By further assuming $\mathbb{E}[n_i] = 0$, n can be removed by using strategy of $\mathbb{E}[\tilde{x}_i] = x^*$. However, we believe n is still dependent on x^* due to the iterative process in MRI reconstruction that is more difficult to remove.

Here, we propose a K-space calibration strategy (Fig. 2), called 'K2Calibrate', to try to mitigate the effect of noise in the unrolled networks. Different from designing a complexity prior of n manually, we speculate that the reconstruction problem can be transferred to balance n and x^* during the iteration process. Let's divide n into two parts, n_s and n_g, denoting noise at location of sampled/non-sampled K-space measurements, respectively. Since DC layers are included in the unrolled networks, $\mathbb{E}[n_s]$ is closed to 0 and is much smaller than $\mathbb{E}[n_g]$. Therefore, if we choose a tiny increment $n_\delta \in n_g$, we have:

$$\mathbb{E}[\tilde{x}_{s+\delta}] = \mathbb{E}[x_{s+\delta}^* + n_s + n_\delta] \approx x_{s+\delta}^* \tag{6}$$

which reduces the scale of n in $\tilde{x}$ comparing to $\mathbb{E}[\tilde{x}_{s+g}] = x_{s+\delta}^* + n_\delta$. Based on this observation, we can prevent the accumulation of noise in each iteration by reducing the size of n generated from the previous iteration. We modified Eq. 3 to achieve this and make sure that noise can be removed iteratively rather than all at once in each iteration:

$$x^{k+1} = \arg\min_x \| Ax - y \|^2 + \lambda \| (x - z^k(x)) \|^2$$
$$z^k = \mathbb{E}_{s+\delta}^k(D_w(x^k)) \tag{7}$$

In experiments, we use Bernoulli-sampling to simulate the incremental $\delta \in g$. By adapting this calibration strategy in K-space measurements, D_w can be optimized to learn more robust representations since the calibration operation reduces the propagation of n_g in the unrolled networks, especially in the initial iteration steps.

3 Experiments and Results

3.1 Dataset

We use an open-source MR multi-coil knee dataset, FastMRI, to verify the effectiveness of the proposed method. FastMRI is a large-scale data collection of clinical MR measurements released by Facebook AI Research [25]. 1,594 scans were collected utilizing the following scanning parameters: Echo train length 4, 15-channels coils, matrix size of 320 × 320, slice thickness 3 mm, in-plane resolution 0.5 mm × 0.5 mm, and no gap between slices. The dataset was split into training, validation, and testing sets. During training, we train the models with 3% (Set-A) and 1% (Set-B) data of the training set to evaluate the performance of different methods when different numbers of training data are utilized.

3.2 Implementation Details

Multiple comparison methods are implemented. Among them, we use Sigpy [26] package to implement L1-Wavelet, SENSE, and TotalVariation (TV). DL-based self-supervised methods include SSDU [18] and Hu et al. [21] and supervised MoDL [12] are also experimented with. By sharing the learning weight of D_w, we unroll the network into 5 and 10 iterations according to the experiments settings, and adopt the proposed K2Calibrate strategy at different steps in the iterations. It is worth noting K2Calibrate is only enabled during model training and it is removed during model testing.

3.3 Results

This section presents various quantitative and qualitative evaluations to verify the effectiveness of the proposed method.

Quantitative Analysis. Two evaluation metrics, peak signal to noise ratio (PSNR) and structural similarity index measure (SSIM), are calculated to quantitatively evaluate the image reconstruction results. Table 1 lists the results of conventional methods and DL-based methods. Both methods do not require ground truth fully sampled reference data for model training. Compared with the conventional methods, DL-based methods show better performance due to the complex denoiser provided by its large number of parameters. When the proposed K2Calibrate in utilized, the metrics of the two self-supervised DL-based methods improve obviously. SSIM is increased from 0.7674 to 0.7803 for

SSDU(8x) and from 0.7680 to 0.7754 for Hu(8x), respectively. Similar performance improvement is observed for other settings, which validates K2Calibrate that can improve the performance of different reconstruction methods.

Table 1. Quantitative results on Set-A with acceleration rates of 4 and 8 of different self-supervised MRI reconstruction methods.

Method	4x		8x	
	PSNR	SSIM	PSNR	SSIM
L1Wavelet	32.172	0.7674	28.704	0.6749
SENSE	35.323	0.9121	29.461	0.7636
TV	31.856	0.7725	29.361	0.7175
SSDU	37.795	0.9332	29.584	0.7674
SSDU-K2C	**38.496**	**0.9402**	**30.303**	**0.7803**
Hu	37.670	0.9341	29.604	0.7680
Hu-K2C	**37.947**	**0.9361**	**29.841**	**0.7754**

We implemented our method on the smaller training set, Set-B, and results are listed in Table 2. Since the conventional methods are not affected by the number of training data, the performance of them is the same as that presented in Table 1. Compared with Table 1, the overall scores in Table 2 are slightly decreased due to that fewer training data are utilized. However, on this smaller-scale dataset, K2Calibrate can still improve the model performance, indicating that the effectiveness of K2Calibrate is not dependent on the amount of training data.

Table 2. Quantitative results on Set-B with acceleration rates of 4 and 8. K2Calibrate can still improve the reconstruction performance of the two self-supervised methods.

Method	4x		8x	
	PSNR	SSIM	PSNR	SSIM
SSDU	36.936	0.9242	29.447	0.7634
SSDU-K2C	**37.693**	**0.9313**	**29.783**	**0.7735**
Hu	36.926	0.9256	29.600	0.7681
Hu-K2C	**37.356**	**0.9301**	**29.642**	**0.7692**

K2Calibrate is a plug-and-play module. To have a clear understanding of the impact of K2Calibrate on the reconstruction performance, we have conducted experiments by enabling K2Calibrate in different network training iterations. SSDU was adopted as the base architecture in this set of experiments. Relatively higher acceleration rates (8x and 10x) were employed to better visualize the improvements made by K2Calibrate. Results are plotted in Fig. 4. In the first 8 iterations, the reconstruction performance is enhanced when more K2Calibrate modules are enabled. Compared to the method without K2Calibrate, utilizing K2Calibrate in the first iteration increases the PSNR value from 28.54 db to 29.08 db under the acceleration rate of 10, which validates the effectiveness of K2Calibrate on noise suppression. When more than 8 K2Calibrate modules are enabled (the number of K2calibrate is 9 or 10 in Fig. 3), the performance becomes worse. This observation is in accordance with our expectations. We have explained that the noise ratio is relatively higher in the initial iterations, and thus utilizing K2Calibrate in these iterations is essential for noise removal. After these iterations, utilizing more K2Calibrate modules becomes ineffective.

The above experiments show that self-supervised MRI reconstruction methods can outperform the conventional methods and our method can effectively improve the performance of the self-supervised model-driven methods regardless of the acceleration rates utilized. Extensive experiments have been conducted by utilizing different numbers of K2Calibrate modules during model optimization with higher acceleration rates of 8x and 10x.

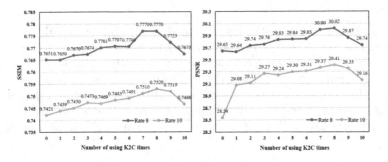

Fig. 3. Reconstruction results when different numbers of K2Calibrate are enabled. Acceleration rates of 8 and 10 are utilized. The number of K2calibrate indicate how many iterations utilized K2Calibrate. For example, if the number of K2Calibrate is 5, it means K2Calibrate is enabled in only the first 5 training iterations.

Qualitative Analysis. Figure 4 depicts the reconstructed images under the acceleration rate of 4 of conventional and DL-based methods. The conventional methods suffer from extensive loss of structure details while both DL-based methods can recover these details more accurately, showing that DL-based methods are more effective for the recovery of high-frequency measurements. Building on two state-of-the-art self-supervised deep learning methods, K2Calibrate can further improve the reconstruction performance. These results demonstrate that the proposed method can successfully remove the residual artifacts, while achieving higher qualitative and quantitative performances compared to the baseline methods.

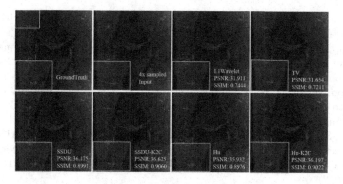

Fig. 4. Qualitative results with the acceleration rate of 4. The enlarged comparison is in the red box. (Color figure online)

All these experimental results validate the performance enhancement of the proposed K2Calibrate for self-supervised DL-based MRI reconstruction.

4   Conclusion

In this study, we provide a fresh perspective to review the optimization process of iterative DL-based reconstruction. We propose K2Calibrate, a plug-and-play module that help the unrolled network gradually reconstruct K-space measurements. Compared to the existing self-supervised learning methods that reconstruct all the K-space measurements at once with high uncertainties and propagate them to the following network training iterations, K2Calibrate can effectively reduce the error accumulation. Experiments on the FastMRI dataset confirm that the proposed method can achieve encouraging performances. It is worth to be noted that K2Calibrate can be easily plugged into different model-driven DL-based methods without any additional operations.

Acknowledgments. This research was partly supported by Scientific and Technical Innovation 2030-"New Generation Artificial Intelligence" Project (2020AAA0104100, 2020AAA0104105), the National Natural Science Foundation of China (61871371), Guangdong Provincial Key Laboratory of Artificial Intelligence in Medical Image Analysis and Application (Grant No. 2022B1212010011), the Basic Research Program of Shenzhen (JCYJ20180507182400762), Shenzhen Science and Technology Program (Grant No. RCYX20210706092104034), AND Youth Innovation Promotion Association Program of Chinese Academy of Sciences (2019351).

References

1. Lustig, M., Donoho, D., Pauly, J.M.: Sparse MRI: the application of compressed sensing for rapid MR imaging. Magn. Reson. Med. Off. J. Int. Soc. Magn. Reson. Med. **58**(6), 1182–1195 (2007)

2. Haldar, J.P., Hernando, D., Liang, Z.-P.: Compressed-sensing MRI with random encoding. IEEE Trans. Med. Imaging **30**(4), 893–903 (2010)
3. Trzasko, J., Manduca, A.: Highly undersampled magnetic resonance image reconstruction via homotopic l_0-minimization. IEEE Trans. Med. Imaging **28**(1), 106–121 (2008)
4. Shahdloo, M., Ilicak, E., Tofighi, M., Saritas, E.U., Çetin, A.E., Çukur, T.: Projection onto epigraph sets for rapid self-tuning compressed sensing MRI. IEEE Trans. Med. Imaging **38**(7), 1677–1689 (2018)
5. Ramani, S., Liu, Z., Rosen, J., Nielsen, J.-F., Fessler, J.A.: Regularization parameter selection for nonlinear iterative image restoration and MRI reconstruction using GCV and sure-based methods. IEEE Trans. Image Process. **21**(8), 3659–3672 (2012)
6. Lee, D., Yoo, J., Tak, S., Ye, J.C.: Deep residual learning for accelerated MRI using magnitude and phase networks. IEEE Trans. Biomed. Eng. **65**(9), 1985–1995 (2018)
7. Wang, S., et al.: Accelerating magnetic resonance imaging via deep learning. In: 2016 IEEE 13th International Symposium on Biomedical Imaging (ISBI), pp. 514–517. IEEE (2016)
8. Zhu, B., Liu, J.Z., Cauley, S.F., Rosen, B.R., Rosen, M.S.: Image reconstruction by domain-transform manifold learning. Nature **555**(7697), 487–492 (2018)
9. Mardani, M., et al.: Deep generative adversarial neural networks for compressive sensing MRI. IEEE Trans. Med. Imaging **38**(1), 167–179 (2018)
10. Han, Y., Sunwoo, L., Ye, J.C.: k-space deep learning for accelerated MRI. IEEE Trans. Med. Imaging **39**(2), 377–386 (2019)
11. Hammernik, K., et al.: Learning a variational network for reconstruction of accelerated MRI data. Magn. Reson. Med. **79**(6), 3055–3071 (2018)
12. Aggarwal, H.K., Mani, M.P., Jacob, M.: MoDL: model-based deep learning architecture for inverse problems. IEEE Trans. Med. Imaging **38**(2), 394–405 (2018)
13. Zhang, J., Ghanem, B.: ISTA-Net: interpretable optimization-inspired deep network for image compressive sensing. In: Proceedings of the IEEE Conference on Computer Vision and Pattern Recognition, pp. 1828–1837 (2018)
14. Sun, J., Li, H., Xu, Z., et al.: Deep ADMM-Net for compressive sensing MRI. In: Advances in Neural Information Processing Systems, vol. 29 (2016)
15. Qin, C., Schlemper, J., Caballero, J., Price, A.N., Hajnal, J.V., Rueckert, D.: Convolutional recurrent neural networks for dynamic MR image reconstruction. IEEE Trans. Med. Imaging **38**(1), 280–290 (2018)
16. Liang, D., Cheng, J., Ke, Z., Ying, L.: Deep magnetic resonance image reconstruction: inverse problems meet neural networks. IEEE Signal Process. Mag. **37**(1), 141–151 (2020)
17. Schlemper, J., Caballero, J., Hajnal, J.V., Price, A.N., Rueckert, D.: A deep cascade of convolutional neural networks for dynamic MR image reconstruction. IEEE Trans. Med. Imaging **37**(2), 491–503 (2017)
18. Yaman, B., Hosseini, S.A.H., Moeller, S., Ellermann, J., Uğurbil, K., Akçakaya, M.: Self-supervised learning of physics-guided reconstruction neural networks without fully sampled reference data. Magn. Reson. Med. **84**(6), 3172–3191 (2020)
19. Yaman, B., Hosseini, S.A.H., Akcakaya, M.: Zero-shot physics-guided deep learning for subject-specific MRI reconstruction. In: NeurIPS 2021 Workshop on Deep Learning and Inverse Problems (2021)

20. Yaman, B., Hosseini, S.A.H., Moeller, S., Ellermann, J, Uğurbil, K., Akçakaya, M.: Ground-truth free multi-mask self-supervised physics-guided deep learning in highly accelerated MRI. In: 2021 IEEE 18th International Symposium on Biomedical Imaging (ISBI), pp. 1850–1854. IEEE (2021)

21. Hu, C., Li, C., Wang, H., Liu, Q., Zheng, H., Wang, S.: Self-supervised learning for MRI reconstruction with a parallel network training framework. In: de Bruijne, M., et al. (eds.) MICCAI 2021. LNCS, vol. 12906, pp. 382–391. Springer, Cham (2021). https://doi.org/10.1007/978-3-030-87231-1_37

22. Cole, E.K., Ong, F., Pauly, J.M., Vasanawala, S.S.: Unsupervised image reconstruction using deep generative adversarial networks. In: ISMRM Work Data Sampling & Image Reconstruction (2020)

23. Krull, A., Buchholz, T.-O., Jug, F.: Noise2void-learning denoising from single noisy images. In: Proceedings of the IEEE/CVF Conference on Computer Vision and Pattern Recognition, pp. 2129–2137 (2019)

24. Lehtinen, J., et al.: Noise2noise: learning image restoration without clean data. In: International Conference on Machine Learning, pp. 2965–2974. PMLR (2018)

25. Zbontar, J., et al.: fastMRI: an open dataset and benchmarks for accelerated MRI. arXiv preprint arXiv:1811.08839 (2018)

26. Ong, F., Lustig, M.: SigPy: a python package for high performance iterative reconstruction. In: Proceedings of the ISMRM 27th Annual Meeting, Montreal, Quebec, Canada, vol. 4819 (2019)

NPB-REC: Non-parametric Assessment of Uncertainty in Deep-Learning-Based MRI Reconstruction from Undersampled Data

Samah Khawaled[1]([✉])[ID] and Moti Freiman[2][ID]

[1] Department of Applied Mathematics, Technion – Israel Institute of Technology, Haifa, Israel
ssamahkh@campus.technion.ac.il
[2] Faculty of Biomedical Engineering, Technion – Israel Institute of Technology, Haifa, Israel
moti.freiman@technion.ac.il

Abstract. Uncertainty quantification in deep-learning (DL) based image reconstruction models is critical for reliable clinical decision making based on the reconstructed images. We introduce "NPB-REC", a non-parametric fully Bayesian framework for uncertainty assessment in MRI reconstruction from undersampled "k-space" data. We use Stochastic gradient Langevin dynamics (SGLD) during the training phase to characterize the posterior distribution of the network weights. We demonstrated the added-value of our approach on the multi-coil brain MRI dataset, from the fastmri challenge, in comparison to the baseline E2E-VarNet with and without inference-time dropout. Our experiments show that NPB-REC outperforms the baseline by means of reconstruction accuracy (PSNR and SSIM of 34.55, 0.908 vs. 33.08, 0.897, $p < 0.01$) in high acceleration rates ($R = 8$). This is also measured in regions of clinical annotations. More significantly, it provides a more accurate estimate of the uncertainty that correlates with the reconstruction error, compared to the Monte-Carlo inference time Dropout method (Pearson correlation coefficient of $R = 0.94$ vs. $R = 0.91$). The proposed approach has the potential to facilitate safe utilization of DL based methods for MRI reconstruction from undersampled data. Code and trained models are available in https://github.com/samahkh/NPB-REC.

Keywords: MRI reconstruction · Uncertainty estimation · Bayesian deep-learning

1 Introduction

Magnetic resonance imaging (MRI) is a noninvasive modality, which provides multi-planar images in-vivo through its sensitivity to the inherent magnetic properties of human tissue [13]. Although MRI is the modality of choice in many

N. Haq et al. (Eds.): MLMIR 2022, LNCS 13587, pp. 14–23, 2022.
https://doi.org/10.1007/978-3-031-17247-2_2

clinical applications due to its excellent sensitivity to soft tissue contrast, its non-invasiveness, and the lack of harmful ionizing radiation, long acquisition times are a major limiting factor to achieve high spatial and temporal resolutions, reduce motion artifacts, improve the patient experience and reduce costs [20].

Reducing MRI acquisition time by under-sampling the "k-space" (i.e. Fourier domain) constitutes a key necessity in enabling advanced MRI applications such as cardiac and fetal imaging. Further, acceleration of MRI will also reduce MRI vulnerability to patient motion during the acquisition process. However, the under-sampled data results in aliasing artefacts in the reconstructed images. Early approaches rely upon Parallel Imaging (PI) [7,14] to reduce the acquisition time. This is done by utilizing multiple receiver coils simultaneously to acquire multiple views and then combining them to construct the image. Other approaches reduce the acquisition time by sampling only a subset of measurements, i.e. under-sampling, and use a non-linear compressed sensing (CS) approach to reconstruct the MRI image from the under-sampled data [3,11].

In the past few years, Deep-neural-networks (DNN) based models overcame classical reconstruction approaches in their ability to reconstruct high-quality MRI images from highly under-sampled data (i.e. 25% or less) [1,5,6,13,16,18]. The Variational Network (VarNet) [8] solves an optimization problem by cascaded design of multiple layers, each solves a single gradient update step. The End-to-End Variational Network (E2E-VarNet) approach [17], extends the VarNet model by estimation of the sensitivity maps within the network, which, in turn improves the quality of the reconstruction significantly at higher accelerations. These models, however, do not provide posterior sampling neither enable uncertainty quantification, which are critical for clinical decision making based on the predicted images [16].

Bayesian methods, such as Variational autoencoders (VAEs) and Monte Carlo dropout, are able to provide probabilistic interpretability and uncertainty quantification in MRI reconstruction [2,5]. The VAE approach, however, is limited to specific DNN architectures. Further, it assumes a parametric distribution of the latent space in the form of a Gaussian distribution.

In this work, we propose a non-parametric Bayesian DNN-based approach [9, 10] for MRI image reconstruction from under-sampled k-space data. Our method is able to provide quantitative measures of uncertainty of the prediction by fully characterizing the entire posterior distribution of the reconstructed high-quality MRI images. We achieve this by adopting the strategy of Stochastic gradient Langevin dynamics (SGLD) [19] to sample from the posterior distribution of the network weights [4]. Specifically, we enable sampling by injecting Gaussian noise to the loss gradients during the training of the model. We save models with weights obtained after the *"burn-in"* iteration, in which the training loss curve exhibits only small variations around its steady-state. Then, at inference time, we estimate the statistics of the reconstructed image by averaging predictions obtained by the model with the saved weights. Our contributions are: (1) the proposed approach can provide quantitative measures of uncertainty correlated with risk of failure in the MRI image predictions, and (2) can improve overall image reconstruction accuracy. These hypotheses were tested by experiments

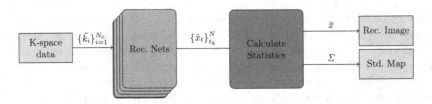

Fig. 1. Block diagram of the proposed NPB-REC system. The result of the SGLD-based training is a set of models with the same backbone network but diffident weights. At inference, the set of under-sampled k-space data, $\{\tilde{k}_i\}_{i=1}^{N_c}$, pass through each one of the backbone models. These models predict a set of reconstructed images, $\{\hat{x}_t\}_{t_b}^{N}$. We then calculate the averaged reconstructed image and the pixel-wise std., $\bar{x}$ and Σ, respectively. The average is used as the most probable reconstruction prediction and the Σ is utilized for uncertainty assessment.

that were conducted on the publicly available fastMRI dataset[1], for accelerated MRI reconstruction with the E2E-VarNet model [17] as the system's backbone. It is important to note that specifically, our main backbone, the E2E-VarNet model, doesn't provide posterior sampling neither enable uncertainty quantification.

2 Methods

2.1 MRI Reconstruction

In multi-coil acquisition, the MRI scanner consists of multiple receiver coils, where each of them partially acquires measurements in the k-space (frequency domain) [12]. Each coil modulates the k-space samples according to its spatial sensitivity map to the MRI signal:

$$k_i = \mathcal{F}(S_i x) + \epsilon_i \ \forall i \in [1, .., N_c] \tag{1}$$

where $\mathcal{F}$ is the Fourier transform, S_i denotes the corresponding sensitivity map and N_c is the overall number of coils. To accelerate the acquisition time, k-space measurements are under-sampled by selecting only a set from the entire k-space data, $\tilde{k}_i = M \circ k_i$, where M is the corresponding binary mask that encodes the under-sampling operator. Restoration of the MRI image from the under-sampled data by performing an inverse Fourier transform on the under-sampled data leads to aliasing artifacts.

2.2 Non-parametric Bayesian MRI Reconstruction

Our goal is to characterize the posterior distribution:

$$\hat{\theta} \sim P\left(\theta | x, \hat{x}, \left\{\tilde{k}_i\right\}_{i=1}^{N_c}\right) \propto P\left(x, \hat{x}, \left\{\tilde{k}_i\right\}_{i=1}^{N_c} | \theta\right) P(\theta) \tag{2}$$

---

[1] https://fastmri.org/.

where, $\hat{x}$, x, and $\{\tilde{k}_i\}_{i=1}^{N_c}$ are the reconstructed image, the ground truth (fully sampled) and the under-sampled k-space measurements, respectively. θ are the network weights that we optimize. We treat the network weights as random variables and aim to sample the posterior distribution of the model prediction. To this end, we incorporate a noise scheduler that injects a time-dependent Gaussian noise to the gradients of the loss during the optimization process. At every training iteration, we add Gaussian noise to the loss gradients. Then, the weights are updated in the next iteration according to the "noisy" gradients. This noise schedule can be performed with any stochastic optimization algorithm during the training procedure. In this work we focused on the formulation of the method for the `Adam` optimizer.

The reconstruction network predicts: $\hat{x} = f_\theta \left(\left\{ \tilde{k}_i \right\}_{i=1}^{N_c} \right)$. We denote the loss gradients by:

$$g^t \triangleq \nabla_\theta L^t \left(x, f_\theta \left(\left\{ \tilde{k}_i \right\}_{i=1}^{N_c} \right) \right) \tag{3}$$

where L^t is the reconstruction loss at the training iteration (epoch) t. At each training iteration, a Gaussian noise is added to g:

$$\tilde{g}^t \leftarrow g^t + \mathbf{N}^t \tag{4}$$

where $\mathbf{N}^t \sim \mathcal{N}(0, s^t)$, s^t is a user-selected parameter that controls the noise variance (can be time-decaying or a constant). We selected s^t equal to the `Adam` learning rate.

Lastly, we save the weights of the network that were obtained in iterations $t \in [t_b, N]$, where N is the overall number of iterations and t_b is the SGLD-parameter, which should be larger than the cut-off point of the *burn-in* phase. One should sample weights obtained in the last $t_b, .., N$ iterations, where the loss curve has converged.

We exploit the network weights that were obtained after the *burn-in* phase, i.e. in the last $t_b, .., N$ iterations, $\{\theta\}_{t_b}^N$. Figure 1 illustrates the operation of the NPB-REC system at the inference phase. We sample a set of reconstructed images $\{\hat{x}\}_{t_b}^N$, obtained by feed-forwarding the under-sampled k-space data $\{\tilde{k}_i\}_{i=1}^{N_c}$ to the reconstitution models with the weights $\{\theta\}_{t_b}^N$. Then, when we have a new image to reconstruct, we estimate the averaged posterior image:

$$\bar{x} = \frac{\sum_{t=t_b}^N \hat{x}_t}{N - t_b} \tag{5}$$

In addition, we quantify the std. of the reconstruction, which is used to characterize the uncertainty.

2.3   The Reconstruction Network

The backbone of our reconstruction system is based on the E2E-VarNet model [17]. E2E-Varnet contains multiple cascaded layers, each applies a refinement step in the k-space according to the following update:

$$k^{m+1} = k^m - \eta^t M\left(k^m - \tilde{k}\right) + G\left(k^m\right) \qquad (6)$$

where k^m and k^{m+1} are the input and output to the m-th layer, respectively. G is the refinement module: $G = \mathcal{F} \circ \mathcal{E} \circ \text{CNN}(\mathcal{R} \circ \mathcal{F}^{-1}(k^m)$. CNN is a DNN-network, which maps a complex image input to a complex output, $\mathcal{E}$ and $\mathcal{R}$ are the expand and reduce operators. $\mathcal{E}$ computes the corresponding image seen by each coil: $\mathcal{E}(x) = (S_1 x, ..., S_{N_c} x)$ and its inverse operator, $\mathcal{R}$, integrates the multiple coil images $\mathcal{R}(x_1, ..., x_{N_c}) = \sum S_i x_i$. Similarly to the design of E2E-VarNet [17], a U-Net is used for the CNN [15]. The sensitivity maps $S_1, ..., S_{N_c}$ are estimated as part of the reconstruction using a CNN that has the same architecture as the CNN in the cascades. After applying a cascaded layers to the k-space input, as described in (6), we obtain the final reconstructed image, $\hat{x}$, by root-sum-squares (RSS) reduction of the image-space representation of the final layer output: $\hat{x} = \sqrt{\sum_{i=1}^{N_c} |\mathcal{F}^{-1} k_i^T|^2}$.

3   Experiments

3.1   Database

In our experiments, we used multi-coil data of brain MRI images, adapted from the publicly available fastMRI database for training our system; we used the validation and training datasets for the brain multi-coil challenge. We excluded a subset from the validation set that contained clinical pathology annotations taken from fastMRI+ [21] and used it in the evaluation of our method, where no overlap between subjects belong to these sets. This is due to the fact that the ground truth of the test set is not publicly available and it is interesting to demonstrate our NPB-REC method on region of interest (ROIs) and to quantify both the reconstruction accuracy and uncertainty in these ROIs.

The training, validation, and inference sets include 4469, 113, and 247 images of size $16 \times 320 \times 320$ and 20 coils. From these datasets, we generate 71504, 1808 2D images and 2141 slices with annotations for the training, validation and the evaluation phases, respectively. The inputs of the network, k^0 in (6), are under-sampled k-space inputs that were generated from the fully-sampled datasets with two types of masks: *equispaced* and *random*. The former samples l low-frequency lines from the center of k-space and every R-th line from the higher frequencies, to make the acceleration rate equal to R. Whereas, the latter samples a fraction of the full width of k-space for the central k-space corresponding to low frequencies and selects uniformly at a subset of a higher frequency line such that the overall acceleration is R.

3.2   Experimental Setup

To conduct a quantitative comparison, we trained three models: (1) E2E-Varnet [17] trained with the proposed NPB-REC method (Sect. 2.2), (2) The baseline E2E-VarNet model [17], and; (3) E2E-VarNet trained with Dropout of probability

0.001 and Monte Carlo averaging used at inference. Higher values of Dropout probabilities led to instabilities in the network loss during training. The three aforementioned models have the same architecture as described in [17] with $T = 8$ cascaded layers. Dropout layers were incorporated only to model (3), whereas the first two configurations where trained without adding it. For the three models, we used $1 - SSIM$ as a training loss and Adam optimizer with learning rate set to $lr = 0.001$. The total number of epochs (training iterations) was set to 40 and the batch size equal to 1. In our experiments, we selected a standard deviation, $s^t = lr$ for the injected noise variance. The network parameters are then updated according to the Adam update rule. In the training, we generated under-sampled inputs by multiplying with *random* masks of acceleration rate $R = 4$. At inference, we use both *random* and *equispaced* masks of acceleration rates $R = 4$ and $R = 8$, to evaluate the ability of the system to generalize.

Hyper-Parameters Selection: At inference, we sample a set of reconstructed images obtained by passing the under-sampled k-space inputs to the models with the weights $\{\theta\}_{t_b}^N$, i.e. obtained in the last $N - t_b$ iterations. t_b should be selected such that the training loss in the last $N - t_b$ is stable and has only slight variations around its steady state value. In our experiments, we performed a hyper-parameter tuning on t_b and selected the last $N - t_b$ that obtained the best quantitative reconstruction performance.

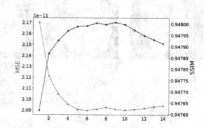

Fig. 2. MSE and SSIM vs. $N - t_b$, the number of models used in the averaging, obtained on subset from the inference set (32 images sampled randomly).

Figure 2 presents the MSE and SSIM metrics for a range of $N - t_b$ that varies from 1 to 10. Although this range of $N - t_b$ values show similar MSE and SSIM metrics, we selected $N - t_b = 9$. This is due to the fact that it shows a slight improvement and with having 9 samples we can calculate robust statistics.

The final reconstructed image is calculated by averaging these 9 samples, predicted from our model, as mentioned in (5). Additionally, we estimate a 2D uncertainty map by calculation of the pixel-wise std. of these predictions. For fair comparison, we used the same number of predictions in Monte Carlo sampling at the inference phase, but with enabled Dropout layers. We assessed the accuracy of the registration models by calculating PSNR and SSIM between the reconstructed and the ground truth, for all pairs of images in the test set.

3.3   Results

Figure 3 presents examples of reconstruction results obtained by (1) our NPB-REC approach, (2) the baseline, and (3) Monte Carlo Dropout, for equispaced masks with two different acceleration rates $R = 4$ and $R = 8$. Table 1 presents the mean PSNR and SSIM metrics, calculated over the whole inference set, for the

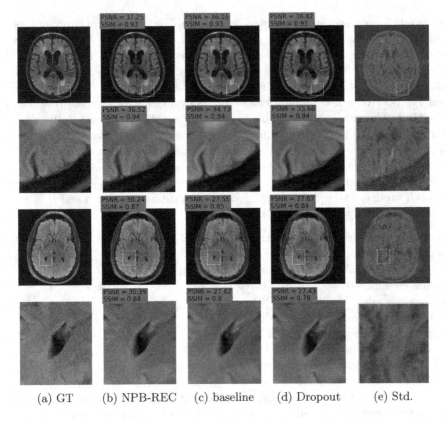

(a) GT   (b) NPB-REC   (c) baseline   (d) Dropout   (e) Std.

Fig. 3. Examples of Reconstruction Results. Rows 1 and 3: The Ground truth (GT) fully sampled image, the reconstructed images obtained by the three models (1–3), NPB-REC, baseline, E2E-VarNet trained with Dropout, and the Std. map derived from our method for acceleration rates $R = 4$, $R = 8$, respectively. Rows 2 and 4: The corresponding annotated ROIS of the edema and resection cavity.

three models. our NPB-REC approach achieved significant improvements over the other methods in terms of PSNR and SSIM (Wilcoxon signed-rank test, p $\ll$ 1e−4). The improvement in the reconstruction performance can be noted both quantitatively from the metrics especially for masks with acceleration rate $R = 8$ and qualitatively via the images of annotations, where our results shows less smoothness than that obtained by Dropout.

Meaning of the Uncertainty Measures: We calculated the mean value of the Std. maps, obtained by our method and Monte Carlo Dropout, for all images in the inference set and utilize it as uncertainty measure. The correlation between these uncertainty measures and reconstruction error (MSE) are depicted in Fig. 4. Compared to Dropout, our NPB-REC uncertainty measure exhibits higher correlation with the Reconstruction error (Pearson correlation coefficient of $R = 0.94$ vs. $R = 0.91$). Further, Fig. 4(c) demonstrates that higher

Table 1. Reconstruction Accuracy. Rows top to bottom: PSNR and SSIM metrics calculated on the annotated anatomical ROIs (denoted by 'A') with mask of acceleration rate $R = 4$, the whole physical images (denoted by 'W') with masks of acceleration rate $R = 4$, $R = 8$, respectively. 'r' and 'e' stands for *random* and *equispaced* mask types.

	R	M	NPB-REC		Baseline		Dropout	
			PSNR	SSIM	PSNR	SSIM	PSNR	SSIM
A	4	r	**30.04 ± 6.78**	**0.87 ± 0.18**	29.91 ± 6.87	0.867 ± 0.182	29.5 ± 6.844	0.858 ± 0.19
		e	**32.22 ± 6.94**	**0.914 ± 0.143**	32.02 ± 7.35	0.911 ± 0.143	31.57 ± 6.89	0.905 ± 0.151
W	4	r	**40.24 ± 6.19**	**0.947 ± 0.081**	40.17 ± 6.19	**0.947 ± 0.081**	39.86 ± 6.10	0.945 ± 0.082
		e	41.61 ± 6.28	**0.955 ± 0.073**	41.64 ± 6.28	0.955 ± 0.074	41.22 ± 6.0	0.953 ± 0.074
W	8	r	**32.23 ± 6.63**	**0.881 ± 0.11**	31.21 ± 6.2	0.87 ± 0.108	30.63 ± 5.91	0.865 ± 0.11
		e	**34.55 ± 5.01**	**0.908 ± 0.09**	33.08 ± 4.82	0.897 ± 0.092	32.25 ± 4.74	0.891 ± 0.09

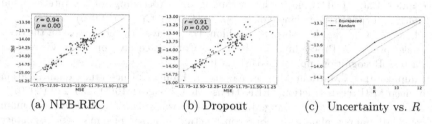

(a) NPB-REC   (b) Dropout   (c) Uncertainty vs. R

Fig. 4. Uncertainty Assessment. Scatter plots of the mean value of Std. estimate versus the MSE metric, calculated between the reconstructed and the ground truth, in log scale, for our NPB-REC method (a) and Monte Carlo Dropout (b). (c) Our measure of uncertainty versus the acceleration rate.

acceleration rates increases the uncertainty measure. These outcomes, in turn, indicate the ability of our uncertainty measure to detect unreliable reconstruction performance.

4   Conclusions

We developed NPB-REC, a non-parametric Bayesian method for the reconstruction of brain MRI images from under-sampled k-space data with uncertainty estimation. Specifically, we used noise injection for the training loss gradients to efficiently sample the true posterior distribution of the network weights. We used the E2E-VarNet network as a baseline. However, the proposed technique is not limited to a specific architecture and can be incorporated to any existing network. The conducted experiments showed that our approach enables uncertainty quantification that exhibits higher correlation with the reconstruction error than that obtained by Monte Carlo Dropout. In addition, it shows a significantly better reconstruction quality over other methods, especially with acceleration rate higher than that used in training. This demonstrates its ability to improve the generalization of the reconstruction over the other methods.

Acknowledgements. Khawaled, S. is a fellow of the Ariane de Rothschild Women Doctoral Program. Freiman, M. is a Taub fellow (supported by the Taub Family Foundation, The Technion's program for leaders in Science and Technology).

References

1. Akçakaya, M., Moeller, S., Weingärtner, S., Uğurbil, K.: Scan-specific robust artificial-neural-networks for k-space interpolation (RAKI) reconstruction: database-free deep learning for fast imaging. Magn. Reson. Med. **81**(1), 439–453 (2019)
2. Avci, M.Y., Li, Z., Fan, Q., Huang, S., Bilgic, B., Tian, Q.: Quantifying the uncertainty of neural networks using Monte Carlo dropout for deep learning based quantitative MRI. arXiv preprint arXiv:2112.01587 (2021)
3. Candès, E.J., et al.: Compressive sampling. In: Proceedings of the International Congress of Mathematicians, vol. 3, pp. 1433–1452. Citeseer (2006)
4. Cheng, Z., Gadelha, M., Maji, S., Sheldon, D.: A Bayesian perspective on the deep image prior. In: Proceedings of the IEEE Conference on Computer Vision and Pattern Recognition, pp. 5443–5451 (2019)
5. Edupuganti, V., Mardani, M., Vasanawala, S., Pauly, J.: Uncertainty quantification in deep MRI reconstruction. IEEE Trans. Med. Imaging **40**(1), 239–250 (2020)
6. Eo, T., Jun, Y., Kim, T., Jang, J., Lee, H.J., Hwang, D.: KIKI-net: cross-domain convolutional neural networks for reconstructing undersampled magnetic resonance images. Magn. Reson. Med. **80**(5), 2188–2201 (2018)
7. Griswold, M.A., et al.: Generalized autocalibrating partially parallel acquisitions (GRAPPA). Magn. Reson. Med. Offi. J. Int. Soc. Magn. Reson. Med. **47**(6), 1202–1210 (2002)
8. Hammernik, K., et al.: Learning a variational network for reconstruction of accelerated MRI data. Magn. Reson. Med. **79**(6), 3055–3071 (2018)
9. Khawaled, S., Freiman, M.: Unsupervised deep-learning based deformable image registration: a Bayesian framework. arXiv preprint arXiv:2008.03949 (2020)
10. Khawaled, S., Freiman, M.: NPBDREG: uncertainty assessment in diffeomorphic brain MRI registration using a non-parametric Bayesian deep-learning based approach. Comput. Med. Imaging Graph. 102087 (2022)
11. Lustig, M., Donoho, D., Pauly, J.M.: Sparse MRI: the application of compressed sensing for rapid MR imaging. Magn. Reson. Med. Offi. J. Int. Soc. Magn. Reson. Med. **58**(6), 1182–1195 (2007)
12. Majumdar, A.: Multi-Coil Parallel MRI Reconstruction, pp. 86–119. Cambridge University Press (2015). https://doi.org/10.1017/CBO9781316217795.005
13. Morris, S.A., Slesnick, T.C.: Magnetic resonance imaging. In: Visual Guide to Neonatal Cardiology, pp. 104–108 (2018)
14. Pruessmann, K.P., Weiger, M., Scheidegger, M.B., Boesiger, P.: Sense: sensitivity encoding for fast MRI. Magn. Reson. Med. Offi. J. Int. Soc. Magn. Reson. Med. **42**(5), 952–962 (1999)
15. Ronneberger, O., Fischer, P., Brox, T.: U-Net: convolutional networks for biomedical image segmentation. In: Navab, N., Hornegger, J., Wells, W.M., Frangi, A.F. (eds.) MICCAI 2015. LNCS, vol. 9351, pp. 234–241. Springer, Cham (2015). https://doi.org/10.1007/978-3-319-24574-4_28
16. Shaul, R., David, I., Shitrit, O., Raviv, T.R.: Subsampled brain MRI reconstruction by generative adversarial neural networks. Med. Image Anal. **65**, 101747 (2020)

17. Sriram, A., et al.: End-to-end variational networks for accelerated MRI reconstruction. In: Martel, A.L., et al. (eds.) MICCAI 2020. LNCS, vol. 12262, pp. 64–73. Springer, Cham (2020). https://doi.org/10.1007/978-3-030-59713-9_7
18. Tezcan, K.C., Baumgartner, C.F., Luechinger, R., Pruessmann, K.P., Konukoglu, E.: MR image reconstruction using deep density priors. IEEE Trans. Med. Imaging **38**(7), 1633–1642 (2018)
19. Welling, M., Teh, Y.W.: Bayesian learning via stochastic gradient langevin dynamics. In: Proceedings of the 28th International Conference on Machine Learning (ICML 2011), pp. 681–688 (2011)
20. Zbontar, J., et al.: fastMRI: an open dataset and benchmarks for accelerated MRI. arXiv preprint arXiv:1811.08839 (2018)
21. Zhao, R., et al.: fastMRI+: clinical pathology annotations for knee and brain fully sampled multi-coil MRI data. arXiv, Computer Vision and Pattern Recognition arXiv:2109.03812, September 2021

Adversarial Robustness of MR Image Reconstruction Under Realistic Perturbations

Jan Nikolas Morshuis[1]([✉]), Sergios Gatidis[2], Matthias Hein[1], and Christian F. Baumgartner[1]

[1] Cluster of Excellence Machine Learning, University of Tübingen, Tübingen, Germany
nikolas.morshuis@uni-tuebingen.de
[2] Max-Planck Institute for Intelligent Systems, Tübingen, Germany

Abstract. Deep Learning (DL) methods have shown promising results for solving ill-posed inverse problems such as MR image reconstruction from undersampled k-space data. However, these approaches currently have no guarantees for reconstruction quality and the reliability of such algorithms is only poorly understood. Adversarial attacks offer a valuable tool to understand possible failure modes and worst case performance of DL-based reconstruction algorithms. In this paper we describe adversarial attacks on multi-coil k-space measurements and evaluate them on the recently proposed E2E-VarNet and a simpler UNet-based model. In contrast to prior work, the attacks are targeted to specifically alter diagnostically relevant regions. Using two realistic attack models (adversarial k-space noise and adversarial rotations) we are able to show that current state-of-the-art DL-based reconstruction algorithms are indeed sensitive to such perturbations to a degree where relevant diagnostic information may be lost. Surprisingly, in our experiments the UNet and the more sophisticated E2E-VarNet were similarly sensitive to such attacks. Our findings add further to the evidence that caution must be exercised as DL-based methods move closer to clinical practice.

Keywords: MRI reconstruction · MR imaging · Adversarial attacks

1 Introduction

MR image acquisition is notoriously limited by long scan times adding to patient discomfort and healthcare costs. By acquiring only a subset of measurements in the k-space this process can be substantially accelerated. However, reconstructing images from such undersampled k-space data requires solving an ill-posed inverse problem. The problem was initially approached using techniques rooted in the theory of compressed sensing which offers provable error bounds (see e.g. [14]). In recent years, it has been shown that MRI reconstruction algorithms based on deep learning (DL) can substantially outperform classical reconstruction methods both in accuracy and speed [7,11,15–17,21]. Such approaches,

N. Haq et al. (Eds.): MLMIR 2022, LNCS 13587, pp. 24–33, 2022.
https://doi.org/10.1007/978-3-031-17247-2_3

however, currently lack provable robustness guarantees. Moreover, their failure cases are not sufficiently understood, putting into question the trustworthiness of such approaches in real-world scenarios.

Recently, there has been an increasing focus on better understanding the robustness properties of DL-based reconstruction algorithms. For instance, in the 2020 fastMRI challenge it was reported that top performing deep learning based methods can sometimes miss small abnormalities at $8\times$ acceleration [2,11]. A priori it is unclear whether the information of these abnormalities is lost in the k-space subsampling step, which would make a correct reconstruction physically impossible, or whether the information is contained in the measurements but reconstruction algorithms fail to retrieve it. Cheng et al. [3] provided compelling evidence that in many cases the latter is the case by inserting adversarially generated false positives which fail to be reconstructed. This suggests that robustness properties of DL-based reconstruction algorithms deserve closer scrutiny. In another line of work, a large analysis of the 2019 fastMRI challenge submissions [8] found that the performance of DL-based reconstruction methods can suffer if a lower SNR is encountered during test-time than during training time. Darestani et al. [18] further showed a sensitivity to different acquisition techniques and different anatomies.

While it seems well documented that clinically relevant failure modes do exist, comparatively little work has been dedicated to understanding the worst case performance. Better understanding the maximum harm an algorithm can do is crucial for any clinical application and an integral part of the medical auditing process [9]. In absence of theoretical guarantees a number of works have attempted to provide empirical bounds on the worst case performance using adversarial attacks. While it is well established that DL-based classification networks are very sensitive to such attacks due to the "vulnerable" decision boundary stemming from the discrete nature of the problem, MR reconstruction algorithms do not necessarily suffer from the same problem [1,6]. Firstly, MR reconstruction can be seen as a regression problem lacking discrete boundaries. Furthermore, many DL-based algorithms, such as the state-of-the-art E2E-VarNet (E2E-VN) [16], which we study in this paper, are inspired by classical algorithms with documented robustness properties.

Antun et al. [1] demonstrated that, indeed, small adversarial perturbations applied to the input of reconstruction algorithms may result in severe reconstruction artifacts. Similarly, Darestani et al. [18] investigated adding adversarial noise to the k-space measurements, observing that DL-based methods can be sensitive to the adversarial noise and that such attacks can also substantially degrade diagnostically relevant regions. Genzel et al. [6] also investigated adversarial attacks with bounded noise on the k-space measurements. Interestingly, the authors came to the conclusion that the investigated reconstruction networks are relatively stable to such attacks, though results varied with different undersampling patterns. In particular, the authors note that diagnostically relevant regions remain largely unaffected. We thus observe that the evidence for adversarial robustness of MR reconstruction algorithms remains inconclusive.

In this paper, we aim to shed further light on this question by analysing adversarial robustness on the commonly investigated fastMRI knee dataset [19,20]. In contrast to prior work we show that when attacking state-of-the-art MRI reconstruction algorithms in a way targeting regions with diagnosed pathologies directly, very small levels of adversarial noise on the k-space (of comparable magnitude to the thermal noise always present in MR acquisition) can substantially degrade those regions and in some instances alter diagnostically relevant features. Going beyond the standard noise based adversarial attacks, we furthermore show that, somewhat worryingly, very small adversarial rotations can have similar effects. These findings add additional evidence that the worst case performance of DL-based MR reconstruction algorithms may currently be unacceptable for clinical use.

2   Methods

Problem Setting. In MR image acquisition typically multiple receiver coils are used to measure the data necessary to produce an image. Each coil i produces a k-space measurement $\mathbf{k}_i \in \mathbb{C}^n$. Given $\mathbf{k}_i$, a coil image $\mathbf{x}_i \in \mathbb{C}^n$ can be calculated using the inverse Fourier transform, such that

$$\mathbf{x}_i = \mathcal{F}^{-1}(\mathbf{k}_i + \mathbf{z}), \tag{1}$$

where $\mathbf{z} \in \mathcal{N}(0, \sigma \cdot \mathbf{I})$ is additive Gaussian thermal noise which is unavoidable in MR image acquisition [10]. In the fastMRI setting only a subset of the k-space data is measured. This can be simulated by applying a mask function $\mathcal{M}$ that sets the unmeasured part of the k-space data to 0, i.e. $\mathcal{M}(\mathbf{k}) = \mathbf{k} \odot M$, for a mask M and with $\odot$ the element-wise matrix multiplication. We employ the usual Cartesian undersampling pattern also used for the fastMRI challenge in all our experiments. Thus, a single undersampled coil-image can be expressed as

$$\tilde{\mathbf{x}}_i = \mathcal{F}^{-1}(\mathcal{M}(\mathbf{k}_i + \mathbf{z})). \tag{2}$$

The acquired coil-images $\mathbf{x}_i$ or $\tilde{\mathbf{x}}_i$ can be combined using the voxelwise root-sum-of-squares (RSS) method [12] to obtain the fully-sampled image $\mathbf{X}$ (or the undersampled image $\tilde{\mathbf{X}}$, respectively):

$$\mathbf{X} = \sqrt{\sum_{i=0}^{N} |\mathbf{x}_i|^2}, \tag{3}$$

where N indicates the number of coils.

MR reconstruction algorithms aim to reconstruct $\mathbf{X}$ given only the undersampled k-space data $\mathcal{M}(\mathbf{k}_i)$ for $i \in \{1, 2, ..., N\}$. DL-based approaches either start by obtaining the image $\tilde{\mathbf{X}}$ created from undersampled measurements according to Eq. (3) and treat the reconstruction as a de-aliasing problem (e.g. [7,15]), or use the k-space data as input directly (e.g. [16,21]). Here, we define the reconstruction network f as a mapping from (partial) k-space to image space.

Investigated Reconstruction Methods. In this paper we investigated two different neural network architectures. Namely a method based on the image-to-image UNet approach proposed in [13] as well as the iterative network E2E-VN [16], which reported state-of-the-art performance on the fastMRI challenge data. Although pretrained weights for both these models exist in the fastMRI-repository [11], they were trained using both train and validation sets of the fastMRI data, and evaluated on a private challenge test set. Since the ground-truth data of the private test set is not publicly available, we conduct our analysis of the model robustness on the validation set. The models therefore had to be retrained using data from the training set only.

Both networks have been trained using a batch-size of 32, like in their original implementation [11]. To train with the original batch-size, the E2E-VN requires 32 GPUs of 32 GB memory each, which was not feasible with our local compute infrastructure. This necessitated adapting the network size such that it could fit into the 11 GB memory of our local GPUs. For the E2E-VN, we reduced the number of unrolled iterations from 12 to 8 and halved the number of channels in each UNet. The size of the UNet for estimating the sensitivity maps was also reduced from 8 top-level channels to 6. Due to the computational constraints, we also halved the number of channels in the baseline UNet approach. The final training of our E2E-VN adjustment was carried out with 32 GPUs in parallel and took around one day to train, our adjusted UNet used 8 GPUs in parallel and also took around one day to train. Other than the reduction of the number of parameters, our version of the two networks is identical to the originals used for the fastMRI challenge and we expect our insights into its robustness properties to carry over to their larger counterparts.

Adversarial Attacks on the Reconstruction Methods. When using adversarial attacks, we are interested in finding a worst-case perturbation according to some attack model and within given boundaries. In this paper we explore two types of attack: 1) Adversarial noise added to the k-space measurements, which is bounded by a maximum L_2-norm, 2) Adversarial rotations where we simulate a slightly rotated position of the patient during acquisition. In the following both methods are described in more detail.

For the first attack model, we aim to find bounded adversarial noise-vectors z_i for every k-space measurement k_i of every coil i, such that the resulting output changes as much as possible in a user-defined target region. More specifically, we have the following optimization problem:

$$\max_z ||S \odot [f(\mathcal{M}(k+z)) - X]||_2 \; : \; ||z_i||_2 \leq \eta \, ||k_i||_2. \qquad (4)$$

Here, k is the vector of all k-space data k_i from all coils i, η defines the L_2-adversarial noise level relative to every coil measurement k_i, and S is a binary region selection mask to limit the attack to diagnostically relevant regions. Specifically, we use the bounding boxes indicating pathologies provided by the fastMRI+ dataset [20] to define S. In contrast to [6,18], we restrict the noise-vector z_i for every coil individually instead of the complete measurement, thereby allowing for differences in the coil-sensitivities.

The proposed realistic rotation attacks can be expressed similarly as

$$\max_\theta ||S \odot [(\mathcal{R}_\theta^{-1} \circ f \circ \mathcal{M} \circ \mathcal{R}_\theta)(k) - X] ||_2 \ : \ d \in [-\theta_{max}, \theta_{max}]. \quad (5)$$

Here, we introduce an operator $\mathcal{R}_\theta$ which denotes a rotation of the MRI data by θ. In practice, we rotate the data in the spatial domain and then Fourier-transform back to obtain k similar to [4]. After a prediction is created by the neural network, the inverse rotation $\mathcal{R}_\theta^{-1}$ is used to transform the image back. It is then compared to the original untransformed target-image.

The optimization process in Eq. (4) was implemented using 10-step projected gradient descent. In every step, the adversarial method adds a noise-vector z_i to the k-space k_i for every coil i, using this transformed k-space data as a new input for the reconstruction method f. After the calculation of the main objective in Eq. (4) and successive backpropagation, the resulting gradients are added to the noise-vector using a step-size of 0.5. The noise-vector z_i is then renormalized to stay within the pre-defined boundaries. The worst-case rotation angle θ in Eq. (5) was found using a grid search using an evenly spaced grid from $-\theta_{max}$ to θ_{max} with a step-size of 0.1°. Our code is publicly be available online[1].

3   Experiments and Results

We investigated adversarial noise and rotation attacks as described in Sect. 2 on the fastMRI knee dataset [19]. We explored attacking the entire center-cropped image, as well as targeted attacks on diagnostically relevant regions, which we obtained from the pathology annotations in the fastMRI+ dataset [20]. We evaluated the adversarial robustness for the E2E-VN [16] as well as the UNet [7] and for acceleration factors of 4× and 8×.

To explore attacks of varying severity, we repeated all experiments for a range of parameters η and θ_{max}. Similar to [6] and [18], we set the upper bound of the noise vector η relative to the k-space norm $||k_i||_2$. We explored a range of $\eta \in [0\%, 2.5\%]$. We empirically verified that the adversarial noise levels have a similar scale to thermal noise in our data, by measuring the real noise in the background regions of the input images as described in [5]. This makes it plausible that similar noise could also occur in practice. For the maximum rotation parameter θ_{max} we explored a range of $[0°, 5°]$.

Figure 1 shows the relative degradation of the structural similarity (SSIM) computed over the diagnostically relevant regions for the noise attack model. Overall E2E-VN yields consistently better results compared to the simpler UNet-based reconstruction method. Nevertheless, the slope of the degradation is similar for both techniques, suggesting that both methods are equally susceptible to the attack. These findings also hold for the rotation attacks shown in Fig. 4a.

---

[1] https://github.com/NikolasMorshuis/AdvRec

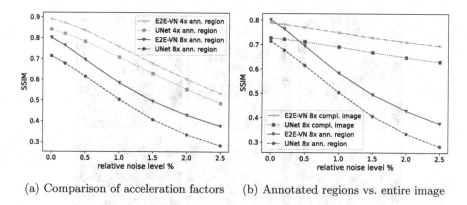

(a) Comparison of acceleration factors   (b) Annotated regions vs. entire image

Fig. 1. SSIM between the full k-space reconstruction and DL-based reconstruction with adversarial noise. (a) shows the behaviour with respect to the acceleration factor, while (b) compares attacks on annotated, diagnostically relevant regions with attacks on the entire image.

The similar sensitivity to adversarial attacks is surprising given that the E2E-VN is implicitly an iterative approach with enforced data consistency.

We further analysed the results qualitatively in collaboration with a senior radiologist. In Fig. 2, reconstructions of the UNet, the E2E-VN as well as reconstructions of both methods with adversarial noise are compared for a sample image. While the fully sampled reconstruction shows a low grade sprain of the anterior cruciate ligament (ACL), the UNet reconstruction with adversarial noise shows a thickening and distention, which could mistakenly be interpreted as an acute injury. The E2E-VN reconstruction with adversarial noise on the other hand could lead to a false diagnosis of an old ACL tear. It can thus be concluded that even small amounts of adversarial noise can lead to a false diagnosis with potential clinical consequences.

Figure 1b compares attacks targeted on annotated regions with attacks on entire images (the latter being the standard approach e.g. [1,6,18]). While [6] reported that diagnostically relevant regions remain relatively unaffected by adversarial noise attacks, we are able to show that when the attack is targeting those regions directly, the effect is much more severe. A qualitative example demonstrating this effect is shown in Fig. 3. While the annotated region noticeably changed when the adversarial attack was focused on it (third column), the effect is much smaller when the attack was performed on the complete image (fourth column). Clinically interpreting the results, we note that when only the annotated region is attacked (third column), it starts to look more defined and homogeneous. This could lead to a failure to detect the ACL rupture which is present in the image.

The SSIM scores after adversarially attacking our models with rotations are shown in Fig. 4. Comparing Fig. 4a with Fig. 1a above, it can be seen that rotation attacks are less severe than attacks with adversarial noise which is not unex-

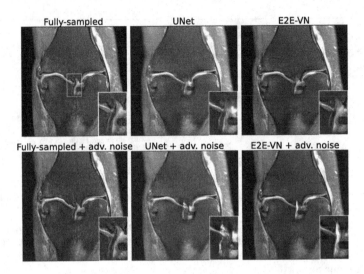

Fig. 2. Comparison of reconstruction algorithms with a relative noise-level of 2% and 8×-acceleration (top row: unperturbed reconstruction, bottom row: reconstruction with adversarial noise). The fully sampled image shows a low grade sprain of the anterior cruciate ligament (ACL). Both the UNet and the E2E-VN reconstructions with adv. noise could lead to clinically relevant misdiagnoses. Note that changes are barely visible if the adversarial noise is added to the fully-sampled k-space (bottom left).

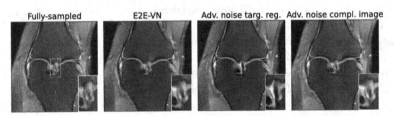

Fig. 3. Comparison of attacking the targeted region only (third column) versus attacking the complete image (fourth column) using the E2E-VN trained for 8× acceleration. Attacking only the annotated region, the ligament appears more homogeneous, which could lead to a misdiagnosis of the ACL rupture.

pected given the much higher degree of freedom of the noise attacks. However, the rotation attacks, although very small and purportedly benign in nature, can still manage to substantially degrade the output of the algorithm. From Fig. 4b it can be observed that the attack is continuous in θ and a non-negligible range of rotation angles leads to substantial drops in SSIM. This indicates that such degradation could realistically occur in clinical practice. A qualitative example of a UNet reconstruction is shown in Fig. 5. While the rotation has negligible effects on the fully-sampled reconstruction (third column), it can be seen that the UNet attacked with the same rotation (fourth column) produces an image where the ACL appears fuzzy (similar to the example in Fig. 3). As in the previous examples, this could potentially lead to a misdiagnosis.

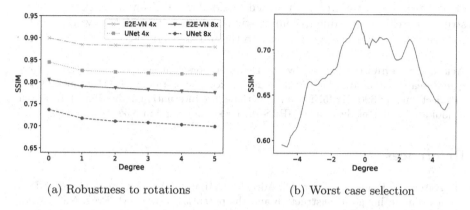

(a) Robustness to rotations   (b) Worst case selection

Fig. 4. Results of adversarial rotation experiments. (a) contains the methods' SSIM with increasing severity of the attack. (b) visualises the sensitivity of the SSIM score with respect to θ for the qualitative example shown in Fig. 5.

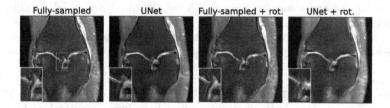

Fig. 5. Effects of small rotation on the reconstruction quality ($8\times$ acceleration). For the worst-case angle of $-4.9°$, the annotated region gets more fuzzy, potentially leading to a misdiagnosis of an ACL tear instead of a low grade sprain.

4   Conclusion

In this work we have shown potential pitfalls of using DL-based MR-reconstruction methods. By creating realistic adversarial changes to the k-space data we have shown that the reconstruction quality of common reconstruction methods declines significantly for both an iterative network (i.e. the E2E-VN) and a UNet-based approach. We observed that both methods, although the architecture and reconstruction method are quite different, encounter similar levels of reconstruction quality decline when adversarial perturbations are applied. By further targeting only specific regions we have shown that diagnostically relevant information can – contrary to the findings of [6] – fall victim to adversarial attacks for the same noise levels. Lastly, we observed that both examined reconstruction algorithms are also sensitive to very small adversarial rotations in some instances also leading to loss of diagnostic information. We believe future work should increasingly incorporate such worst case analyses and focus on the creation of models that are relatively stable under such perturbations. A limitation of our work is that we explored reduced versions of the UNet and E2E-VN reconstruction architectures due to computational constraints. In future work, we aim to verify that our insights carry-over to the full size models.

Acknowledgements. Funded by the Deutsche Forschungsgemeinschaft (DFG, German Research Foundation) under Germany's Excellence Strategy - EXC number 2064/1 - Project number 390727645. The authors thank the International Max Planck Research School for Intelligent Systems (IMPRS-IS) for supporting Jan Nikolas Morshuis.

References

1. Antun, V., Renna, F., Poon, C., Adcock, B., Hansen, A.C.: On instabilities of deep learning in image reconstruction and the potential costs of AI. Proc. Natl. Acad. Sci. **117**(48), 30088–30095 (2020). https://doi.org/10.1073/pnas.1907377117
2. Calivá, F., Cheng, K., Shah, R., Pedoia, V.: Adversarial robust training of deep learning MRI reconstruction models. arXiv preprint arXiv:2011.00070 (2020)
3. Cheng, K., Calivá, F., Shah, R., Han, M., Majumdar, S., Pedoia, V.: Addressing the false negative problem of deep learning MRI reconstruction models by adversarial attacks and robust training. In: Arbel, T., Ben Ayed, I., de Bruijne, M., Descoteaux, M., Lombaert, H., Pal, C. (eds.) Proceedings of the Third Conference on Medical Imaging with Deep Learning. Proceedings of Machine Learning Research, vol. 121, pp. 121–135. PMLR, 06–08 July 2020. https://proceedings.mlr.press/v121/cheng20a.html
4. Fabian, Z., Heckel, R., Soltanolkotabi, M.: Data augmentation for deep learning based accelerated MRI reconstruction with limited data. In: Meila, M., Zhang, T. (eds.) Proceedings of the 38th International Conference on Machine Learning. Proceedings of Machine Learning Research, vol. 139, pp. 3057–3067. PMLR, 18–24 July 2021. https://proceedings.mlr.press/v139/fabian21a.html
5. Firbank, M., Coulthard, A., Harrison, R., Williams, E.: A comparison of two methods for measuring the signal to noise ratio on MR images. Phys. Med. Biol. **44**(12), N261 (1999)
6. Genzel, M., Macdonald, J., März, M.: Solving inverse problems with deep neural networks - robustness included? (2020). https://doi.org/10.48550/ARXIV.2011.04268. https://arxiv.org/abs/2011.04268
7. Hyun, C.M., Kim, H.P., Lee, S.M., Lee, S., Seo, J.K.: Deep learning for undersampled MRI reconstruction. Phys. Med. Biol. **63**(13), 135007 (2018). https://doi.org/10.1088/1361-6560/aac71a
8. Johnson, P.M., et al.: Evaluation of the robustness of learned MR image reconstruction to systematic deviations between training and test data for the models from the fastMRI challenge. In: Haq, N., Johnson, P., Maier, A., Würfl, T., Yoo, J. (eds.) MLMIR 2021. LNCS, vol. 12964, pp. 25–34. Springer, Cham (2021). https://doi.org/10.1007/978-3-030-88552-6_3
9. Liu, X., Glocker, B., McCradden, M.M., Ghassemi, M., Denniston, A.K., Oakden-Rayner, L.: The medical algorithmic audit. Lancet Digit. Health **4**(5), e384–e397 (2022)

10. Macovski, A.: Noise in MRI. Magn. Reson. Med. **36**(3), 494–497 (1996)
11. Muckley, M.J., et al.: Results of the 2020 fastMRI challenge for machine learning MR image reconstruction. IEEE Trans. Med. Imaging **40**(9), 2306–2317 (2021). https://doi.org/10.1109/TMI.2021.3075856
12. Roemer, P.B., Edelstein, W.A., Hayes, C.E., Souza, S.P., Mueller, O.M.: The NMR phased array. Magn. Reson. Med. **16**(2), 192–225 (1990)
13. Ronneberger, O., Fischer, P., Brox, T.: U-Net: convolutional networks for biomedical image segmentation. In: Navab, N., Hornegger, J., Wells, W.M., Frangi, A.F. (eds.) MICCAI 2015. LNCS, vol. 9351, pp. 234–241. Springer, Cham (2015). https://doi.org/10.1007/978-3-319-24574-4_28
14. Rudin, L.I., Osher, S., Fatemi, E.: Nonlinear total variation based noise removal algorithms. Phys. D Nonlinear Phenom. **60**(1–4), 259–268 (1992)
15. Schlemper, J., Caballero, J., Hajnal, J.V., Price, A., Rueckert, D.: A deep cascade of convolutional neural networks for MR image reconstruction. In: Niethammer, M., et al. (eds.) IPMI 2017. LNCS, vol. 10265, pp. 647–658. Springer, Cham (2017). https://doi.org/10.1007/978-3-319-59050-9_51
16. Sriram, A., et al.: End-to-end variational networks for accelerated MRI reconstruction. In: Martel, A.L., et al. (eds.) MICCAI 2020. LNCS, vol. 12262, pp. 64–73. Springer, Cham (2020). https://doi.org/10.1007/978-3-030-59713-9_7
17. Tezcan, K.C., Baumgartner, C.F., Luechinger, R., Pruessmann, K.P., Konukoglu, E.: MR image reconstruction using deep density priors. IEEE Trans. Med. Imaging **38**(7), 1633–1642 (2018)
18. Darestani, M.Z., Chaudhari, A.S., Heckel, R.: Measuring robustness in deep learning based compressive sensing. In: International Conference on Machine Learning (ICML) (2021)
19. Zbontar, J., et al.: fastMRI: an open dataset and benchmarks for accelerated MRI (2018)
20. Zhao, R., et al.: fastMRI+, clinical pathology annotations for knee and brain fully sampled magnetic resonance imaging data. Sci. Data **9**(1), 152 (2022). https://doi.org/10.1038/s41597-022-01255-z
21. Zhu, B., Liu, J.Z., Cauley, S.F., Rosen, B.R., Rosen, M.S.: Image reconstruction by domain-transform manifold learning. Nature **555**(7697), 487–492 (2018)

High-Fidelity MRI Reconstruction with the Densely Connected Network Cascade and Feature Residual Data Consistency Priors

Jingshuai Liu$^{(\boxtimes)}$, Chen Qin, and Mehrdad Yaghoobi

IDCOM, School of Engineering, University of Edinburgh, Edinburgh, UK
{J.Liu,Chen.Qin,m.yaghoobi-vaighan}@ed.ac.uk

Abstract. Since its advent in the last century, magnetic resonance imaging (MRI) provides a radiation-free diagnosis tool and has revolutionized medical imaging. Compressed sensing (CS) methods leverage the sparsity prior of signals to reconstruct clean images from under-sampled measurements and accelerate the acquisition process. However, it is challenging to reduce strong aliasing artifacts caused by under-sampling and produce high-quality reconstructions with fine details. In this paper, we propose a novel GAN-based framework to recover the under-sampled images, which is characterized by a novel data consistency block and a densely connected network cascade used to improve the model performance in visual inspection and evaluation metrics. The role of each proposed block has been challenged in the ablation study, in terms of reconstruction quality metrics, using texture-rich FastMRI Knee image dataset.

Keywords: MRI reconstruction · GAN-based framework · Dense network connections · Data consistency

1 Introduction

Magnetic resonance imaging (MRI) provides a non-invasive diagnosis tool in medical imaging. However, the long acquisition time hinders its growth and development in time-critic applications. The acquisition process can be accelerated by sampling fewer data. Under-sampling in k-space below the Nyquist-Shannon rate leads to aliasing artifacts in image domain, which restricts the acceleration factor in scanning. Many methods have been proposed to recover the under-sampled signals. Compressed sensing (CS) leverages the sparsity prior of signals to solve the ill-posed problems. Assuming sparsity representations in image domain [5] or in some transformed space [10,14], CS methods retrieve reconstructions by solving sparsity regularized optimization. Nevertheless, the sparsity assumption can be difficult to hold in real-world scenarios and potentially fails to capture complicated features. Parallel imaging (PI) [8] unfolds

N. Haq et al. (Eds.): MLMIR 2022, LNCS 13587, pp. 34–43, 2022.
https://doi.org/10.1007/978-3-031-17247-2_4

aliasing artifacts in image domain and produce clean images by incorporating coil sensitivity priors. However, it is still difficult to remove strong artifacts and provide high-quality reconstructions under very low sampling rates.

In recent years, deep neural networks have achieved notable success in image tasks and show potential to benefit the development of modern MRI [9,21,22]. The work in [13] retrieves promising reconstructions using dual magnitude and phase networks. The method in [2] adopts a neural network to predict the missing k-space points. A primal-dual network is introduced in [25] to solve the conventional CS-MRI problem. VS-Net is proposed in [4] to find more accurate solutions. The method in [20] adopts a neural network to estimate the coil sensitivity maps used for parallel imaging. Despite their success, those methods still struggle to preserve sharp structures and local subtleties.

Generative adversarial networks (GAN) [7] model the data distribution via an adversarial competition between a generator and a discriminator. A GAN-based framework is introduced in [21] to yield more realistic images. The method in [18] incorporates a pre-trained generative network in the iterative reconstruction pipeline. A self-attention layer is used in [23] to improve the capacity of the generator and achieve better results. However, GAN-based methods can potentially produce unwanted artifacts and hallucinations and fail to capture diagnostic information. How to recover high-fidelity images from a few sampled data is still challenging, which is directly linked with the maximum MRI acceleration factor.

In this paper, we propose to reconstruct alias-free images from the under-sampled data in an end-to-end manner. We introduce a novel GAN-based reconstruction framework, which incorporates the data consistency prior and dense skip-connections to produce high-quality reconstructions with more accurate structures and local details. To evaluate the proposed framework, we compare it with other deep learning methods. It is demonstrated that the proposed method shows superiority in terms of visual quality and relevance metrics. The ablation studies show that the proposed model is able to deliver enhanced performance.

2   Method

2.1   Problem Formulation

The high-quality image s is under-sampled as follows,

$$y = A(s) = m \odot F(s), \tag{1}$$

where y is the measurement, A is the under-sampling operator, m is the sampling mask, F denotes the Fourier transform, and $\odot$ refers to the element-wise multiplication. CS methods recover the signal by solving the optimization below,

$$\min_x \|A(x) - y\|^2 + \lambda R(x), \tag{2}$$

where $R(x)$ denotes a regularization. Existing optimization solvers can be computationally expensive and hard to handle complex image features [21]. We instead provide an end-to-end solution using a trained neural network model.

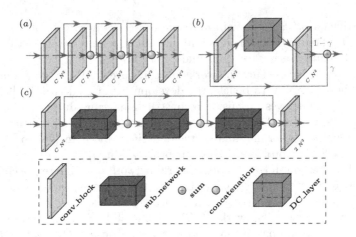

Fig. 1. Illustration of network features where the channel and spatial size of output features are denoted by C and N^2. a) Densely connected layers, b) FR-DCB, and c) densely connected network cascade.

2.2 Reconstruction Framework

In this section, we first introduce the data consistency block and network cascade, and then describe the model design.

Feature Residual Data Consistency Block (FR-DCB). We propose to leverage data consistency (DC) blocks to "correct" the intermediate predictions and provide more faithful results. However, conventional DC blocks inevitably require to collapse the feature channels to fit the complex-valued data, which can have a damaging effect on final performance due to the bottleneck design. To benefit feature propagation and alleviate the bottleneck problem, we take the advantage of residual learning at the feature level and implement the DC operation by,

$$h \leftarrow \gamma h + (1 - \gamma) f^*(DC(f(h))), \tag{3}$$

where h denotes the output features, f and f^* are two convolutional layers used for channel collapse and expansion, and DC refers to the data consistency update given by,

$$DC(x) = F^{-1}(m \odot y + (1 - m) \odot F(x)), \tag{4}$$

where F^{-1} denotes the inverse Fourier transform. The resultant block, dubbed feature residual data consistency block (FR-DCB), is illustrated in Fig. 1.

Densely Connected Network Cascade. Deep cascade of neural networks are widely used for MRI reconstruction [1,4,13,19], which potentially yield higher performance due to the powerful representations learned with a deep structure. Inspired by densely connected layers introduced in [11], we propose a densely connected reconstruction framework, see Figs. 1 and 2, to enable feature transmission and reuse by dense skip-connections between sub-networks. It is noteworthy that the outputs of each sub-network are feature volumes rather than 2-channel images, e.g. in [1,17], which potentially resists the bottleneck problem. The predictions from all preceding sub-networks are collected together with the current output via channel concatenation and fed to the following sub-network as input. The feature maps from all sub-networks are fused together to produce the final outcome, as illustrated in Figs. 1 and 2.

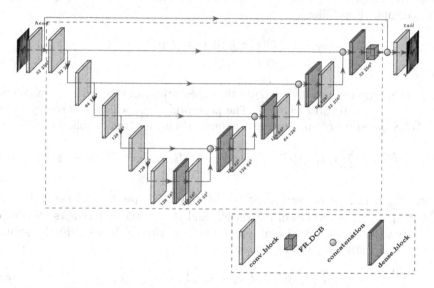

Fig. 2. Illustration of the model architecture where a single sub-network is displayed for brevity. The zero-filled as input is first mapped by a head layer. The output features from all preceding sub-networks are collected to form dense bypass connections. The final result is given via a tail layer.

Model Design. We adopt the U-shaped structure, displayed in Fig. 2, as sub-networks to form the reconstruction framework where 5 sub-networks are deployed. Densely connected layers [11] are embedded in all decoding levels to refine feature representations and the FR-DCB blocks are appended to each sub-network. We use the zero-filled $z = F^{-1}(y)$ as input to the framework, which is first mapped via a convolutional layer and subsequently fed to sub-networks. The features from each sub-network are consecutively used to construct a densely connected cascade. The reconstruction G is given by fusing all collected features.

2.3 Objective Function

We use the L_1 metric and structural similarity index (SSIM) to measure the reconstruction errors. The loss is given by,

$$L_{rec} = (1 - \alpha)L_1(G, s) + \alpha L^{SSIM}(G, s), \tag{5}$$

where we set $\alpha = 0.4$. We adopt the Least Squares GAN (LSGAN) [16] to encourage realistic details. It can prevent the saturation issue and provide more stable and faster convergences [16], compared to vallina GAN. The adversarial loss is computed as follows,

$$
\begin{aligned}
L_{adv}^D &= E[\|D(s) - b\|_2^2] + E[\|D(G) - a\|_2^2] \\
L_{adv}^G &= E[\|D(G) - c\|_2^2],
\end{aligned}
\tag{6}
$$

where D is a discriminator, E denotes the expectation, and the hyper-parameters are set to be $a = 0$ and $b = c = 1$. The perceptual loss, which is normally used in a GAN-based framework to resist hallucinations, is given as follows,

$$L_{vgg} = \sum_i (\|f_{vgg}^i(G) - f_{vgg}^i(s)\|_1 + \beta\|f_{gram}^i(G) - f_{gram}^i(s)\|_1), \tag{7}$$

where f_{vgg}^i is the pre-activations at the i-th layer of a pre-trained network, e.g. VGG [21], f_{gram}^i is the Gram matrix [6], and $\beta = 0.005$. It leverages the deep structure to learn more consistent representations with the human visual system. The total objective is given as below,

$$L = E_{\{(G,s)\}}[\lambda_{rec}L_{rec} + \lambda_{adv}L_{adv} + \lambda_{vgg}L_{vgg}], \tag{8}$$

where we set $\lambda_{rec} = 10$, $\lambda_{adv} = 0.05$, and $\lambda_{vgg} = 0.5$.

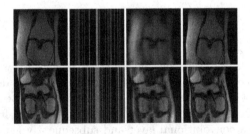

Fig. 3. Illustration of 8× and 4× under-sampling and reconstruction. First) fully sampled, second) sampling pattern, third) zero-filled, and last) reconstruction.

3   Experiment

We conduct experiments on single-coil knee MR images which contain rich structures and textures. We extract 2800 samples from the FastMRI Knee database [24] for training and 164 samples from different cases for test. A fixed random mask is adopted in the under-sampling operation, as presented in Fig. 3, where the total reduction factor is respectively set to 8 and 4 with 4% and 8% central lines preserved. The model is trained for 30 epochs with a batch size of 4. An Adam optimizer is used with $\beta_1 = 0.5$, $\beta_2 = 0.999$, and a learning rate of 1e−5. We use two channels to handle complex-valued data, e.g. inputs and outputs.

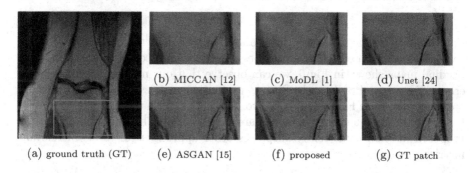

(a) ground truth (GT)   (b) MICCAN [12]   (c) MoDL [1]   (d) Unet [24]

(e) ASGAN [15]   (f) proposed   (g) GT patch

Fig. 4. Comparison results of 8× accelerated single-coil MRI reconstruction.

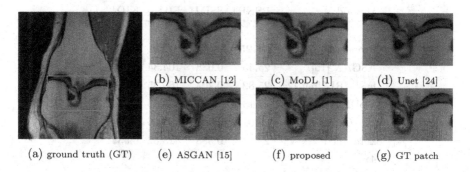

(a) ground truth (GT)   (b) MICCAN [12]   (c) MoDL [1]   (d) Unet [24]

(e) ASGAN [15]   (f) proposed   (g) GT patch

Fig. 5. Comparison results of 4× accelerated single-coil MRI reconstruction.

3.1   Comparison Results

We compare the proposed method with other state-of-the-art approaches: MIC-CAN [12], MoDL [1], FastMRI Unet [24], and ASGAN [15]. The reconstruction results are displayed in Figs. 4 and 5. From Fig. 4, we found that the proposed method produces superior reconstructions with rich textural and structural details, which leads to more realistic and visually promising results. We can observe that ASGAN generates fine local subtleties, whereas it can suffer

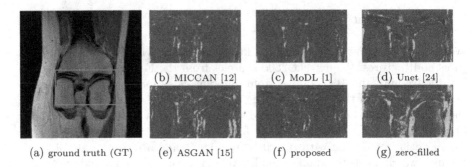

(a) ground truth (GT)   (e) ASGAN [15]   (f) proposed   (g) zero-filled

Fig. 6. Residual maps (2× amplified) of 8× accelerated single-coil MRI reconstruction.

from textural artifacts, see Fig. 5(e), and disrupted structures, see Fig. 4(e). By contrast, the proposed method provides more faithful reconstructions. From the residual maps shown in Fig 6, we can observe that our method produces fewer errors. We adopt PSNR and SSIM as evaluation metrics, where higher values are better, and use FID and KID [3] to measure the visual quality, which prefer lower scores. The quantitative results are shown in Table 1, which shows that the proposed method consistently surpasses other approaches in terms of relevant metrics.

Table 1. Quantitative evaluation on accelerated MRI reconstruction.

Method	PSNR↑	SSIM↑	FID↓	KID↓
8×				
Proposed	**27.25**	**0.720**	**81.06**	**0.014**
ASGAN [15]	25.45	0.638	104.34	0.036
FastMRI Unet [24]	25.82	0.703	160.35	0.121
MoDL [1]	27.13	0.620	143.65	0.080
MICCAN [12]	26.61	0.642	180.66	0.146
Zero-filled	20.54	0.388	423.32	0.533
4×				
Proposed	**31.11**	**0.824**	**63.74**	**0.006**
ASGAN [15]	27.73	0.711	82.18	0.016
FastMRI Unet [24]	28.35	0.771	118.07	0.061
MoDL [1]	30.34	0.745	98.86	0.042
MICCAN [12]	30.11	0.711	99.44	0.040
Zero-filled	23.94	0.486	255.06	0.239

Table 2. Ablation studies on model components using 8× acceleration.

Method	PSNR↑	SSIM↑	FID↓	KID↓
Proposed	**27.25**	**0.720**	**81.06**	**0.014**
W/o FR-DCB	25.72	0.687	94.12	0.028
W/o dense cascade	27.02	0.713	85.82	0.019

3.2 Ablation Studies on Model Components

We conduct ablation studies to verify the effectiveness of the proposed model features. We remove the FR-DCB modules from the framework and compare it with the proposed model. For simplicity, the acceleration factor is selected to 8 for ablation studies. The ablation results are presented in Table 2. We found that the removal of FR-DCB leads to performance drop in all evaluation metrics by a large margin. To testify the efficacy of the densely connected cascade, we remove the dense bypasses between sub-networks and repeat the feature volumes to fit the input channel size. From Table 2, we observed that the densely connected cascade provides better reconstruction results. It is demonstrated that the proposed model features are all able to obtain improved performance.

Table 3. Ablation on feature connection in FR-DCB Using 8× acceleration.

Method	PSNR↑	SSIM↑	FID↓	KID↓
Proposed	**27.25**	**0.720**	**81.06**	**0.014**
W/o DC shortcut	26.91	0.713	88.81	0.023

3.3 Ablation Studies on Bottleneck Design in DC Blocks

To further verify the effectiveness of FR-DCB and show the influence of the bottleneck design in conventional DC blocks, we remove the feature residual shortcut in FR-DCB and implement the update rule as shown below,

$$h \leftarrow f^*(\gamma f(h) + (1 - \gamma)DC(f(h))), \tag{9}$$

which is mathematically equivalent to those used in [1,12,19], where f^* and f can be omitted and absorbed into sub-networks. We present the results in Table 3. It shows that the update rule in (9) reduces PSNR and SSIM scores and concomitantly increases FID and KID, which indicates the adverse impact of the bottleneck design in conventional DC blocks and confirms the efficacy of the proposed FR-DCB.

4   Conclusions and Discussion

A novel GAN-based deep neural network framework is introduced in this paper to provide an end-to-end solution to the high-fidelity MRI reconstruction problem. The framework incorporates a novel data consistency block and a densely connected cascade structure to improve the model performance in recovering accelerated MR images with rich structural and textural details. In experiments, the proposed approach achieves superior high-quality reconstruction results with a high acceleration factor in a comparison with other deep learning-based methods both qualitatively and quantitatively, using FastMRI Knee dataset. The future researches include extending the method to parallel imaging, accelerating model deployments, and applying it to other texture-rich MRI imaging modalities.

References

1. Aggarwal, H., Mani, M., Jacob, M.: MoDL: model-based deep learning architecture for inverse problems. IEEE Trans. Med. Imaging **38**(2), 394–405 (2019). https://doi.org/10.1109/TMI.2018.2865356
2. Anuroop, S., Jure, Z., Tullie, M., Lawrence, Z., Aaron, D., K.S., D.: GrappaNet: combining parallel imaging with deep learning for multi-coil MRI reconstruction. In: 2020 IEEE/CVF Conference on Computer Vision and Pattern Recognition (CVPR), pp. 14303–14310 (2020). https://doi.org/10.1109/CVPR42600.2020.01432
3. Bińkowski, M., Sutherland, D., Arbel, M., Gretton, A.: Demystifying MMD GANs. In: International Conference on Learning Representations (2018)
4. Duan, J., et al.: VS-Net: variable splitting network for accelerated parallel MRI reconstruction. In: Shen, D., et al. (eds.) MICCAI 2019. LNCS, vol. 11767, pp. 713–722. Springer, Cham (2019). https://doi.org/10.1007/978-3-030-32251-9_78
5. Fair, M., Gatehouse, P., DiBella, E., Firmin, D.: A review of 3D first-pass, whole-heart, myocardial perfusion cardiovascular magnetic resonance. J. Cardiovasc. Magn. Reson. **17**, 68 (2015). https://doi.org/10.1186/s12968-015-0162-9
6. Gatys, L., Ecker, A., Bethge, M.: Image style transfer using convolutional neural networks. 2016 IEEE Conference on Computer Vision and Pattern Recognition (CVPR), pp. 2414–2423 (2016). https://doi.org/10.1109/CVPR.2016.265
7. Goodfellow, I., Pouget, A., Mirza, M., Xu, B., Warde, F., Ozair, S., Courville, A., Bengio, Y.: Generative adversarial networks. Adv. Neural. Inf. Process. Syst. **27**, 2672–2680 (2014)
8. Griswold, M., Jakob, P., Heidemann, R.M., Nittka, M., Jellus, V., Wang, J., Kiefer, B., Haase, A.: Generalized autocalibrating partially parallel acquisitions (GRAPPA). Magn. Reson. Med. **47**(6), 1202–1210 (2002). https://doi.org/10.1002/mrm.10171
9. Hammernik, k., et al.: Learning a variational network for reconstruction of accelerated MRI data. Magn. Reson. Med. **79**(6), 3055–3071 (2018). https://doi.org/10.1002/mrm.26977
10. Hong, M., Yu, Y., Wang, H., Liu, F., Crozier, S.: Compressed sensing MRI with singular value decomposition-based sparsity basis. Phys. Med. Biol. **56**, 6311–6325 (2021)

11. Huang, G., Liu, Z., Van Der Maaten, L., Weinberger, K.Q.: Densely connected convolutional networks. In: 2017 IEEE Conference on Computer Vision and Pattern Recognition (CVPR), pp. 2261–2269 (2017)
12. Huang, Q., Yang, D., Wu, P., Qu, H., Yi, J., Metaxas, D.: MRI reconstruction via cascaded channel-wise attention network. In: 2019 IEEE 16th International Symposium on Biomedical Imaging (ISBI 2019), pp. 1622–1626 (2019). https://doi.org/10.1109/ISBI.2019.8759423
13. Lee, D., Yoo, J., Tak, S., Ye, J.: Deep residual learning for accelerated MRI using magnitude and phase networks. IEEE Trans. Biomed. Eng. **65**(9), 1985–1995 (2018)
14. Lingala, S., Jacob, M.: Blind compressive sensing dynamic MRI. IEEE Trans. Med. Imaging **32**(6), 1132–1145 (2013)
15. Liu, J., Yaghoobi, M.: Fine-grained MRI reconstruction using attentive selection generative adversarial networks. In: ICASSP 2021–2021 IEEE International Conference on Acoustics, Speech and Signal Processing (ICASSP), pp. 1155–1159 (2021)
16. Mao, X., Li, Q., Xie, H., Lau, R., Wang, Z., Smolley, S.: Least squares generative adversarial networks. In: 2017 IEEE International Conference on Computer Vision (ICCV), pp. 2813–2821 (2017)
17. Mardani, M., Gong, E., Cheng, J.Y., Vasanawala, S.S., Zaharchuk, G., Xing, L., Pauly, J.M.: Deep generative adversarial neural networks for compressive sensing MRI. IEEE Trans. Med. Imaging **38**(1), 167–179 (2019). https://doi.org/10.1109/TMI.2018.2858752
18. Narnhofer, D., Hammernik, K., Knoll, F., Pock, T.: Inverse GANs for accelerated MRI reconstruction. Wavel. Sparsity XVIII **11138**, 111381A (2019). https://doi.org/10.1117/12.2527753
19. Schlemper, J., Caballero, J., Hajnal, J., Price, A., Rueckert, D.: A deep cascade of convolutional neural networks for dynamic MR image reconstruction. IEEE Trans. Med. Imaging **37**(2), 491–503 (2018). https://doi.org/10.1109/TMI.2017.2760978
20. Sriram, A., et al.: End-to-end variational networks for accelerated MRI reconstruction. In: Martel, A.L., et al. (eds.) MICCAI 2020. LNCS, vol. 12262, pp. 64–73. Springer, Cham (2020). https://doi.org/10.1007/978-3-030-59713-9_7
21. Yang, G., et al.: DAGAN: deep de-aliasing generative adversarial networks for fast compressed sensing MRI reconstruction. IEEE Trans. Med. Imaging **37**(6), 1310–1321 (2018)
22. Yang, Y., Sun, J., Li, H., Xu, Z.: Deep ADMM-Net for compressive sensing MRI. Adv. Neural Inf. Process. Syst. **29**, 1–9 (2016)
23. Yuan, Z., et al.: SARA-GAN: self-attention and relative average discriminator based generative adversarial networks for fast compressed sensing MRI reconstruction. Front. Neuroinform. **14**, 1–12 (2020). https://doi.org/10.3389/fninf.2020.611666
24. Zbontar, J., et al.: FastMRI: an open dataset and benchmarks for accelerated MRI. CoRR abs/1811.08839 (2018)
25. Zhang, C., Liu, Y., Shang, F., Li, Y., Liu, H.: A novel learned primal-dual network for image compressive sensing. IEEE Access **9**, 26041–26050 (2021). https://doi.org/10.1109/ACCESS.2021.3057621

Metal Artifact Correction MRI Using Multi-contrast Deep Neural Networks for Diagnosis of Degenerative Spinal Diseases

Jaa-Yeon Lee[1], Min A Yoon[2], Choong Guen Chee[2], Jae Hwan Cho[2], Jin Hoon Park[2], and Sung-Hong Park[1(✉)]

[1] Korea Advanced Institute of Science and Technology (KAIST), Daejeon, South Korea
{jaayeon,sunghongpark}@kaist.ac.kr
[2] Seoul Asan Medical Center, Seoul, South Korea
spinejhpark@naver.com

Abstract. Our research aims to accelerate Slice Encoding for Metal Artifact Correction (SEMAC) MRI using multi-contrast deep neural networks for patients with degenerative spine diseases. To reduce the scan time of SEMAC, we propose multi-contrast deep neural networks which can produce high SEMAC factor data from low SEMAC factor data. We investigated acceleration in k-space along the SEMAC encoding direction as well as phase encoding direction to reduce the scan time further. To leverage the complementary information of multi-contrast images, we downsampled the data at different k-space positions. The output of multi-contrast SEMAC reconstruction provided great performance for correcting metal artifacts. The developed networks potentially enable clinical use of SEMAC in a reduced scan time with reasonable quality.

Keywords: SEMAC · Degenerative spinal diseases · Multi-contrast MR · Deep learning

1 Introduction

Degenerative spine diseases are about gradual loss of structure and function of the spine over time. To diagnose the diseases more effectively, multi-contrast MRI is often required. The patients with degenerative spine diseases often carry metallic objects in the disease core, which hamper the accurate diagnosis of the diseases using MRI. There are a few methods for correcting metal artifacts in MRI. One of the popular methods is slice encoding for metal artifact correction (SEMAC) MRI [3]. SEMAC is performed as 2D multi-slice imaging, where metal-induced distortion is additionally encoded along the slice direction providing information of the metal-induced distortion and thus the way of its correction. Clinical application of SEMAC is often hampered by the long scan time associated with the SEMAC encoding, which is worsened in case of multi-contrast MRI.

N. Haq et al. (Eds.): MLMIR 2022, LNCS 13587, pp. 44–52, 2022.
https://doi.org/10.1007/978-3-031-17247-2_5

There has been a trial to decrease the scan time of SEMAC using convolutional neural network by undersampling along the SEMAC encoding direction, which was demonstrated in phantoms and brain surgical patients [5]. Often spinal diseases induce metal artifacts more severely than brain surgical patients, requiring SEMAC MRI more extensively. Nonetheless, acceleration of SEMAC MRI on diagnosis of spinal diseases has not been investigated yet. Also, multi-contrast MRI can be accelerated better through joint acceleration [1], but it has not been investigated for SEMAC MRI yet.

In this study, we propose joint acceleration of multi-contrast SEMAC MRI for diagnosis of degenerative spinal diseases. The multi-contrast MRI information was gathered through multiple encoders for better acceleration and the results were compared with their corresponding single-contrast MRI. The acceleration was applied not only to the SEMAC encoding dimension but also to the phase-encoding dimension for higher accelerations.

2   Method

2.1   Data Preprocessing

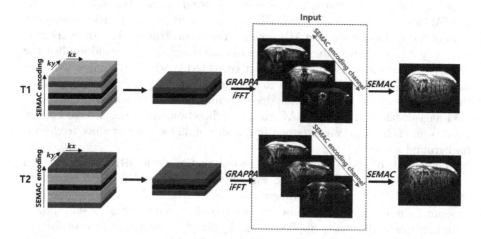

Fig. 1. The overall preprocessing steps. We downsampled the SEMAC encoding lines along k_x, k_y, and slice directions in different positions between multi-contrast data. After reconstructing the MR images with GRAPPA and inverse Fourier transform, we used multichannel downsampled spatial MR images as network input.

The L-spines of eighteen patients with degenerative spinal diseases with metallic implants were scanned using the SEMAC techniques on 3T Siemens Skyra scanners. T1 and T2-weighted images were acquired for each patient with SEMAC factors 6 and 7. To speed up SEMAC MRI, we designed a network that reconstructed the full SEMAC encoding lines from the downsampled SEMAC data.

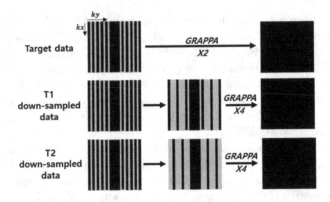

Fig. 2. Details of phase-encoding line donwsampling and reconstruction with GRAPPA. The black lines indicate the sampled lines. Similar to SEMAC factor downsampling, we used uniformly sampled lines at different positions between multi-contrast data.

Figure 1 shows the overall preprocessing steps. To match the SEMAC factor of two target contrast images at 7, we zero-padded the additional k-space SEMAC encoding line of T1-weighted images. The k-space data was downsampled to the SEMAC factor 3 as input. Then, GRAPPA [2] and inverse Fourier transform were performed to reconstruct MR images. The reconstructed data were 4D data with x, y, SEMAC encoding direction and slice direction. We could applied the SEMAC algorithm to get metal artifact corrected spatial MR images with the downsampled SEMAC factor, but to get better corrected images, we increased the SEMAC encoding factor using deep learning. The input was constructed as 3D images with x, y, and SEMAC encoding direction. After the inverse Fourier transform, each image was cropped into a size of 320 × 320 to reduce irrelevant background space.

The details of phase encoding line reconstruction with GRAPPA are shown in Fig. 2. Because the original data was obtained with $X2$ GRAPPA factor, we set the $X2$ GRAPPA as the target data. Since the SEMAC factor obtained was not large enough to compose a more strictly downsampled version, downsampling was additionally applied along k_y direction uniformly except for the autocalibration region, resulting in $X4$ GRAPPA. Likewise, acceleration factor can be increased simultaneously by incorporating SEMAC acceleration and other traditional in-plane acceleration techniques. Instead of using downsampled data immediately, we filled the zero-filled phase encoding line to plausible data with GRAPPA algorithm to avoid severe aliasing artifacts in spatial image that can degrade the acceleration network performance. Therefore, two types of downsampled data were used in this study, SEMAC only downsampled data with acceleration factor 2 and SEMAC, phase-encoding downsampled data with total acceleration factor 4 compared to the target data.

To leverage the complementary information of multi-contrast images in joint acceleration, we downsampled the SEMAC encoding lines at different positions between the multi-contrast data. Also, in the same reason, we downsampled k_y phase-encoding lines at different positions between the multi-contrast data.

2.2 Multi-contrast SEMAC Acceleration

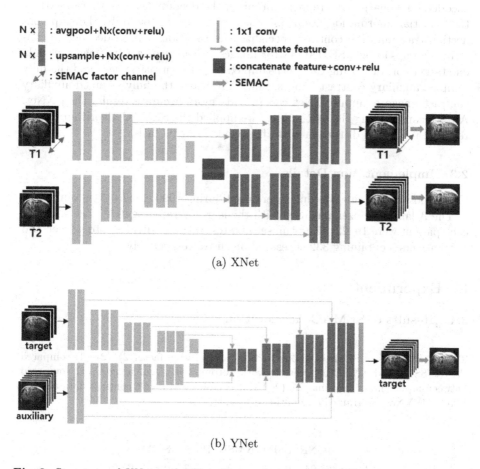

(a) XNet

(b) YNet

Fig. 3. Structure of XNet and YNet. To accelerate multi-contrast images simultaneously, we used multi-contrast images in pairs as input. XNet takes downsampled multi-contrast images as input and provides fully sampled images as output for both contrasts. YNet takes one downsampled target contrast image as input and another fully sampled contrast image as a guide (auxiliary), and provides the fully sampled target contrast images as output.

To accelerate the SEMAC MRI, we developed two types of Convolutional Neural Network (CNN) that can correct metal-induced distortions with a lower

SEMAC factor. In this study, we used XNet and YNet structures from [1], which used multi-contrast T1, T2-weighted images in MR reconstruction based on UNet structure [4]. Figure 3 shows the overall architecture of XNet and YNet in SEMAC acceleration.

XNet and YNet used paired multi-contrast images as input. XNet simultaneously generates an upsampled SEMAC factor from a downsampled SEMAC factor in both contrast images. By learning the representation with separate encoders and sharing the representation on the deepest feature, we can extract the essential information useful for both contrasts. Incidentally, the skip connection transmits the contrast specialized information to each decoder to construct the upsampled SEMAC factor images. YNet reconstructs images of only one target contrast using the downsampled target contrast images and the fully sampled auxiliary contrast images. Since YNet uses the fully sampled auxiliary contrast image as input, YNet can provide more accurate results than XNet. After reconstructing the MR images, we applied the SEMAC algorithm to correct metal-induced distortion with the higher SEMAC factor.

2.3 Implementation Details

The L1 loss and cosine scheduler were used during 1000 epochs with mini-batch 4. The Adam optimizer was used with the learning rate 2×10^{-4}. The slices for each patient were 19–22. The train set and test set were divided into sixteen and two patients, containing 332 slices and 38 slices, respectively.

3   Experiment

3.1   Results of SEMAC Acceleration

Table 1. Results of SEMAC reconstruction (acceleration factor 2). (2)–(4) compared PSNR, SSIM and NMSE between network output and target images. (1) compared between input and output images. (2) UNet is trained on single contrast data and (3) XNet, (4) YNet are trained on multi-contrast data.

	T1			T2		
	PSNR	SSIM	NMSE	PSNR	SSIM	NMSE
(1) Input	27.04	0.864	0.013	26.07	0.826	0.021
(2) UNet	35.73	0.944	0.001	35.00	0.926	0.002
(3) XNet	36.05	0.946	0.002	35.37	0.927	0.002
(4) YNet	**36.57**	0.947	0.001	**35.90**	0.930	0.002

We compared the reconstruction performance of the SEMAC factor between single-contrast and multi-contrast networks. We used UNet as a single contrast network. The input and output of UNet is the same as the proposed method

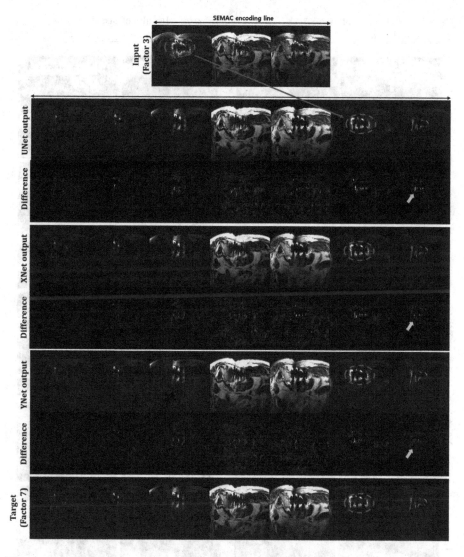

Fig. 4. Demonstration of the aliasing artifact caused by the downsampled SEMAC factor and the performance of the networks to correct the artifacts. The channel of the SEMAC encoding line is shown individually to confirm the aliasing effect. The differences between the network outputs and the target images are also given.

which contains the multi SEMAC encoding channels. Table 1 shows the output of PSNR, SSIM and NMSE in both contrasts. The multi-contrast network XNet (3) outperformed the single contrast networks UNet (2), and the multi-contrast network YNet (4) further outperformed the other networks. To visualize the meaning of reconstructing the SEMAC factor, Fig. 4 shows how the reconstructed SEMAC factor can provide better metal artifact correction. When the SEMAC

Results of Sec. 3.1   Results of Sec. 3.2
    T1   T2   T1   T2

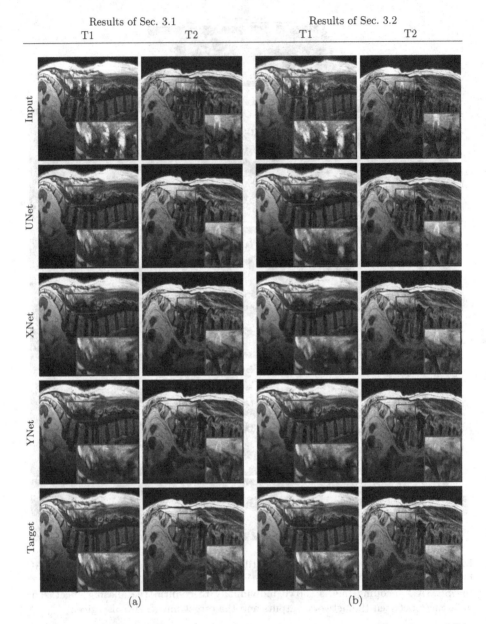

(a)   (b)

Fig. 5. The results of the MR acceleration. (a) indicates the results of Sect. 3.1, and (b) indicates the results of Sect. 3.2. Each row displays input, UNet, XNet, YNet output and target images, from the top to the bottom.

factor is downsampled, aliasing occurred through the SEMAC encoding line and all networks were able to successfully reconstruct full SEMAC encoding lines. The networks could correctly identify the aliasing artifact and non-aliasing artifact of input images. The multi-contrast networks were able to improve fine structures far from the center images (due to bigger metal-induced distortion) better than the single-contrast network. Figure 5(a) shows the representative images of Table 1 that applied the SEMAC algorithm to output images. The metal artifact slightly remained in the UNet output of Fig. 5, but decreased in the XNet and YNet outputs.

3.2   Results of SEMAC/Phase-Encoding Acceleration

Table 2. Results of SEMAC/Phase-encoding reconstruction (total acceleration factor 4). (2)–(4) compared PSNR, SSIM and NMSE between network output and target images. Because of the higher acceleration factor than that in Table 1, these PSNR, SSIM, and NMSE were recorded relatively low.

	T1			T2		
	PSNR	SSIM	NMSE	PSNR	SSIM	NMSE
(1) Input	24.41	0.690	0.024	24.46	0.722	0.030
(2) UNet	31.39	0.886	0.004	31.36	0.879	0.006
(3) XNet	31.80	0.891	0.004	31.72	0.882	0.006
(4) YNet	**32.53**	0.899	0.004	**32.64**	0.893	0.005

To evaluate the network performance under more stringent conditions, down-sampled data in both SEMAC/Phase-encoding was used as input. The total acceleration rate 4 with $X2$ SEMAC and $X2$ Phase-encoding. Table 2 shows PSNR, SSIM and NMSE of the output images. In accordance with Sect. 3.1, the multi-contrast network XNet (3) outperformed the single-contrast UNet (2), and the multi-contrast network YNet (4) further outperformed the other networks. Figure 5(b) shows the representative images of Table 2. Although the overall images are blurry compared to (a) due to the higher acceleration factor, it is clearly demonstrated that the metal artifact correction was performed better in XNet and YNet than UNet.

4   Discussion and Conclusion

In this study, we introduced deep learning networks for multi-contrast SEMAC MRI acceleration to correct metal artifact in metal-implanted patients with degenerative spinal diseases. To the best of our knowledge, this is the first study approaching joint multi-contrast MR acceleration in SEMAC encoding steps. Multi-contrast acceleration outperformed single-contrast acceleration, yielding metal artifact corrected images that were quantitatively and perceptually comparable to the full SEMAC factor images. Even with phase-encoding downsampled images, multi-contrast SEMAC factor acceleration successfully corrected the metal artifact and improved the quality of the output images.

SEMAC is a powerful metal artifact correction algorithm, but a longer scan time is a barrier to real clinical use. This study may facilitate the clinical use of SEMAC in a reduced scan time. By using multi-contrast images, we can simultaneously produce a high SEMAC factor of multiple contrasts. In particular, L-spine MR scans of degenerative spinal disease patients with metallic implants inevitably need a metal artifact reduction process due to severe metal-induced distortions. At this point, this study is meaningful for the diagnosis of degenerative spinal disease.

This study can be further developed with self-supervised learning using multiple contrast images of various low SEMAC factor data. Given enough data, it can also be developed to achieve more powerful performance with a state-of-the-art network architecture that has better complexity and increased generalizability to multiple regions.

References

1. Do, W.J., Seo, S., Han, Y., Ye, J.C., Choi, S.H., Park, S.H.: Reconstruction of multicontrast MR images through deep learning. Med. Phys. **47**(3), 983–997 (2020)
2. Griswold, M.A., et al.: Generalized autocalibrating partially parallel acquisitions (GRAPPA). Magn. Reson. Med. Off. J. Int. Soc. Magn. Reson. Med. **47**(6), 1202–1210 (2002)
3. Lu, W., Pauly, K.B., Gold, G.E., Pauly, J.M., Hargreaves, B.A.: SEMAC: slice encoding for metal artifact correction in MRI. Magn. Reson. Med. Off. J. Int. Soc. Mag. Reson. Med. **62**(1), 66–76 (2009)
4. Ronneberger, O., Fischer, P., Brox, T.: U-Net: convolutional networks for biomedical image segmentation. In: Navab, N., Hornegger, J., Wells, W.M., Frangi, A.F. (eds.) MICCAI 2015. LNCS, vol. 9351, pp. 234–241. Springer, Cham (2015). https://doi.org/10.1007/978-3-319-24574-4_28
5. Seo, S., Do, W.J., Luu, H.M., Kim, K.H., Choi, S.H., Park, S.H.: Artificial neural network for slice encoding for metal artifact correction (SEMAC) MRI. Magn. Reson. Med. **84**(1), 263–276 (2020)

Segmentation-Aware MRI Reconstruction

Mert Acar[1,2(✉)], Tolga Çukur[1,2], and İlkay Öksüz[3]

[1] Department of Electrical and Electronics Engineering, Bilkent University,
Ankara, Turkey
mert.acar@bilkent.edu.tr
[2] National Magnetic Resonance Research Center, Bilkent University, Ankara, Turkey
[3] Department of Computer Engineering, Istanbul Technical University,
Istanbul, Turkey

Abstract. Deep learning models have been broadly adopted for accelerating MRI acquisitions in recent years. A common approach is to train deep models based on loss functions that place equal emphasis on reconstruction errors across the field-of-view. This homogeneous weighting of loss contributions might be undesirable in cases where the diagnostic focus is on tissues in a specific subregion of the image. In this paper, we propose a framework for segmentation-aware reconstruction based on segmentation as a proxy task. We leverage an end-to-end model comprising reconstruction and segmentation networks; and leverage backpropagation of segmentation error to devise a pseudo-attention effect to focus the reconstruction network. We introduce a novel stabilization method to prevent convergence onto a local minima with unacceptably poor reconstruction or segmentation performance. Our stabilization approach initiates learning on fully-sampled acquisitions, and gradually increases the undersampling rate assumed in the training set to its desired value. We validate our approach for cardiac MR reconstruction on the publicly available OCMR dataset. Segmentation-aware reconstruction significantly outperforms vanilla reconstruction for cardiac imaging.

Keywords: Cardiac MRI · Reconstruction · Segmentation ·
Convolutional neural networks

1 Introduction

Magnetic resonance imaging (MRI) is an essential part of routine clinical practice for noninvasive disease detection and monitoring. Yet, its prolonged scan times limit broad utilization. Shortening scan durations can improve patient throughput and lower motion-based image artifacts. However, undersampled k-space acquisitions elicit well-known aliasing artifacts that must be suppressed to obtain diagnostic-quality images. Artifact suppression involves an inverse problem solution where high-quality images are reconstructed from undersampled k-space data [1].

In recent years, deep learning (DL) models have become a preferred approach for accelerated MRI reconstruction [1–4]. DL models are trained to recover

N. Haq et al. (Eds.): MLMIR 2022, LNCS 13587, pp. 53–61, 2022.
https://doi.org/10.1007/978-3-031-17247-2_6

high-quality images consistent with fully-sampled acquisitions given as input undersampled acquisitions. Training is typically performed with a global loss function expressed over the entire image. However, such global loss functions are often dominated by diagnostically-irrelevant background tissues.

Self-attention mechanisms have been proposed to help focus the model's attention on subregions where there is greater tendency for introducing reconstruction errors [5]. Note that vanilla attention mechanisms are not explicitly informed regarding the underlying anatomy. Other studies have considered more direct guidance from segmentation maps to focus on reconstruction performance in regions of interest [6–8]. Pre-trained segmentation models have been transferred to mitigate problems associated with joint training of the reconstruction-segmentation network. Few recent studies have considered joint training of reconstruction-segmentation models, where an alternating optimization is performed between the two networks [9]. However, such alternative optimization is prone to premature stopping of learning where one of the networks performs unacceptably poorly.

In this work, we propose a segmentation-aware reconstruction method. The proposed method is based on a sequential architecture containing two networks for reconstruction and segmentation. To avoid premature stopping of learning, a stabilization approach is introduced for end-to-end training of the model. In particular, the undersampling rate is gradually decreased during the course of training. A composite reconstruction-segmentation loss is used, and errors back-propagated from the segmentation stage are used to focus the reconstruction on critical image regions. Experiments were conducted on a public cardiac MRI dataset [10]. Our results clearly indicate that the proposed segmentation-aware reconstruction improves focal image quality over solo reconstruction methods and unstabilized joint reconstruction-segmentation methods.

2   Methods

2.1   Proposed Framework

We propose an end-to-end training of reconstruction and segmentation networks to enable high reconstruction quality for a target region of interest (ROI). Figure 1 illustrates the proposed framework for segmentation-aware reconstruction for cardiac MRI reconstruction. Our framework is general in the sense that many different state-of-the-art architecture for reconstruction and segmentation modules can be utilized. The specific pairs of architectures that we examine in the current study are described in implementation details.

2.2   Stabilization

Our framework rests on the key notion of employing segmentation loss to focus the reconstruction process on tissues of high diagnostic interest. Accordingly, we perform end-to-end training of a sequential cascade of reconstruction and

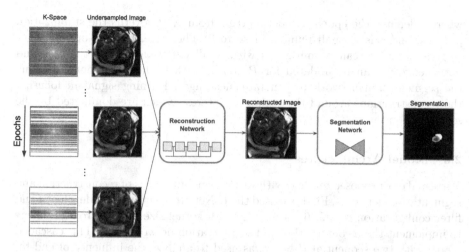

Fig. 1. Segmentation-aware reconstruction framework. During training the network is trained end-to-end with stabilization. During inference an image is recollected from only the reconstruction network, along with an auxiliary segmentation map. Stabilization technique is illustrated by the sample inputs on the left across epochs

segmentation networks. Training of such compound networks is prone to undesirable convergence onto local minima where either network yields undesirably poor performance. During initial stages of training, the segmentation network receives an input computed by an insufficiently trained reconstruction network, so the input will contain a high degree of reconstruction artifacts. This will inevitably compromise the learning process for the segmentation stage, resulting in inaccurate segmentation maps. Note that the segmentation maps are then provided as guidance to the reconstruction network, so a vicious circle can be created where both network are compromised.

To address this critical issue, we propose to use a novel stabilization method where the undersampling rate of the acquisitions are gradually ramped up during the course of training. In the initial stages, the reconstruction network receives lightly undersampled data that is easy to reconstruct with few artifacts. Thus, the segmentation network receives as input high-quality reconstructions that will improve its learning capabilities. Once both network adapt to the instant acceleration rate, then the degree of undersampling can be elevated. Overall, the learning signals generated from the high-quality inputs in earlier epochs are propagated back to "warm-up" the model for the increasingly lower quality samples that are to come in later epochs. In particular, we impose an epoch-specific undersampling rate starting from $1 - \epsilon$ reaching to the desired undersampling rate r in an exponential manner as follows:

$$r_i = \begin{cases} (1 - \epsilon) \left(\frac{r}{1-\epsilon} \right)^{(i-1)/P} & 1 \leq i \leq P \\ r & i > P \end{cases} \tag{1}$$

where i denotes the epoch number starting from 1, P governs the stabilization patience and ϵ is a small number close to 0. Therefore, the sub-optimal convergence problem can be mitigated with small perturbations on the task and both networks can be updated for P epochs with healthy gradients to prime the segmentation network to generate meaningful learning signal in focusing the reconstructions around the regions of interest which are dominated by the segmentation maps.

2.3   Model Architectures

We tested our proposed method with various configurations of reconstruction and segmentation networks. First, we used the U-Net architecture with depth of 4 and filter configuration of (32, 64, 128, 256) with kernel size 3×3 across all layers to implement the reconstruction and segmentation networks [11]. This cascaded model with two sequential U-Nets was used to analyze the influence of end-to-end training and stabilization. For enhanced performance, we then adopted the Cascade Network for reconstruction and Multiscale Attention Network (MANet) for segmentation [12,13]. Cascade Network follows an unrolled architecture with interleaved data consistency and regularization blocks, and progressively suppresses aliasing artifacts in reconstructions. The regularization blocks include residual connections to carry the input signal to the output and force the network to learn required the residual information [12]. In our setup, we used 6 cascades with 5 layers of 64 filters each. MANet improves upon UNet with multiscale information extraction achieved by point-wise and multiscale attention blocks [11,13]. Using dilated convolutions in the decoder distills multiscale information processed with the squeeze-and-excitation attention mechanism to capture dependencies among feature maps [14]. We used ResNet34 in the encoder with a depth of 4 and filter sizes (32, 64, 128, 256) for MANet [15]. Finally, a multi-decoder architecture where the decoder head is split to separately perform reconstruction and segmentation is added to the experiments as an additional baseline [16]. For Multi-Decoder UNet, a common encoder of depth 4 with filter configuration (32, 64, 128, 256) is created for reconstruction and segmentation tasks, taking the undersampled images as input. The encoder is used to obtain disentangled feature representations which are then fed to the first decoder head to reconstruct the underlying image and to the second decoder to create the segmentation map.

2.4   Implementation Details

All networks were trained using the Adam optimizer with parameters $\beta_1 = 0.99$ and $\beta_2 = 0.999$, a learning rate of 10^{-4} and batch size of 16. Models were implemented using PyTorch library and executed on NVIDIA RTX 3090 GPUs. Experiments were conducted on fully-sampled MRI data from the public OCMR dataset containing CINE scans from 74 subjects [10]. Subjects had varying number of slices and frames, yielding a total of 183 slices, which were coil combined to simulate single-coil data acquisition. Data were split into independent training (155 slices) and test (28 slices) sets, with no subject overlap between the two

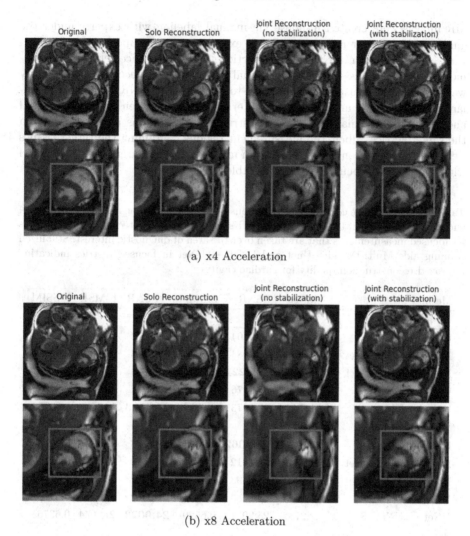

(a) x4 Acceleration

(b) x8 Acceleration

Fig. 2. Representative reconstructions from competing techniques at (a) 4-fold, (b) 8-fold acceleration. The second row displays the localized reconstruction around the heart. The area on which the local performance calculations are taken is indicated with the red rectangle. First column displays Fourier reconstructions of fully-sampled data. In remaining columns, reconstruction with no help from the segmentation maps, joint reconstruction without stabilization and joint reconstruction with stabilization is shown respectively. (Color figure online)

sets. MRI data were retrospectively undersampled to achieve acceleration rates of 4 and 8. A Gaussian sampling density with an autocalibration region containing 8 lines was used. Magnitude images for the resulting reconstructions are used to generate segmentation map predictions. Ground-truth segmentation maps for

MR images were created in-house via manual labeling with experts under the guidance of a senior radiologist. In all experiments, a composite loss function with an $\ell_1 - \ell_2$ term for the reconstruction task, and a Dice term for the segmentation task [17] is employed with equal weights. Global reconstruction quality was assessed by measuring peak signal-to-noise ratio (PSNR), structural similarity index (SSIM) and mean-squared error (MSE) between the reconstructed and ground-truth images. Local reconstruction quality was also measured via the same metrics, albeit the measurement regions containing the target tissues were selected based on the segmentation maps. Local measurements are denoted with the 'F' (for 'Focused') prefix in Table 2.

Table 1. Performance comparisons of various baselines on cardiac MRI data across ×4 and ×8 acceleration rates. (S) suffix signifies the stabilization technique. "F" stands for focused measurements that are taken over the area of diagnostic interest. Stabilized training aids Multi-Decoder Unet and UNet → UNet in focused metrics indicating improved reconstruction quality for cardiac cavity.

Method	MSE	PSNR	SSIM	F-PSNR	F-MSE	F-SSIM
×4 acceleration						
UNet	1.7693	26.9204	0.6247	25.5002	1.9009	0.5926
Multi-Decoder UNet	1.9693	26.3084	0.6651	25.3396	2.0209	0.6318
Multi-Decoder UNet (S)	1.7530	**27.1221**	**0.7082**	25.8338	**1.7109**	**0.6735**
UNet → UNet	1.9509	25.4176	0.5227	24.6887	2.5709	0.5488
UNet → UNet (S)	**1.7474**	27.0973	0.6729	**26.4023**	1.8174	0.6475
×8 acceleration						
UNet	**2.2378**	**25.4062**	**0.6583**	24.3128	2.7243	0.6033
Multi-Decoder UNet	2.4312	25.1512	0.6532	24.0712	2.9125	0.6219
Multi-Decoder UNet (S)	2.2441	25.2193	0.6646	24.7312	2.6217	**0.6422**
UNet → UNet	3.1743	23.2683	0.5491	23.0352	3.4719	0.5428
UNet → UNet (S)	2.2782	25.2931	0.6529	**24.9023**	**2.4174**	0.6375

3   Experimental Results

Figure 2 illustrates reconstructions for a representative test subject at ×4 and 8x acceleration along with the fully-sampled ground truth. PSNR, SSIM and MSE of all tested methods are presented in Tables 1 and 2 along with the localized measurements around the heart. Table 1 underlines the results of the experiments done on the UNet architecture which is taken as a baseline for both the reconstruction and segmentation tasks. Additionally Multi-Decoder UNet is introduced to the experiments to compare against the segmentation-aware reconstruction framework. We see that in a stabilized setting, aided by segmentation, reconstruction of the diagnostically-relevant areas improve compared to single UNet. Multi-Decoder UNet seems to surpass the reconstruction-segmentation network performance at ×4 acceleration task in MSE and SSIM measures around the regions of interest. However, when tasked with harsher undersampling rates, Table 1 highlights the effect of an end-to-end architecture as it yields better quality reconstructions in terms of PSNR and MSE metrics around the heart.

Table 2 shows, while Cascade Network performs better at solo reconstruction task in terms of global performance metrics, segmentation-aware reconstruction with stabilization outperforms competing methods in terms of localized metrics. Note that the jointly trained compound model for segmentation-aware reconstruction greatly suffer in the absence of stabilization. When supplied with high quality reconstructions, segmentation network is able learn the mapping to create accurate segmentation maps. However, in the case of an insufficiently trained reconstruction network in the model, the segmentation network is exposed to heavy undersampling artifacts which in turn misguide the resulting segmentation output. Therefore, inaccurate segmentation information propagating into the reconstruction network damages overall quality of the reconstructions, leading to poor performance on both networks. As loss functions typically utilized for reconstruction is expressed over the entire image the learning signal coming directly from the reconstruction output largely governs the performance for the overall image in the global setting. However, such loss functions are mainly dominated by bright bone structures, diagnostically irrelevant body parts and overall low-frequency information. Back-propagating the errors from the segmentation network into the reconstruction network, indirectly emphasizes the areas of interest during training since the segmentation loss is concentrated around such diagnostically-relevant areas. Therefore, end-to-end training of a reconstruction-segmentation network creates a pseudo-attention effect to focus the efforts of the reconstruction network which in turn improves the localized performance around regions of interest.

Table 2. Performance comparisons (MSE, PSNR and SSIM) on cardiac MRI data with ×4 and ×8 acceleration rates across experiment setups. MSE is scaled with 10^3. (S) suffix indicates the stabilization technique. "F" stands for focused measurements that are taken over the area of diagnostic interest. Stabilized training improves the focused metrics indicating improved reconstruction quality for cardiac cavity.

Method	MSE	PSNR	SSIM	F-MSE	F-PSNR	F-SSIM
×4 acceleration						
CascadeNet	**0.6698**	**32.1988**	**0.9113**	1.0342	29.1253	0.8331
CascadeNet → MANet	0.7640	31.5884	0.8563	1.1980	28.3712	0.8131
CascadeNet → MANet (S)	0.7114	31.4328	0.8991	**0.9731**	**30.0000**	**0.8828**
×8 acceleration						
CascadeNet	**1.2825**	**28.4301**	**0.8259**	1.7826	25.5156	0.7728
CascadeNet → MANet	1.7603	25.2837	0.7265	2.4456	23.3219	0.6673
CascadeNet → MANet (S)	1.3226	27.4895	0.8217	**1.5453**	**26.3421**	**0.7931**

4 Conclusion

Here we proposed a segmentation-aware reconstruction framework for cardiac MRI acquisitions. Experiments were conducted to systematically demonstrate the proposed method against solo reconstruction methods. As expected, solo reconstruction with global loss terms yields higher performance in global quality metrics. That said, our results clearly demonstrate that the segmentation-aware reconstruction outperform solo reconstruction in local quality metrics focused on the target ROI. Furthermore, we observe that stabilization of the acceleration rate during the course of joint network training is highly effective in mitigating convergence onto local minima with unacceptably poor reconstruction or segmentation performance.

Acknowledgements. This paper has been produced benefiting from the 2232 International Fellowship for Outstanding Researchers Program of TUBITAK (Project No: 118C353). However, the entire responsibility of the publication/paper belongs to the owner of the paper. The financial support received from TUBITAK does not mean that the content of the publication is approved in a scientific sense by TUBITAK.

References

1. Dar, S.U.H., Yurt, M., Shahdloo, M., Ildız, M.E., Tınaz, B., Çukur, T.: Prior-guided image reconstruction for accelerated multi-contrast MRI via generative adversarial networks. IEEE J. Sel. Top. Sig. Process. **14**(6), 1072–1087 (2020)
2. Oksuz, I., et al.: Cardiac MR motion artefact correction from K-space using deep learning-based reconstruction. In: Knoll, F., Maier, A., Rueckert, D. (eds.) MLMIR 2018. LNCS, vol. 11074, pp. 21–29. Springer, Cham (2018). https://doi.org/10.1007/978-3-030-00129-2_3
3. Wang, S., et al.: Accelerating magnetic resonance imaging via deep learning. In: 2016 IEEE 13th International Symposium on Biomedical Imaging (ISBI), pp. 514–517 (2016)
4. Fuin, N., et al.: A multi-scale variational neural network for accelerating motion-compensated whole-heart 3D coronary MR angiography. Magn. Reson. Imaging **70**, 155–167 (2020)
5. Yan, W., Ma, Y., Liu, J., Jiang, D., Xing, L.: Self-attention convolutional neural network for improved MR image reconstruction. Inf. Sci. **490**, 317–328 (2019)
6. Huang, Q., Yang, D., Wu, P., Qu, H., Yi, J., Metaxas, D.: MRI reconstruction via cascaded channel-wise attention network. In: 2019 IEEE 16th International Symposium on Biomedical Imaging (ISBI 2019), pp. 1622–1626 (2019)
7. Yuan, Z., et al.: SARA-GAN: self-attention and relative average discriminator based generative adversarial networks for fast compressed sensing MRI reconstruction. Front. Neuroinform. **14**, 611666 (2020)
8. Pramanik, A., Jacob, M.: Reconstruction and segmentation of parallel MR data using image domain Deep-SLR (2021)
9. Huang, Q., Yang, D., Yi, J., Axel, L., Metaxas, D.: FR-Net: joint reconstruction and segmentation in compressed sensing cardiac MRI. In: Coudière, Y., Ozenne, V., Vigmond, E., Zemzemi, N. (eds.) FIMH 2019. LNCS, vol. 11504, pp. 352–360. Springer, Cham (2019). https://doi.org/10.1007/978-3-030-21949-9_38

10. Chen, C., et al.: OCMR (v1.0)-open-access multi-coil k-space dataset for cardio-vascular magnetic resonance imaging (2020)
11. Ronneberger, O., Fischer, P., Brox, T.: U-Net: convolutional networks for biomedical image segmentation. In: Navab, N., Hornegger, J., Wells, W.M., Frangi, A.F. (eds.) MICCAI 2015. LNCS, vol. 9351, pp. 234–241. Springer, Cham (2015). https://doi.org/10.1007/978-3-319-24574-4_28
12. Schlemper, J., Caballero, J., Hajnal, J.V., Price, A.N., Rueckert, D.: A deep cascade of convolutional neural networks for dynamic MR image reconstruction. IEEE Trans. Med. Imaging **37**(2), 491–503 (2018)
13. Fan, T., Wang, G., Li, Y., Wang, H.: MA-NET: a multi-scale attention network for liver and tumor segmentation. IEEE Access **8**, 179656–179665 (2020)
14. Hu, J., Shen, L., Albanie, S., Sun, G., Wu, E.: Squeeze-and-excitation networks (2017)
15. He, K., Zhang, X., Ren, S., Sun, J.: Deep residual learning for image recognition (2015)
16. Amyar, A., Modzelewski, R., Li, H., Ruan, S.: Multi-task deep learning based CT imaging analysis for COVID-19 pneumonia: classification and segmentation. Comput. Biol. Med. **126**, 104037 (2020)
17. Sudre, C.H., Li, W., Vercauteren, T., Ourselin, S., Jorge Cardoso, M.: Generalised dice overlap as a deep learning loss function for highly unbalanced segmentations. In: Cardoso, M.J., et al. (eds.) DLMIA/ML-CDS -2017. LNCS, vol. 10553, pp. 240–248. Springer, Cham (2017). https://doi.org/10.1007/978-3-319-67558-9_28

MRI Reconstruction with Conditional Adversarial Transformers

Yilmaz Korkmaz[1,2(✉)], Muzaffer Özbey[1,2], and Tolga Cukur[1,2]

[1] Department of Electrical and Electronics Engineering, Bilkent University, Ankara, Turkey
[2] National Magnetic Resonance Research Center (UMRAM), Bilkent University, Ankara, Turkey
korkmaz@ee.bilkent.edu.tr

Abstract. Deep learning has been successfully adopted for accelerated MRI reconstruction given its exceptional performance in inverse problems. Deep reconstruction models are commonly based on convolutional neural network (CNN) architectures that use compact input-invariant filters to capture static local features in data. While this inductive bias allows efficient model training on relatively small datasets, it also limits sensitivity to long-range context and compromises generalization performance. Transformers are a promising alternative that use broad-scale and input-adaptive filtering to improve contextual sensitivity and generalization. Yet, existing transformer architectures induce quadratic complexity and they often neglect the physical signal model. Here, we introduce a model-based transformer architecture (MoTran) for high-performance MRI reconstruction. MoTran is an adversarial architecture that unrolls transformer and data-consistency blocks in its generator. Cross-attention transformers are leveraged to maintain linear complexity in terms of the feature map size. Comprehensive experiments on MRI reconstruction tasks show that the proposed model improves the image quality over state-of-the-art CNN models.

Keywords: MRI Reconstruction · Transformer · Generative · Attention

1 Introduction

Magnetic resonance imaging (MRI) is a non-invasive modality that can produce unparalleled tissue contrast. Yet, the slow data acquisition process in MRI reduces its applicability. Thus, reconstruction methods that recover high-quality images from accelerated scans with k-space undersampling are direly needed. In recent years, deep learning (DL) methods have enabled performance leaps in MRI reconstruction over traditional methods [1–3, 6, 10, 11, 13, 18, 19, 22, 23, 27, 28, 30, 33].

The majority of state-of-the-art reconstruction methods are based on convolutional neural network (CNN) backbones [2, 15, 19, 28, 29]. These CNN models are used to map undersampled data at input onto fully-sampled data at output.

N. Haq et al. (Eds.): MLMIR 2022, LNCS 13587, pp. 62–71, 2022.
https://doi.org/10.1007/978-3-031-17247-2_7

The mapping is achieved through a series of convolutional filters that have limited receptive fields. As such, CNNs extract local features in MR images, and so they are suboptimal in capturing long-range context over broad spatial distances. Transformer models have recently been introduced as a powerful alternative free from the inductive biases of CNNs [14, 20]. Promising results have readily been demonstrated in multiple medical imaging tasks including segmentation [4], synthesis [5], analysis [24–26], and reconstruction [7, 8, 17, 31, 32]. Although transformer models offer higher precision in detecting long-range interactions in MRI, they are also notoriously complex due to exhaustive self-attention and multi-layer perceptron calculations [8, 32]. Furthermore, many previous transformer-based methods for MRI reconstruction are purely data-driven, not giving consideration to the underlying physical signal model, so they may show suboptimal generalization performance [7].

Here we propose a model-based adversarial transformer (MoTran) for MRI reconstruction with enhanced computational efficiency and reconstruction performance. Unlike vanilla transformers, MoTran leverages cross-attention transformer blocks with cross-attention layers to replace self-attention and modulated convolution layers to replace fully-connected layers. As such, MoTran maintains linear complexity in terms of the image size unlike vanilla transformers with quadratic complexity. Cross-attention transformers implicitly characterize long-range interactions between a small set of learnable latent variables and image pixels. To incorporate the physical signal model, MoTran interleaves cross-attention transformer blocks with data-consistency blocks across its generator. Lastly, MoTran is trained adversarially for improved realism in MRI reconstructions. Experiments on brain MRI demonstrate that MoTran achieves higher image quality than state-of-the-art traditional and CNN-based methods.

2   Theory

2.1   Deep MRI Reconstruction

Accelerated MRI can be achieved via performing undersampled acquisitions in k-space:

$$F_k C m = y_s \tag{1}$$

where F_k is the partial Fourier operator, C denotes coil sensitivity, m is the MR image and y_s are acquired k-space data. Reconstruction of m from y_s is an underdetermined problem. Deep learning methods address this issue by incorporating a data-driven prior to regularize the solution:

$$\widehat{m} = \operatorname*{argmin}_m \frac{1}{2} \|y_s - F_k C m\|_2^2 + R(m) \tag{2}$$

where $\widehat{m}$ is the reconstruction, and $R(m)$ is the regularization term. Regularization is typically achieved by projecting acquired data through a CNN architecture in order to suppress aliasing artifacts.

2.2 Conditional Adversarial Transformers

Existing deep reconstruction methods are primarily based on CNN architectures. CNN backbones offer sensitivity to local features and relatively low model complexity [15,28,29], but they are poor in capturing long-range interactions among image pixels. While transformer backbones use self-attention operators to improve contextual sensitivity, they suffer from quadratic complexity [12], and many prior methods neglect the underlying physical signal model [7]. To address these limitations, here we propose a model-based transformer architecture, MoTran (Fig. 1). MoTran uses cross-attention transformers between latent variables and image features to capture long range dependencies with linear computational cost, and interleaves transformer and data-consistency blocks in its generator for compatibility with the physical model.

Network Architecture: MoTran is an adversarial network with a generator and a discriminator. The generator is composed of cross-attention transformer blocks interleaved with data-consistency blocks, as inspired by [2]. To avoid quadratic complexity of self-attention, MoTran employs cross-attention transformers where long-range interactions are characterized by attention between a small set of latent vectors (W) and image pixels [14]. The discriminator distinguishes actual MR images corresponding to fully-sampled acquisitions from predicted images from the generator. The discriminator is trained to minimize the least-square adversarial loss [21], while the generator minimizes a compound loss containing least-squared adversarial loss and pixel-wise $\mathcal{L}_1$ loss. The composition of the transformer and data-consistency blocks are detailed below.

A) Transformer Blocks: MoTran offers the contextual sensitivity of transformers while avoiding the quadratic computational burden. To do this, it leverages transformer blocks composed of convolution and cross-attention layers as opposed to fully-connected and self-attention layers in vanilla transformers. Each transformer block first starts with a modulated convolution layer. Let $X_{input}^i \in \mathbb{R}^{(h \times w) \times n}$ be the input feature map to the ith transformer block, where h and w the height and width of the image, and n denotes the number of feature channels. X_{input}^i is modulated with the affine-transformed global latent vector ($W_g \in \mathbb{R}^s$) via a modulated-convolution operation [16]. Assuming that the modulated-convolution kernel is given as h_G^i, this operation is expressed as:

$$X_{output}^i = \begin{bmatrix} \sum_m X_{input}^{i,m} \circledast h_G^{i,m,1} \\ \vdots \\ \sum_m X_{input}^{i,m} \circledast h_G^{i,m,v} \end{bmatrix} \tag{3}$$

where $h_G^{i,u,v} \in \mathbb{R}^{3 \times 3}$ is the convolution kernel for the uth input channel and v^{th} output channel, and m is the channel index.

Next, the cross-attention layer follows where cross-attention is calculated between local latent vectors ($W_l \in \mathbb{R}^{k \times s}$) and feature maps within the jth transformer block ($X^j \in \mathbb{R}^{h \times w \times n}$). Let $X_{2D}^j \in \mathbb{R}^{(h \times w) \times n}$ be the vectorized form of

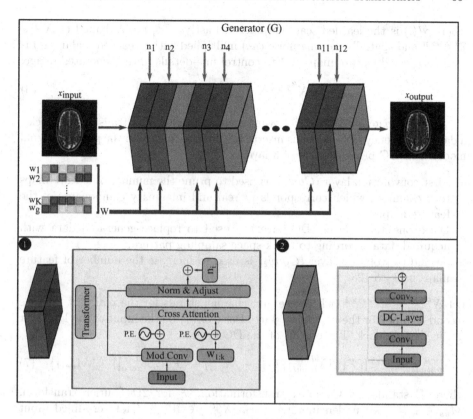

Fig. 1. MoTran is a model-based architecture that unrolls projections through cross-attention transformer blocks (blue, see 1) and data-consistency blocks (red, see 2). The generator is trained to map undersampled images (x_{input}) onto ground-truth images (x_{output}). It includes learnable latent (W) and noise (n) variables for controlling the statistics and fine details of feature maps. (Color figure online)

feature maps across the two spatial dimensions in the jth transformer block. Cross-attention maps $att^j \in \mathbb{R}^{(h \times w) \times k}$ between W_l and X_{2D}^j are computed as:

$$att^j = softmax\left(\frac{Q^j(X_{2D}^j + PE_x)K^j(W_l + PE_w)^T}{\sqrt{n}}\right)V^j(W_l) \qquad (4)$$

where $Q^j(.) \in \mathbb{R}^{(h \times w) \times n}$, $K^j(.) \in \mathbb{R}^{k \times n}$, $V^j(.) \in \mathbb{R}^{k \times n}$, $PE_x \in \mathbb{R}^{(w \times h) \times n}$, $PE_w \in \mathbb{R}^{k \times s}$ are queries, keys, values and positional encoding variables respectively. Next, X_{2D}^j is normalized and scaled with a learnable projection of attention maps att^j:

$$X_{2D}^{'j} = \gamma^j(att^j) \odot \left(\frac{X_{2D}^j - \mu(X_{2D}^j)}{\sigma(X_{2D}^j)}\right) \qquad (5)$$

where $\gamma^j(.)$ is the learned scale parameter. Lastly, $X_{2D}^{'j}$ are reshaped to $X^{'j} \in \mathbb{R}^{h \times w \times n}$ and spatially varying noise (n^j) multiplied with a learned scalar (α^j) is added to scaled feature maps $X^{'j}$ to control fine-details in the generated image:

$$X^{''j} = X^{'j} + (\alpha^j \times n^j) \tag{6}$$

B) Data-Consistency Blocks: Following a consecutive pair of transformer blocks, a data-consistency (DC) block is inserted to enforce fidelity to the physical signal model. The DC block consists of 3 layers:

- First convolution layer $(Conv_1)$ is used to prune the number of feature maps to 2 channels, which corresponds to real and imaginary components of the feature map.
- Data-consistency layer (DC-Layer) is used to replace generated data with acquired data according to the k-space sampling pattern.
- Second convolution layer $(Conv_2)$ is used to increase the number of feature maps back to 128.

Let $X_{input}^{dc,i} \in \mathbb{R}^{h \times w \times 2}$ (where the first channel stands for the real part and the second channel for the imaginary part after $Conv_1$) be the input of the DC layer in the ith DC block. The output of the DC layer is:

$$X_{output}^{dc,i} = \mathcal{F}^{-1}\{(\mathcal{F}\{\mathbb{C}[X_{input}^{dc,i}]\} \odot [1 - \mathcal{M}_{us}]) + (\mathcal{F}\{\mathbb{C}[X_{zero}^{dc,i}]\} \odot [\mathcal{M}_{us}])\} \tag{7}$$

where $\mathbb{C}$ stands for Complex transformation, $\mathcal{F}$ for 2D Fourier transform, $\mathcal{M}_{us} \in \mathbb{R}^{h \times w}$ for undersampling mask, $X_{zero}^{dc} \in \mathbb{R}^{h \times w \times 2}$ for zero-filled input image (X_{input} in Fig. 1), and $\mathcal{F}^{-1}$ for inverse 2D Fourier transform.

3   Methods

Datasets. Demonstrations were performed on a public brain MRI dataset, IXI (http://brain-development.org/). T_1- and T_2-weighted images of 40 subjects were analyzed (25 reserved for training, 5 for validation, 10 for testing). Variable-density random undersampling was implemented. The sampling density followed a two-dimensional (2D) normal distribution to achieve acceleration factors $R = 4,8$. Fully-sampled acquisitions in the dataset were retrospectively subsampled to obtain undersampled acquisitions.

Baselines. MoTran was compared against state-of-the-art traditional and CNN-based reconstruction methods.

1. **LORAKS:** A traditional method that regularizes the reconstructions via low-rank matrix approximation was considered [9].
2. **cGAN:** A conditional GAN method based on a CNN architecture was considered [6]. The cGAN method used adversarial and pixel-wise losses during model training as described in [6].

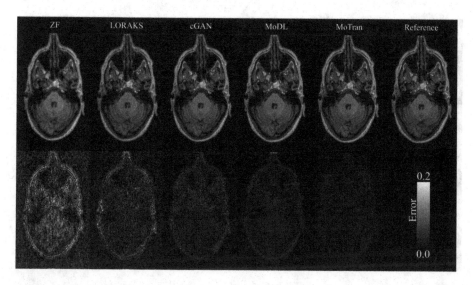

Fig. 2. Reconstructions of a T_1-weighted acquisition in IXI at $R = 4$. Results are shown along with the reference image and respective error maps.

3. **MoDL:** A model-based CNN method that interleaves convolutional and data-consistency blocks was considered [2]. The model architecture and loss functions were adopted for single-coil reconstruction by assuming unit coil sensitivities from [2].

Experiments. The proposed method and competing baselines were used to reconstruct undersampled acquisitions at $R = 4,8$. LORAKS is a scan-specific method that is directly applied on test data without a priori training. Learning-based methods were trained to map zero-filled Fourier transform of undersampled acquisitions onto the Fourier transform of fully-sampled acquisitions. For all methods, hyperparameter optimization was conducted to maximize peak signal-to-noise ratio (PSNR) performance on the validation set. Eventual model performance was assessed on the test set in terms of PSNR and structural similarity index (SSIM) between the reconstructed and ground-truth images.

4   Results

MoTran was compared against state-of-the-art traditional and deep-learning methods, including LORAKS, cGAN and MoDL. Quantitative performance metrics for $T_{1,2}$-weighted reconstructions at $R = 4$ and 8 are listed in Table 1. On average across reconstruction tasks, MoTran achieves 2.40 dB higher PSNR and % 1.13 higher SSIM than the second-best competing baseline.

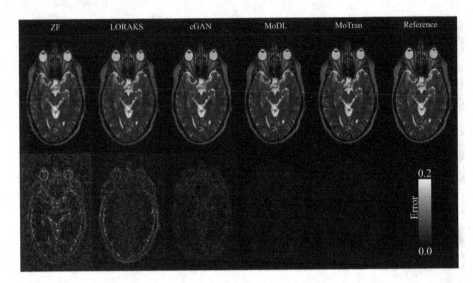

Fig. 3. Reconstructions of a T_2-weighted acquisition in IXI at $R = 4$. Results are shown along with the reference image and respective error maps.

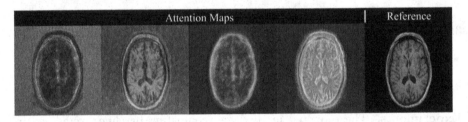

Fig. 4. Attention maps generated by the last transformer block in MoTran during reconstruction are illustrated along with the reference image. These maps show how the similar intensity pixels over distant areas of the image are coupled via cross-attention to be used in reconstruction.

Representative reconstructions via competing methods are displayed in Fig. 2 for T_1-weighted images and in Fig. 3 for T_2-weighted images. LORAKS suffers from noise amplification, and cGAN and MoDL have notable residual reconstruction artifacts. In contrast, MoTran maintains high visual acuity, with the highest overall similarity to the ground-truth images.

We also extracted attention maps in MoTran to diagnose the spatial interactions that it captures. Sample attention maps during the reconstruction of a cross-section are shown in Fig. 4. The attention maps are broadly distributed across the image, with focal attention regions carrying a semantically meaningful distribution of tissue with correlated signals.

Table 1. Reconstruction performance for T_1- and T_2-weighted acquisitions at $R = 4$ and 8.

	LORAKS		cGAN		MoDL		MoTran	
	PSNR	SSIM(%)	PSNR	SSIM(%)	PSNR	SSIM(%)	PSNR	SSIM(%)
T_1, $R = 4$	30.7 ± 1.2	91.7 ± 1.0	36.9 ± 0.5	97.7 ± 0.2	43.1 ± 0.6	98.1 ± 1.1	$\mathbf{45.9 \pm 0.8}$	$\mathbf{99.3 \pm 0.4}$
T_1, $R = 8$	26.8 ± 0.9	87.3 ± 1.1	32.5 ± 0.7	95.5 ± 0.3	36.6 ± 0.6	97.3 ± 0.8	$\mathbf{38.0 \pm 0.7}$	$\mathbf{98.5 \pm 0.3}$
T_2, $R = 4$	35.4 ± 0.5	92.3 ± 1.2	38.6 ± 0.5	96.7 ± 0.2	44.4 ± 0.6	98.2 ± 1.0	$\mathbf{47.8 \pm 0.8}$	$\mathbf{99.2 \pm 0.9}$
T_2, $R = 8$	31.4 ± 0.4	88.2 ± 1.3	34.8 ± 0.7	94.5 ± 0.3	38.4 ± 0.7	97.3 ± 0.8	$\mathbf{40.4 \pm 0.8}$	$\mathbf{98.4 \pm 0.7}$

Ablation Experiments

Ablation experiments were conducted to show the importance of the main elements in the cross-attention transformer blocks in MoTran. In particular, cross-attention layers were ablated from the transformer blocks to obtain a convolutional variant (w.o. Transformer), and learnable latents that control the modulation statistics of feature maps were ablated (w.o. Latent). Quantitative metrics listed in Table 2 clearly indicate that each element contributes significantly to reconstruction performance.

Table 2. Performance for MoTran and ablated variants in T_1- and T_2-weighted reconstruction at $R = 4$ and 8.

	w.o. Latent		w.o. Transformer		MoTran	
	PSNR	SSIM(%)	PSNR	SSIM(%)	PSNR	SSIM(%)
T_1, $R = 4$	44.9 ± 0.8	98.9 ± 0.6	42.1 ± 0.8	93.1 ± 2.3	$\mathbf{45.9 \pm 0.8}$	$\mathbf{99.3 \pm 0.4}$
T_1, $R = 8$	36.7 ± 0.7	98.1 ± 0.3	36.1 ± 0.7	80.7 ± 0.8	$\mathbf{38.0 \pm 0.7}$	$\mathbf{98.5 \pm 0.3}$
T_2, $R = 4$	47.4 ± 0.9	99.0 ± 1.0	43.0 ± 1.5	91.6 ± 4.1	$\mathbf{47.8 \pm 0.8}$	$\mathbf{99.2 \pm 0.9}$
T_2, $R = 8$	40.1 ± 0.8	98.3 ± 0.8	38.1 ± 0.8	96.5 ± 1.0	$\mathbf{40.4 \pm 0.8}$	$\mathbf{98.4 \pm 0.7}$

5   Discussion

Here, we proposed a model-based architecture with cross-attention transformers for MRI reconstruction. Cross-attention transformers enable capture of long-range dependencies in MR images without suffering from the quadratic complexity of vanilla self-attention transformers. Meanwhile, interleaved transformer and data-consistency blocks in the generator enable guidance from the physical signal model.

6   Conclusion

The proposed model-based transformer offers improved contextual sensitivity over CNNs, and enhanced computational efficiency over vanilla transformers. Therefore, MoTran is a promising candidate in high-performance and efficient MRI reconstruction.

References

1. Adler, J., Öktem, O.: Learned primal-dual reconstruction. IEEE Trans. Med. Imaging **37**(6), 1322–1332 (2018)
2. Aggarwal, H.K., Mani, M.P., Jacob, M.: MoDL: model-based deep learning architecture for inverse problems. IEEE Trans. Med. Imaging **38**(2), 394–405 (2019)
3. Bakker, T., Muckley, M., Romero-Soriano, A., Drozdzal, M., Pineda, L.: On learning adaptive acquisition policies for undersampled multi-coil MRI reconstruction. arXiv preprint arXiv:2203.16392 (2022)
4. Chen, J., et al.: TransUNet: Transformers make strong encoders for medical image segmentation. arXiv preprint arXiv:2102.04306 (2021)
5. Dalmaz, O., Yurt, M., Çukur, T.: ResViT: residual vision transformers for multimodal medical image synthesis. arXiv preprint arXiv:2106.16031 (2021)
6. Dar, S.U., Yurt, M., Shahdloo, M., Ildız, M.E., Tınaz, B., Çukur, T.: Prior-guided image reconstruction for accelerated multi-contrast MRI via generative adversarial networks. IEEE J. Sel. Topics Signal Process. **14**(6), 1072–1087 (2020)
7. Feng, C.M., Yan, Y., Chen, G., Fu, H., Xu, Y., Shao, L.: Accelerated multi-modal MR imaging with transformers. arXiv preprint arXiv:2106.14248 (2021)
8. Guo, P., Mei, Y., Zhou, J., Jiang, S., Patel, V.M.: ReconFormer: accelerated MRI reconstruction using recurrent transformer. arXiv preprint arXiv:2201.09376 (2022)
9. Haldar, J.P., Zhuo, J.: P-LORAKS: low-rank modeling of local k-space neighborhoods with parallel imaging data. Magn. Reson. Med. **75**(4), 1499–1514 (2016)
10. Hammernik, K., et al.: Learning a variational network for reconstruction of accelerated MRI data. Magn. Reson. Med. **79**(6), 3055–3071 (2017)
11. Hammernik, K., Pan, J., Rueckert, D., Küstner, T.: Motion-guided physics-based learning for cardiac MRI reconstruction. In: 2021 55th Asilomar Conference on Signals, Systems, and Computers, pp. 900–907. IEEE (2021)
12. Huang, J., et al.: Swin transformer for fast MRI. Neurocomputing **493**, 281–304 (2022)
13. Huang, W., et al.: Rethinking the optimization process for self-supervised model-driven MRI reconstruction. arXiv preprint arXiv:2203.09724 (2022)
14. Hudson, D.A., Zitnick, C.L.: Generative adversarial transformers. arXiv preprint arXiv:2103.01209 (2021)
15. Hyun, C.M., Kim, H.P., Lee, S.M., Lee, S., Seo, J.K.: Deep learning for undersampled MRI reconstruction. Phys. Med. Biol. **63**(13), 135007 (2018). https://doi.org/10.1088/1361-6560/aac71a
16. Karras, T., Laine, S., Aittala, M., Hellsten, J., Lehtinen, J., Aila, T.: Analyzing and improving the image quality of StyleGAN. In: Proceedings of the IEEE/CVF Conference on Computer Vision and Pattern Recognition (CVPR), pp. 8107–8116 (2020)
17. Korkmaz, Y., Dar, S.U., Yurt, M., Özbey, M., Cukur, T.: Unsupervised MRI reconstruction via zero-shot learned adversarial transformers. IEEE Trans. Med. Imaging (2022)
18. Kwon, K., Kim, D., Park, H.: A parallel MR imaging method using multilayer perceptron. Med. Phys. **44**(12), 6209–6224 (2017). https://doi.org/10.1002/mp.12600
19. Lee, D., Yoo, J., Tak, S., Ye, J.C.: Deep residual learning for accelerated MRI using magnitude and phase networks. IEEE Trans. Biomed. Eng. **65**(9), 1985–1995 (2018)

20. Liu, Z., et al.: Swin transformer: hierarchical vision transformer using shifted windows. In: Proceedings of the IEEE/CVF International Conference on Computer Vision, pp. 10012–10022 (2021)

21. Mao, X., Li, Q., Xie, H., Lau, R.Y.K., Wang, Z., Smolley, S.P.: Least squares generative adversarial networks. In: IEEE International Conference on Computer Vision, pp. 2813–2821 (2017). https://doi.org/10.1109/ICCV.2017.304

22. Mardani, M., et al.: Deep generative adversarial neural networks for compressive sensing MRI. IEEE Trans. Med. Imaging **38**(1), 167–179 (2019)

23. Narnhofer, D., Effland, A., Kobler, E., Hammernik, K., Knoll, F., Pock, T.: Bayesian uncertainty estimation of learned variational MRI reconstruction. IEEE Trans. Med. Imaging **41**(2), 279–291 (2021)

24. Niu, C., Wang, G.: Unsupervised contrastive learning based transformer for lung nodule detection. arXiv preprint arXiv:2205.00122 (2022)

25. Oh, Y., Bae, G.E., Kim, K.H., Yeo, M.K., Ye, J.C.: A hybrid 2-stage vision transformer for AI-assisted 5 class pathologic diagnosis of gastric endoscopic biopsies. arXiv preprint arXiv:2202.08510 (2022)

26. Park, S., Kim, G., Kim, J., Kim, B., Ye, J.C.: Federated split task-agnostic vision transformer for COVID-19 CXR diagnosis. Adv. Neural. Inf. Process. Syst. **34**, 24617–24630 (2021)

27. Schlemper, J., Caballero, J., Hajnal, J.V., Price, A., Rueckert, D.: A deep cascade of convolutional neural networks for MR image reconstruction. In: Niethammer, M., et al. (eds.) IPMI 2017. LNCS, vol. 10265, pp. 647–658. Springer, Cham (2017). https://doi.org/10.1007/978-3-319-59050-9_51

28. Wang, S., et al.: Accelerating magnetic resonance imaging via deep learning. In: IEEE 13th International Symposium on Biomedical Imaging (ISBI), pp. 514–517 (2016). https://doi.org/10.1109/ISBI.2016.7493320

29. Yoon, J., et al.: Quantitative susceptibility mapping using deep neural network: QSMnet. Neuroimage **179**, 199–206 (2018)

30. Yu, S., et al.: DAGAN: deep de-aliasing generative adversarial networks for fast compressed sensing MRI reconstruction. IEEE Trans. Med. Imaging **37**(6), 1310–1321 (2018)

31. Zhang, L.: Spatial adaptive and transformer fusion network (STFNet) for low-count pet blind denoising with MRI. Med. Phys. **49**(1), 343–356 (2022)

32. Zhou, B., et al.: DSFormer: a dual-domain self-supervised transformer for accelerated multi-contrast MRI reconstruction. arXiv preprint arXiv:2201.10776 (2022)

33. Zhu, B., Liu, J.Z., Rosen, B.R., Rosen, M.S.: Image reconstruction by domain transform manifold learning. Nature **555**(7697), 487–492 (2018)

Deep Learning for General Image Reconstruction

A Noise-Level-Aware Framework for PET Image Denoising

Ye Li[1]([✉]), Jianan Cui[2], Junyu Chen[3], Guodong Zeng[4], Scott Wollenweber[5], Floris Jansen[5], Se-In Jang[1], Kyungsang Kim[1], Kuang Gong[1], and Quanzheng Li[1]

[1] MGH/HMS, Boston, USA
gary.li@mgh.harvard.edu
[2] Massachusetts General Hospital, Boston, USA
[3] Johns Hopkins University, Baltimore, USA
[4] University of Bern, Bern, Switzerland
[5] GE Healthcare, Chicago, USA

Abstract. In PET, the amount of relative (signal-dependent) noise present in different body regions can be significantly different and is inherently related to the number of counts present in that region. The number of counts in a region depends, in principle and among other factors, on the total administered activity, scanner sensitivity, image acquisition duration, radiopharmaceutical tracer uptake in the region, and patient local body morphometry surrounding the region. In theory, less amount of denoising operations is needed to denoise a high-count (low relative noise) area than images a low-count (high relative noise) area, and vice versa. The current deep-learning-based methods for PET image denoising are predominantly trained on whole images using image appearance only and have not taken into account any prior knowledge about the spatially varying noise in PET. Our hypothesis is that by explicitly providing the relative noise level of each local area of a PET image to a deep convolutional neural network (DCNN), the DCNN learn noise-level-specific denoising features at different noise-levels and apply these features to areas with different denoising needs, thus outperforming the DCNN trained on whole images using image appearance only. To this end, we propose a noise-level-aware framework denoising framework that allows embedding of local noise level into a DCNN. The proposed is trained and tested on 30 and 15 patient PET images acquired on a GE Discovery MI PET/CT system. Our experiments showed that the increases in both PSNR and SSIM from our backbone network with relative noise level embedding (NLE) versus the same network without NLE were statistically significant with $p < 0.001$, and the proposed method significantly outperformed a strong baseline method by a large margin.

Keywords: Denoising · Local relative noise level · PET · Depp learning · Neural network

1 Introduction

In recent years, due to the fast development of deep convolutional neural networks (DCNN), we have witnessed rapid progress in DCNN-based PET image denoising, with

N. Haq et al. (Eds.): MLMIR 2022, LNCS 13587, pp. 75–83, 2022.
https://doi.org/10.1007/978-3-031-17247-2_8

the goal to reduce the patient's administered activity (AA) or shorten the image acquisition duration while maintaining sufficient diagnostic image quality. Many of these deep-learning-based methods for PET image denoising have achieved better performance than traditional image enhancement methods in recovering the PSNR and SSIM [1–10].

Depending on the radiotracer used and the pharmacokinetics, the activity uptake concentration can differ in different organs/parts of the same patient and other patients. These different radiotracer uptakes intrinsically lead to varying number of counts (coincidence events) being generated at different regions of the body. Besides the tracer uptakes being distributed differently within the patient body, the total amount of AA to the patient, the scan acquisition duration, the patient local body morphometry surrounding the region, and scanner sensitivity can also affect the number of counts received by the detector in that region. Together, these factors lead to very different noise levels in different areas of a patient's PET image and in images acquired for different patients, using different imaging protocols and on different scanners.

In sinogram domain, the amount of Poisson noise can be quantified by considering the coefficient of variation (COV), defined as the standard deviation divided by the mean, which describes the relative level of noise in a sinogram bin and is given by

$$COV = \frac{\sqrt{m}}{m} = \frac{1}{\sqrt{m}}, \tag{1}$$

which shows that Poisson noise, while growing in absolute terms with the signal, is relatively smaller at higher count levels. These different noise levels lead to drastically different appearances of the images. Furthermore, we observe that the ranking of the relative noise levels is likely correlated with the amount of denoising operations needed for each image pair shown in Fig. 1. Specifically, less amount of denoising is needed for images with high counts as compared to the images with low counts. However, most of the current DCNN-based PET denoising methods are trained on the whole image, consisting of a hodgepodge of noise levels, resulting in learned filters to contain a mix of features present in different noise levels.

In this paper, we propose a noise-level-aware denoising framework that embeds a surrogate for the local noise level of the input image to condition the network to perform a denoising operation for a specified noise level. Specifically, the embedded noise level features enable the network to learn a specific set of filters needed for such specified noise-level mapping (from a high to low level of noise), as opposed to learning all the noise-level mappings altogether only from image appearance. The proposed framework was evaluated on two denoising tasks (1/8 to full and 1/4 to full) using a real patient dataset consisted of 45 images acquired with three different tracers (FDG, Fluciclovine and DOTATATE). The results show that a backbone network with noise level embedding (NLE) can outperform (p < 0.001) the same network without NLE as measured by both the PSNR and SSIM.

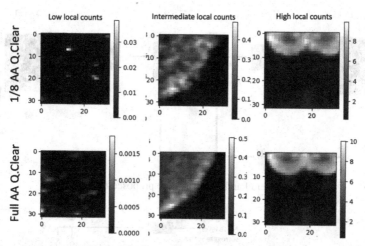

Fig. 1. Sample of coronal slices of patches cropped at three different regions of the same patient acquired with 1/8 AA and full AA. The images were reconstructed with GE's Q. Clear reconstruction algorithm and were normalized to SUV value by dividing (AA/weight). The scale bars indicate the range of counts present in each patch.

2 Noise-Level-Aware Framework

As illustrated in Fig. 2, a surrogate scalar for the local relative noise level is embedded into a backbone denoising network to modulate the network for different denoising needs for input images with different relative noise levels. For the backbone network, we adopted the original resolution subnetwork (ORSNet) from the MPRNet [11]. The ORSNet does not employ any downsampling operation and generates spatially-enriched high-resolution features. The ORSNet consists of multiple original-resolution-blocks. Each of the ORB blocks further contains a channel-attenuation-block (CAB). A noise level embedding (NLE) layer is proposed to encode the noise level scalar to the CAB. The encoded feature vector is fed to multiple CABs to condition the importance of the feature maps on the relative noise level of the input image. The conditioning is done by first multiplying the feature vector obtained from an adaptive max pooling layer with the first half of feature vector from the NLE layer and then add the resulting feature vector with the second half of feature vector from the NLE layer.

The schematic of the proposed NLE layer and CAB block with noise level embedding are illustrated in Fig 3(a) and (b), respectively.

2.1 Quantification of Local Relative Noise Level

In Fig. 1, we showed that images of different relative noise levels have very different appearances. This indicates that the filters learned from these images, if trained together with one network, may contain a mix of features present in these images, e.g., a feature that is present in images of one relative noise level can be learned together with a feature present in the images of another relative noise level. This would, in theory, lead to features learned images from a different relative noise level to emerge in one image. In attempt

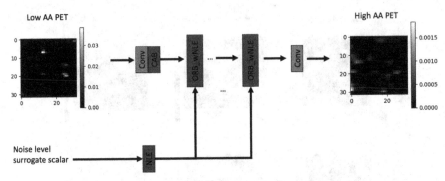

Fig. 2. Overall architecture of the proposed framework

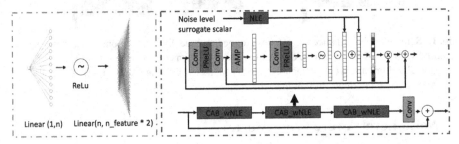

Fig. 3. The detailed architecture of the noise level embedding (NLE) block and modified channel attention block with NLE

to solve this issue, we propose to split the image patches into groups that have similar appearances as categorized by the patches' relative noise level and its background. We hypothesize that the noise level embedding conditioned on each convolutional layer would help the network represent the importance of each feature map more accurately according to the input image's relative noise level, providing an extra aid to the DCNN in addition to its learning solely based on the image appearance.

In theory, the noise in each patch can be quantified by the patch count density [12], i.e., the number of detected coincidence pairs emitted from the objects contained in the patch divided by the volume of the objects. However, we did not have access to sinogram data of this dataset so we used the reconstructed image for this calculation as a surrogate. Specifically, we applied Otsu's segmentation [13] on each patch, followed by computing the patch count density within the resulting 3D mask. The patch count density was then used to quantify the relative noise level present in each patch using Eq. 1.

The patches were grouped into bins that fall in a range of relative noise levels. The ensembles of patches in these bins were expected to have similar noise level and image appearance. We used 4 bins with widths determined by visual inspection of the patches. The bins represent four types of patches: (1) high relative noise with clean background, (2) low relative noise with clean background, (3) high relative noise with lumpy background, and (4) low relative noise with lumpy background (Fig. 4).

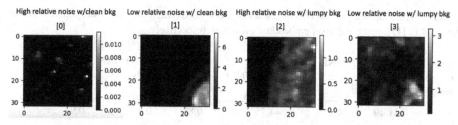

Fig. 4. Samples of patches that have different relative noise levels and image appearances.

3 Experiments

3.1 Experimental Setup

Datasets. A multi-tracer PET/CT dataset containing 45 patients was used to evaluate the proposed method. The dataset was split into a train and test dataset of 30 and 15 images, respectively. The range of administered activity of the dataset is 372 to 559 MBq. All patients were scanned with a GE Discovery MI 5-ring PET/CT system. 1/8 AA images were generated using listmode data of the full AA image. The random scatter correctors were generated based on the downsampled listmode data. PET images (matrix size: 352 × 224 × 128; voxel dimension: 2.8 × 2.734 × 2.734 2 mm^3) were reconstructed using GE's Q. Clear iterative reconstruction algorithm with beta of 750 for the full AA images and beta of 550 for the 1/8 AA images. Both the 1/8 AA and full AA images were normalized to the standard uptake value (SUV) by dividing the corresponding AA over the patient's weight.

3.2 Implementation Details

The proposed framework is end-to-end trainable and requires no pre-training. The network was trained on 32 × 32 × 32 patches with a batch size of 16 for 100 iterations. For data augmentation, horizontal and vertical flips are randomly applied. We used Adam [14] optimizer with initial learning rate of 1×10^{-5}, which is steadily decreased to 1×10^{-6} using the cosine annealing strategy [15].

3.3 Results and Analysis

Ablation Study. To examine the contribution of the NLE module, we conducted an ablation study using the same backbone network with and without NLE. The same train and test dataset was used to train and test these two networks. For the backbone network, we used the ORN as described in Sect. 2. With the aid from the relative noise level embedding conditioned on each convolution operation, we expect that the feature maps to be modulated for the corresponding relative noise level of the image. This will enable the filters of the next convolutional layer to learn appropriate features (i.e., scattered points, sharp edges, and bright spots in lumpy background, etc.) for the images of that relative noise level (Table 1).

Table 1. Ablation study on the 1/8 AA test dataset. ORN and NLE represent the original resolution network in [11], and noise level embedding proposed, respectively.

Test image number	PSNR (input)	PSNR ORN only	PSNR ORNw/NLE	SSIM (input)	SSIM ORN only	SSIM ORNw/NLE
59	41.49	44.17	44.75	0.88	0.93	0.93
66	43.67	46.03	46.6	0.89	0.94	0.94
67	43.93	45.9	46.05	0.88	0.93	0.93
68	52.79	54.68	54.83	0.9	0.95	0.95
69	53.64	54.8	55.06	0.93	0.96	0.96
70	40.44	43.53	43.79	0.9	0.94	0.95
71	42.62	44.95	45.46	0.87	0.93	0.93
72	57.62	58.45	58.92	0.92	0.95	0.96
73	57.61	59.44	59.69	0.89	0.94	0.94
74	47.43	48.67	48.89	0.88	0.93	0.93
77	49.8	51.4	51.95	0.93	0.96	0.96
78	53.52	55.91	56.01	0.9	0.94	0.95
80	55.9	56.64	57.15	0.91	0.95	0.95
81	41.36	44.84	45.05	0.85	0.92	0.93
84	42.38	45.12	45.18	0.87	0.92	0.93
Mean	48.28	50.302	50.625	0.893	0.939	0.943

A paired t-test was conducted to verify the statistical significance of the performance gain of the proposed method (ORN w/ NLE) versus ORN only. The p-values were $9.7e-6$ and $9.6e-3$ for PSNR and SSIM, respectively. To visualize the performance gain from the NLE module, we show a few inferenced patches from the ORN network trained with and without the NLE module. We observed that the improvements are more significant for patches of high and intermediate relative noise levels than those of low relative noise levels. This observation agrees with our hypothesis that patches of low relative noise level (high counts) needs less amount of denoising operations. The PSNR and SSIM improvements are likely attributed to the NLE module's ability to recover the noise-level-specific details shown in Fig. 5. Specifically, the noise-level-specific details missed by the backbone network are highlighted in the red circle and those recovered with addition of the NLE module are highlighted in the green circle.

Comparison with State-of-the-Art. We compared the proposed method with a state-of-the-art image denoising method (MPRNet). To make the comparison fair, we modified the original 2D MRPNet to a 3D network. Furthermore, we adopted a strong baseline method as described in [4], which has been shown to outperform several reference methods commonly used in PET image denoising such as the Gaussian, NLM, BM4D, and Deep Decoder.

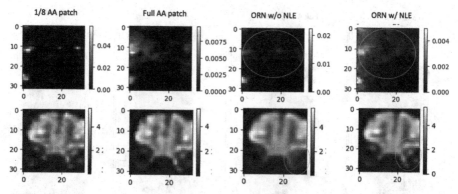

Fig. 5. Qualitative comparisons of sample testing slices with and without NLE. From left to right, 1/8 AA patch (input), Full AA patch (ground truth), predicted image without and with NLE. The scale bars indicate the ranges of voxel values present in the patches. Note that, as shown in the scale bars, the top row and bottom row show a high and low relative noise level sample, respectively. (Color figure online)

Figure 6 summarizes the quantitative performance gains of the baseline, SOTA method and the proposed method. In addition, we quantified the performance gain by ΔPSNR and ΔSSIM between the proposed and baseline (organ) method. The results show that the 95% CI of the ΔPSNR and ΔSSIM between the proposed and baseline method, are [1.04, 2.26], [0.015, 0.025] and [0.916, 2.180] [0.009, 0.019], for the 1/8- and 1/4-full AA denoising task, respectively, under the assumption that the ΔPSNR and ΔSSIM were normally distributed. Figure 7 shows sample images generated using the baseline and proposed method.

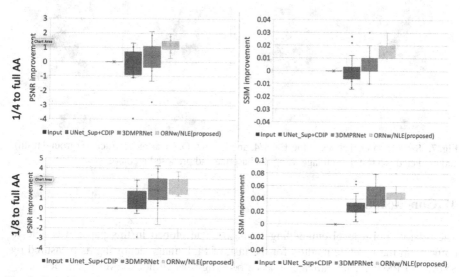

Fig. 6. Box plot of PSNR and SSIM improvement of the baseline method, 3DMPRNet, and proposed method.

1/8 Q.Clear	Full AA Q.Clear	Baseline	Proposed

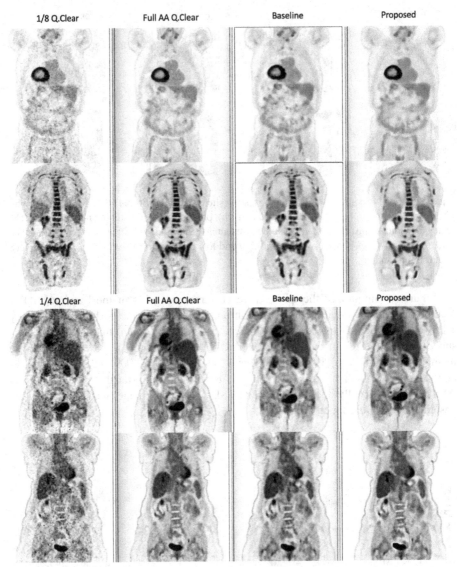

Fig. 7. Sample coronal slices of the 1/8, 1/4, and full AA Q. Clear reconstruction (ground truth), and predicted (on test data) image using the baseline and proposed method.

4 Conclusion

The relative noise level embedding framework developed in this paper was able to outperform the baseline method for the task of PET image denoising as measured by SSIM and PSNR. This indicates that embedding relative noise level into a denoising network may help assist the network in recognizing and subsequently processing patterns that are specific to a pre-specified relative noise level. The proposed framework could be readily adapted to perform denoising task for other nuclear medicine imaging modality such as SPECT.

References

1. Gong, K., et al.: PET image denoising using a deep neural network through fine tuning. IEEE Trans. Radiat. Plasma Med. Sci. **3**(2), 153–161 (2019)
2. Dutta, J., Leahy, R.M., Li, Q.: Non-local means denoising of dynamic PET images. PLoS ONE **8**(12), e81390 (2013)
3. Chan, C., et al.: Postreconstruction nonlocal means filtering of whole-body PET with an anatomical prior. IEEE Trans. Med. Imaging **33**(3), 636–650 (2014)
4. Cui, J., et al.: PET image denoising using unsupervised deep learning. Eur. J. Nucl. Med. Mol. Imaging **46**(13), 2780–2789 (2019). https://doi.org/10.1007/s00259-019-04468-4
5. Ouyang, J.H., et al.: Ultra-low-dose PET reconstruction using generative adversarial network with feature matching and task-specific perceptual loss. Med. Phys. **46**(8), 3555–3564 (2019)
6. Cui, J.A., et al.: Populational and individual information based PET image denoising using conditional unsupervised learning. Phys. Med. Biol. **66**(15) (2021)
7. Zhou, L., et al.: Supervised learning with cyclegan for low-dose FDG PET image denoising. Med. Image Anal. **65** (2020)
8. Zhou, B., et al.: MDPET: a unified motion correction and denoising adversarial network for low-dose gated PET. IEEE Trans. Med. Imaging **40**(11), 3154–3164 (2021)
9. Song, T.A., Yang, F., Dutta, J.: Noise2Void: unsupervised denoising of PET images. Phys. Med. Biol. **66**(21) (2021)
10. Onishi, Y., et al., Anatomical-guided attention enhances unsupervised PET image denoising performance. Med. Image Anal. **74** (2021)
11. Zamir, S.W., et al.: Multi-Stage Progressive Image Restoration. in CVPR (2021)
12. Li, Y., et al.: A projection image database to investigate factors affecting image quality in weight-based dosing: application to pediatric renal SPECT. Phys. Med. Biol. **63**(14), 145004 (2018)
13. Otsu, N.: A Threshold Selection Method from Gray-Level Histograms. IEEE Trans. Syst. Man Cybern. **9**(1) (1979)
14. Ba, J., Kingma, D.P.: Adam: a method for stochastic optimization. arXiv:1412.6980 (2014)
15. Hutter, F., Loshchilov, I.: SGDR: Stochastic gradient descent with warm restarts, in ICLR (2017)

DuDoTrans: Dual-Domain Transformer for Sparse-View CT Reconstruction

Ce Wang[1,2], Kun Shang[3], Haimiao Zhang[4], Qian Li[1,2], and S. Kevin Zhou[1,5(✉)]

[1] Key Lab of Intelligent Information Processing of Chinese Academy of Sciences
(CAS), Institute of Computing Technology, CAS, Beijing, China
[2] Suzhou Institute of Intelligent Computing Technology,
Chinese Academy of Sciences, Suzhou, China
[3] Research Center for Medical AI, Shenzhen Institutes of Advanced Technology,
Chinese Academy of Sciences, Shenzhen, China
[4] Institute of Applied Mathematics, Beijing Information Science and Technology
University, Beijing, China
[5] Medical Imaging, Robotics, and Analytic Computing Laboratory and Engineering
(MIRACLE) Center, School of Biomedical Engineering and Suzhou Institute for
Advanced Research, University of Science and Technology of China, Suzhou, China
skevinzhou@ustc.edu.cn

Abstract. While Computed Tomography (CT) is necessary for clinical diagnosis, ionizing radiation in the imaging process induces irreversible injury, thereby driving researchers to study sparse-view CT reconstruction. Iterative models are proposed to alleviate the appeared artifacts in sparse-view CT images, but their computational cost is expensive. Deep-learning-based methods have gained prevalence due to the excellent reconstruction performances and computation efficiency. However, these methods ignore the mismatch between the CNN's **local** feature extraction capability and the sinogram's **global** characteristics. To overcome the problem, we propose **Dual-Domain Transformer (DuDoTrans)** to simultaneously restore informative sinograms via the long-range dependency modeling capability of Transformer and reconstruct CT image with both the enhanced and raw sinograms. With such a novel design, DuDoTrans even with fewer involved parameters is more effective and generalizes better than competing methods, which is confirmed by reconstruction performances on the NIH-AAPM and COVID-19 datasets. Finally, experiments also demonstrate its robustness to noise.

Keywords: CT Reconstruction · Sparse view · Sinogram restoration

1 Introduction and Motivation

Computed Tomography (CT) is a widely used clinically diagnostic imaging procedure aiming to reconstruct a clean CT image $\mathbf{X}$ from observed sinograms $\mathbf{Y}$, but its accompanying radiation heavily limits its practical usage. To decrease the induced radiation dose and reduce the scanning time, Sparse-View (SV)

N. Haq et al. (Eds.): MLMIR 2022, LNCS 13587, pp. 84–94, 2022.
https://doi.org/10.1007/978-3-031-17247-2_9

CT is commonly applied. However, the deficiency of sinograms brings severe artifacts in the reconstructed images, especially when common methods such as analytical Filtered Backprojection (FBP) and algebraic reconstruction technique (ART) [21] are used, which poses a significant challenge to image reconstruction.

To tackle the artifacts, iterative methods are proposed to impose the well-designed prior knowledge (ideal image properties) via additional regularization terms $R(\mathbf{X})$, such as Total Variation (TV) based methods [19,22], Nonlocal-based methods [29], and sparsity-based methods [2,14]. Although these models have achieved better qualitative and quantitative performances, they suffer from over-smoothness. Besides, the iterative optimization procedure is often computationally expensive and requires careful case-by-case hyperparameter tuning, which is practically less applicable.

With the success of CNNs in various vision tasks [12,26,35,36], CNN-based models are carefully designed and exhibit potential to a fast and efficient CT image reconstruction [1,6–8,10,11,13,27]. These methods render the potential to learn a better mapping between low-quality images, such as reconstructed results of FBP, and ground-truth images. Recently, Vision Transformer [4,5,9,16] has gained attention with its long-range dependency modeling capability, and numerous models have been proposed in medical image analysis [3,5,28,30,34]. Especifically, TransCT [31] is proposed as an efficient method for low-dose CT reconstruction, while it suffers from memory limitation with involved patch-based operations. Besides, these involved deep learning-based methods ignore the informative sinograms, which makes their reconstruction inconsistent with the observed sinograms.

To alleviate the problem, various dual-domain (DuDo) reconstruction models [17,23,32,33] are proposed to simultaneously enhance raw sinograms and reconstruct CT images with both enhanced and raw sinograms, experimentally showing that enhanced sinograms contribute to the latter reconstruction. Although these methods have shown satisfactory performances, **they neglect the global nature of the sinogram's sampling process** as in Fig. 1, which is inherently difficult to be captured by CNNs that are known for extracting local spatial features. This motivates us to go a step further and design a more suitable architecture for sinogram restoration.

Inspired by the long-range dependency modeling capability & shifted window self-attention mechanism of Swin Transformer [18], we specifically design the Sinogram Restoration Transformer (SRT) by considering the time-dependent characteristics of sinograms, which restores informative sinograms and overcome the mismatch between the global characteristics of sinograms and local feature modeling of CNNs. Based on the SRT module, we finally propose **Dual-Domain Transformer (DuDoTrans)** to reconstruct CT image. Compared with previous reconstruction methods, we summarize several benefits of DuDoTrans as follows:

- Considering the global sampling process of sinograms, we introduce the SRT module, which has the advantages of both Swin-Transformer and CNNs. It has the desired long-range dependency modeling ability, which helps better restore the sinograms and has been experimentally verified in CNN-based, Transformer-based, and deep-unrolling-based reconstruction framework.

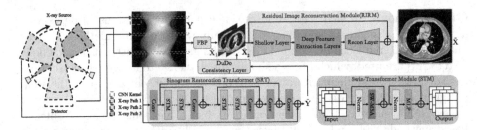

Fig. 1. The left part depicts the global nature of the sinogram's sampling process, which shows that any two sampled projections have overlap information of the patient even they are distant in the resulted sinogram. The global nature is hard to be modeled by a local CNN kernel and motivates the design of DuDuTrans. The right part shows the framework of DuDoTrans for CT image reconstruction. When under-sampled sinograms are given, our DuDoTrans first restores clean sinograms with SRT, followed by RIRM to reconstruct the CT image with both restored and raw sinograms.

- With the powerful SRT module for sinogram restoration, we further propose Residual Image Reconstruction Module (RIRM) for image-domain reconstruction. To compensate for the drift error between the dual-domain optimization directions, we utilize the differentiable DuDo Consistency Layer to keep dual-domain consistency and propose the final DuDoTrans.
- Reconstruction performances on the NIH-AAPM and COVID-19 datasets experimentally confirm the effectiveness, robustness, and generalizability of the proposed method. Besides, by adaptively employing Swin-Transformer and CNNs, our DuDoTrans has achieved better performance with fewer parameters and similar FLOPs, making the model practical useful.

2   Method

In this section, we introduce details of our method as in Fig. 1. Specifically, we build DuDoTrans with three modules: (a) Sinogram Restoration Transformer (SRT), (b) DuDo Consistency Layer, and (c) Residual Image Reconstruction Module (RIRM). Assume that a sparse-view sinogram $\mathbf{Y} \in \mathcal{R}^{H_s \times W_s}$ is given, we first use FBP [21] to reconstruct a low-quality CT image $\tilde{\mathbf{X}}_1$. Simultaneously, the SRT module is introduced to output an enhanced sinogram $\tilde{\mathbf{Y}}$, followed by the DuDo Consistency Layer to yield another estimation $\tilde{\mathbf{X}}_2$. At last, these low-quality images $\tilde{\mathbf{X}}_1$ and $\tilde{\mathbf{X}}_2$ are concatenated and fed into RIRM to predict the CT image $\tilde{\mathbf{X}}$. We next introduce the above-involved modules in detail.

2.1   Network Architecture

Sinogram Restoration Transformer. Sinogram restoration is extremely challenging since the intrinsic information not only contains spatial structures of human bodies, but follows the global sampling process. Specifically, each line

$\{\mathbf{Y}_i\}_{i=1}^{H_s}$ of a sinogram $\mathbf{Y}$ are sequentially sampled with overlapping information of surrounding sinograms. In other words, 1-D components of sinograms
heavily correlate with each other. The global characteristic makes it difficult
to be captured with traditional CNNs, which are powerful in local feature
extraction. For this reason, we equip this module with the Swin-Transformer
structure, which enables it with long-range dependency modeling ability. As
shown in Fig. 1, SRT consists of m successive residual blocks, and each block
contains n normal Swin-Transformer Module (STM) and a spatial convolutional layer, which have the capacity of both global and local feature extraction. Given the degraded sinograms, we first use a convolutional layer to
extract the spatial structure $\mathbf{F}_{conv}$. Considering it as $\mathbf{F}_{STM_0}$, then m STM
components of each residual block output $\{\mathbf{F}_{STM_i}\}_{i=1}^{m}$ with the formulation:
$\mathbf{F}_{STM_i} = M_{conv}(\prod_{j=1}^{n} M_{swin}^j(\mathbf{F}_{STM_{i-1}})) + \mathbf{F}_{STM_{i-1}}$, where M_{conv} denotes a
convolutional layer, $\{M_{swin}^j\}_{j=1}^{n}$ denotes n Swin-Transformer layers, and $\prod$ rep-
resents the successive Swin-Transformer Layers. Finally, the enhanced sinograms
are estimated with: $\tilde{\mathbf{Y}} = \mathbf{Y} + M_{conv}(M_{conv}(\mathbf{F}_{STM_m}) + \mathbf{F}_{STM_0})$. As a restoration
block, $\mathcal{L}_{SRT}$ is used to supervise the output of the SRT:

$$\mathcal{L}_{SRT} = \|\tilde{\mathbf{Y}} - \mathbf{Y}_{gt}\|_2, \tag{1}$$

where $\mathbf{Y}_{gt}$ is the ground truth sinogram, and it should be given when training.

DuDo Consistency Layer. Although input sinograms have been enhanced via
the SRT module, directly learning from the concatenation of $\tilde{\mathbf{X}}_1$ and $\tilde{\mathbf{X}}_2$ leaves
a drift between the optimization directions of SRT and RIRM. To compensate
for the drift, we make use of a differentiable DuDo Consistency Layer M_{DC} to
back-propagate the gradients of RIRM. Specifically, given the input fan-beam
sinogram $\tilde{\mathbf{Y}}$, the DuDo Consistency Layer first converts it into parallel-beam
geometry, followed with Filtered Backprojection: $\tilde{\mathbf{X}}_2 = M_{DC}(\tilde{\mathbf{Y}})$. To additionally keep the restored sinograms consistent with the ground-truth CT image
$\mathbf{X}_{gt}$, $\mathcal{L}_{DC}$ is proposed as follows:

$$\mathcal{L}_{DC} = \|\tilde{\mathbf{X}}_2 - \mathbf{X}_{gt}\|_2. \tag{2}$$

Residual Image Reconstruction Module. As a long-standing clinical problem, the final goal of CT image reconstruction is to recover a high-quality CT
image for diagnosis. With the initially estimated low-quality images that help
rectify the geometric deviation between the sinogram and image domains, we
next employ Shallow Layer M_{sl} to obtain shallow features of input low-quality
images $\tilde{\mathbf{X}}$: $\mathbf{F}_{sl} = M_{sl}([\tilde{\mathbf{X}}_1, \tilde{\mathbf{X}}_2])$. Then a series of Deep Feature Extraction Layers $\{M_{df}^i\}_{i=1}^{n}$ are introduced to extract deep features: $\mathbf{F}_{df}^i = M_{df}^i(\mathbf{F}_{df}^{i-1})$, $i =
1, 2, \ldots, n$, where $\mathbf{F}_{df}^0 = \mathbf{F}_{sl}$. Finally, we utilize a Recon Layer M_{re} to predict
the clean CT image with residual learning: $\tilde{\mathbf{X}} = M_{re}(\mathbf{F}_{df}^n) + \tilde{\mathbf{X}}_1$. To supervise
our network optimization, the below $\mathcal{L}_{RIRM}$ loss is used for this module:

$$\mathcal{L}_{RIRM} = \|\tilde{\mathbf{X}} - \mathbf{X}_{gt}\|_2. \tag{3}$$

Table 1. Performances of models w/ v.s. w/o SRT module. Obviously, SRT improves performances of CNN-based, Transformer-based, and deep-unrolling-based methods.

	Method	PSNR	SSIM
w/o SRT	FBPConvNet [13]	31.47	.8878
	PDNet [1]	31.62	.8894
	ImgTrans	32.50	.9010
w/ SRT	**FBPConvNet+SRT**	**32.13**	**.8989**
	PDNet+SRT	**32.38**	**.9045**
	DuDoTrans	**32.68**	**.9047**

The full objective of our model is:

$$\mathcal{L} = \mathcal{L}_{SRT} + \lambda_1 \mathcal{L}_{DC} + \lambda_2 \mathcal{L}_{RIRM}, \tag{4}$$

where λ_1 and λ_2 are blending coefficients, which are both empirically set as 1 in experiments. Note that the intermediate convolutional layers are used to communicate between image space $\mathcal{R}^{H_I \times W_I}$ and patch-based feature space $\mathcal{R}^{\frac{H_I}{w} \times \frac{W_I}{w} \times w^2}$. Further, by dynamically tuning the depth m and width n, SRT modules are flexible in practice depending on the balance between memory and performance.

3   Experimental Results

Datasets. We first train and test our model with the "NIH-AAPM-Mayo Clinic Low Dose CT Grand Challenge" [20] dataset. Specifically, we choose a total of 1746 slices (512×512) from five patients to train our models, and use 314 slices of another patient for testing. We employ a scanning geometry of Fan-Beam X-Ray source with 800 detector elements. There are four SV scenarios, corresponding to $\alpha_{max} = [24]$ views uniformly distributed around the patient. To simulate the photon noise numerically, we add mixed noise that is by default composed of 5% Gaussian noise and Poisson noise with an intensity of $5e^6$.

Implementation Details and Training Settings. Our models are implemented using the PyTorch framework. We use the Adam optimizer [15] with $(\beta_1, \beta_2) = (0.9, 0.999)$ to train these models. The learning rate starts from 0.0001. Models are all trained on a Nvidia 3090 GPU card for 100 epochs with a batch size of 1.

Evaluation Metrics. Reconstructed CT images are quantitatively measured by the multi-scale SSIM [24,25] and PSNR.

3.1   Ablation Study and Analysis

We first verify the effectiveness of our SRT module and exhaust the best structure for DuDoTrans, followed by analysis. Concretely, we conduct the experiments with the six models: (a) FBPConvNet [13], (b) PDNet [1], (c) ImgTrans, replacing the

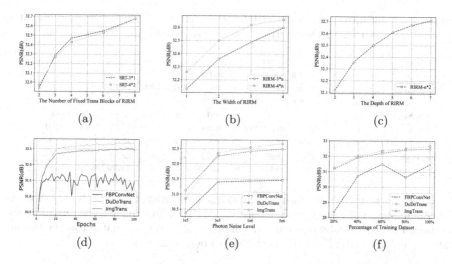

Fig. 2. The first row searches the suitable architecture, and the second row inspects the convergence, robustness on noise, and the effect of training dataset scale on DuDoTrans.

U-Net architecture in (a) with Swin-Transformer [18], (d) FBPConvNet+SRT, (e) PDNet+SRT, and (f) our DuDoTrans. The latter three models are modified versions of (a)–(c) with the proposed SRT module. The experimental settings are by default with $\alpha_{max} = 96$, and the results are shown in Table 1.

The Effectiveness of SRT. Comparing models (a)–(c) versus the corresponding version (d)–(f) in Table 1, the performances are all improved, which confirms that the SRT module output $\tilde{\mathbf{Y}}$ indeed provides useful information for the image-domain reconstruction no matter when the image domain reconstruction architecture is CNN, Transformer or deep-unrolling design.

RIRM and SRT Architecture. Comparing (a) and (c), the achieved 1 dB improvement confirms that the Transformer helps characterize deep features of images, and we therefore equip it as RIRM in DuDoTrans. Then we investigate each sub-module architecture in detail: we first explore the most suitable architecture for the SRT module (depth n and width m are introduced in Sect. 2.1). Specifically, with fixed RIRM structure, we increase (m, n) from $(3, 1)$ to $(4, 2)$, the performance is not influenced as in Fig 2 (a). Therefore, we set SRT depth and width to $(3, 1)$ as default. Similarly, Fig 2 (b–c) shows the corresponding effects of the RIRM width and RIRM depth on the performance. After balancing the computational cost and performance, we set RIRM width and depth to $(4, 2)$.

Convergence, Robustness, and Training Dataset Scale. Next, we first plot the convergence curve of FBPConvNet, ImgTrans, and DuDoTrans in Fig. 2 (d), and the Transformer structure indeed stabilizes the training process. Then we use different Poisson noise levels $[1e^5, 5e^5, 1e^6, 5e^6]$ to test the robustness of these three models, and DuDoTrans still performs the best, except when noise level is $1e^5$, which noise is extremely hard to be suppressed for all three models.

Table 2. Quantitative results on NIH-AAPM dataset. Our DuDoTrans consistently achieves the best results. The inferring time is tested when α_{max} is fixed as 96.

NIH-AAPM	Param(M)	$\alpha_{max} = 24$		$\alpha_{max} = 72$		$\alpha_{max} = 96$		$\alpha_{max} = 144$		Time(ms)
		PSNR	SSIM	PSNR	SSIM	PSNR	SSIM	PSNR	SSIM	
FBP [21]	–	14.58	.2965	17.61	.5085	18.13	.5731	18.70	.6668	–
FBPCovNet [13]	13.39	27.10	.8158	30.80	.8671	31.47	.8878	32.74	.9084	155.53
DuDoNet [17]	25.80	26.47	.7977	30.94	.8816	31.57	.8920	32.96	.9106	145.65
PDNet [1]	0.25	26.86	.8291	30.83	.8788	31.62	.8894	32.76	.9061	129.01
PDNet+SRT	0.66	26.85	.8363	31.69	.8940	32.38	.9045	33.44	.9188	280.32
ImgTrans	0.22	27.46	.8405	31.76	.8899	32.50	.9010	33.50	.9157	225.56
DuDoTrans	0.44	27.55	.8431	31.91	.8936	32.68	.9047	33.70	.9191	243.81

Table 3. We test the robustness of DuDoTrans and compared models with a more difficult Poisson noise level (with intensity $1e^6$ (H1)), and DuDoTrans almost keeps the best. For generalizability, we use the unobserved COVID-19 dataset as the testing dataset, and our DuDoTrans still performs the best in all cases.

Noise-H1	$\alpha_{max} = 24$		$\alpha_{max} = 72$		$\alpha_{max} = 96$		$\alpha_{max} = 144$		Time(ms)
	PSNR	SSIM	PSNR	SSIM	PSNR	SSIM	PSNR	SSIM	
FBP [21]	14.45	.2815	17.52	.4898	18.04	.5541	18.63	.6483	–
FBPCovNet [13]	27.12	.8171	30.74	.8798	31.44	.8874	32.65	.9070	148.58
DuDoNet [17]	26.40	.7932	30.84	.8792	31.47	.8900	32.87	.9090	146.36
PDNet [1]	26.82	.8274	30.69	.8779	31.53	.8876	32.64	.9040	122.04
PDNet+SRT	26.83	.8356	31.58	.8919	32.24	.9014	33.20	.9143	289.24
ImgTrans	27.35	.8395	31.65	.8882	32.42	.8993	33.36	.9133	244.64
DuDoTrans	27.45	.8411	31.80	.8911	32.55	.9021	33.48	.9156	242.38
COVID-19 Test Dataset									
FBP [21]	14.82	.3757	18.16	.5635	18.81	.6248	19.36	.7070	–
FBPCovNet [13]	26.43	.8015	32.84	.9407	33.72	.9409	34.62	.9651	149.48
DuDoNet [17]	26.97	.8558	33.10	.9429	32.57	.9380	36.13	.9722	153.25
PDNet [1]	22.53	.6760	33.09	.9396	35.73	.9610	37.65	.9722	112.40
PDNet+SRT	22.59	.6380	34.80	.9558	37.19	.9710	38.47	.9758	325.12
ImgTrans	27.24	.8797	35.58	.9580	37.31	.9699	39.90	.9801	222.14
DuDoTrans	27.74	.8897	35.62	.9596	37.83	.9727	40.20	.9794	244.46

At last, to test if DuDoTrans needs large-scale data to exhibit performance as ViTs, we train these models with [20%, 40%, 60%, 80%, 100%] of our original training dataset, and show the performance in Fig. 2 (f). Obviously, the reconstruction performance of DuDoTrans is very stable till we decrease the training dataset to 20%, where training data is too less for all models to perform well and DuDoTrans still achieves the best performance.

3.2 Sparse-View CT Reconstruction Analysis

We next conduct thorough experiments to test the performance of DuDoTrans on various sparse-view scenarios. Specifically, we first train and test models when α_{max} is [24], respectively. The results are shown in Table 2, and DuDoTrans have

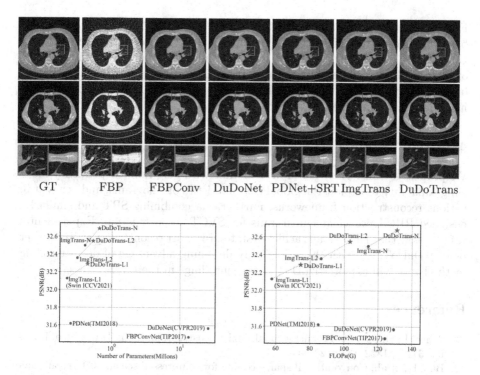

Fig. 3. The first two rows are qualitative comparisons on NIH-AAPM and COVID-19 datasets with $\alpha_{max} = [72, 96]$, respectively. The display window is $[-1000, 800]$ HU. We outline the improvements of images with bounding boxes and show zoom-in sub-images in the third row, where DuDoTrans shows better performance. The last row compares involved parameters and flops of DuDoTrans and convolution-based methods.

achieved consistently better results. Furthermore, the improvement of DuDo-Trans over ImgTrans becomes larger when the α_{max} increases, which confirms the usefulness of the restored sinograms in the latter reconstruction.

Robustness and Generalizability. As the clinical environment and patients are different, we next test model robustness with Poisson noise level $1e^6$ (H1) as in Table 3. Obviously, DuDoTrans still performs best. Similarly, for generalizability, we reconstruct from sinograms simulated from the unobserved COVID-19 dataset. Surprisingly, DuDoTrans have achieved a larger improvement of about 4–5 dB over CNN-based methods, which confirms its powerful performance.

Qualitative Comparison. We also visualize the reconstructed images of these methods in Fig. 3 with $\alpha_{max} = [72, 96]$. In both rows, corresponding to NIH-AAPM and COVID-19 datasets, our DuDoTrans shows better details recovery, and sparse-view artifacts are suppressed.

Parameters and FLOPs. As a practical problem, reconstruction speed is crucial when deployed in modern CT machines. Therefore, we plot the parameters and

FLOPs versus performances in the third row of Fig 3. We find that Transformer-based methods have achieved better performances with fewer parameters, and our DuDoTrans exceeds ImgTrans with only a few additional parameters. For FLOPs of these methods, light versions (DuDoTrans-L1, DuDoTrans-L2) have achieved 0.8–1 dB improvement with fewer FLOPs, and DuDoTrans-N with default size has enlarged the improvement by 1.2 dB.

4 Conclusion

We propose a transformer-based SRT module with long-range dependency modeling capability to exploit the global characteristics of sinograms, and verify it in various reconstruction frameworks. Further, via combining SRT and similarly-designed RIRM, we yield DuDoTrans for SVCT reconstruction. Experimental results show that DuDoTrans achieves state-of-the-art reconstruction. To further benefit DuDoTrans with the accordingly designing advantage of deep-unrolling methods, we will explore "DuDoTrans + unrolling" in the future.

References

1. Adler, J., Öktem, O.: Learned primal-dual reconstruction. IEEE Trans. Med. Imaging **37**(6), 1322–1332 (2018)
2. Bao, P., et al.: Convolutional sparse coding for compressed sensing CT reconstruction. IEEE Trans. Med. Imaging **38**(11), 2607–2619 (2019)
3. Cao, H., et al.: Swin-Unet: Unet-like pure transformer for medical image segmentation. arXiv preprint arXiv:2105.05537 (2021)
4. Carion, N., Massa, F., Synnaeve, G., Usunier, N., Kirillov, A., Zagoruyko, S.: End-to-end object detection with transformers. In: Vedaldi, A., Bischof, H., Brox, T., Frahm, J.-M. (eds.) ECCV 2020. LNCS, vol. 12346, pp. 213–229. Springer, Cham (2020). https://doi.org/10.1007/978-3-030-58452-8_13
5. Chen, H., et al.: Pre-trained image processing transformer. In: Proceedings of the IEEE/CVF Conference on Computer Vision and Pattern Recognition, pp. 12299–12310 (2021)
6. Chen, H., et al.: Learn: learned experts- assessment-based reconstruction network for sparse-data CT. IEEE Trans. Med. Imaging **37**(6), 1333–1347 (2018)
7. Chen, H., et al.: Low-dose CT with a residual encoder-decoder convolutional neural network. IEEE Trans. Med. Imaging **36**(12), 2524–2535 (2017)
8. Cheng, W., Wang, Y., Li, H., Duan, Y.: Learned full-sampling reconstruction from incomplete data. IEEE Trans. Comput. Imaging **6**, 945–957 (2020)
9. Dosovitskiy, A., et al.: An image is worth 16x16 words: transformers for image recognition at scale. arXiv preprint arXiv:2010.11929 (2020)
10. Gupta, H., Jin, K.H., Nguyen, H.Q., McCann, M.T., Unser, M.: CNN-based projected gradient descent for consistent CT image reconstruction. IEEE Trans. Med. Imaging **37**(6), 1440–1453 (2018)
11. Han, Y., Ye, J.C.: Framing U-Net via deep convolutional framelets: application to sparse-view CT. IEEE Trans. Med. Imaging **37**(6), 1418–1429 (2018)
12. He, K., Zhang, X., Ren, S., Sun, J.: Deep residual learning for image recognition. In: Proceedings of the IEEE Conference on Computer Vision and Pattern Recognition, pp. 770–778 (2016)

13. Jin, K.H., McCann, M.T., Froustey, E., Unser, M.: Deep convolutional neural network for inverse problems in imaging. IEEE Trans. Image Process. **26**(9), 4509–4522 (2017)
14. Kim, K., et al.: Sparse-view spectral CT reconstruction using spectral patch-based low-rank penalty. IEEE Trans. Med. Imaging **34**(3), 748–760 (2014)
15. Kingma, D.P., Ba, J.: Adam: a method for stochastic optimization. arXiv preprint arXiv:1412.6980 (2014)
16. Li, Y., Zhang, K., Cao, J., Timofte, R., Van Gool, L.: LocalViT: bringing locality to vision transformers. arXiv preprint arXiv:2104.05707 (2021)
17. Lin, W.A., et al.: DuDoNet: dual domain network for CT metal artifact reduction. In: Proceedings of the IEEE/CVF Conference on Computer Vision and Pattern Recognition, pp. 10512–10521 (2019)
18. Liu, Z., et al.: Swin transformer: hierarchical vision transformer using shifted windows. arXiv preprint arXiv:2103.14030 (2021)
19. Mahmood, F., Shahid, N., Skoglund, U., Vandergheynst, P.: Adaptive graph-based total variation for tomographic reconstructions. IEEE Signal Process. Lett. **25**(5), 700–704 (2018)
20. McCollough, C.: TU-FG-207a-04: overview of the low dose CT grand challenge. Med. Phys. **43**(6Part35), 3759–3760 (2016)
21. Natterer, F.: The Mathematics of Computerized Tomography. SIAM (2001)
22. Sidky, E.Y., Pan, X.: Image reconstruction in circular cone-beam computed tomography by constrained, total-variation minimization. Phys. Med. Biol. **53**(17), 4777 (2008)
23. Wang, C., et al.: Improving generalizability in limited-angle CT reconstruction with sinogram extrapolation. In: de Bruijn, M., et al. (eds.) MICCAI 2021. LNCS, vol. 12906, pp. 86–96. Springer, Cham (2021). https://doi.org/10.1007/978-3-030-87231-1_9
24. Wang, Z., Bovik, A.C., Sheikh, H.R., Simoncelli, E.P.: Image quality assessment: from error visibility to structural similarity. IEEE Trans. Image Process. **13**(4), 600–612 (2004)
25. Wang, Z., Simoncelli, E.P., Bovik, A.C.: Multiscale structural similarity for image quality assessment. In: The Thirty-Seventh Asilomar Conference on Signals, Systems & Computers 2003, vol. 2, pp. 1398–1402. IEEE (2003)
26. Xiu, Z., Chen, J., Henao, R., Goldstein, B., Carin, L., Tao, C.: Supercharging imbalanced data learning with energy-based contrastive representation transfer. In: Advances in Neural Information Processing Systems. Curran Associates, Inc. (2021)
27. Yang, Q., et al.: Low-dose CT image denoising using a generative adversarial network with Wasserstein distance and perceptual loss. IEEE Trans. Med. Imaging **37**(6), 1348–1357 (2018)
28. Yu, S., et al.: MIL-VT: multiple instance learning enhanced vision transformer for fundus image classification. In: de Bruijne, M., et al. (eds.) MICCAI 2021. LNCS, vol. 12908, pp. 45–54. Springer, Cham (2021). https://doi.org/10.1007/978-3-030-87237-3_5
29. Zeng, D., et al.: Spectral CT image restoration via an average image-induced non-local means filter. IEEE Trans. Biomed. Eng. **63**(5), 1044–1057 (2015)
30. Zhang, Y., Pei, Y., Zha, H.: Learning dual transformer network for diffeomorphic registration. In: de Bruijne, M., et al. (eds.) MICCAI 2021. LNCS, vol. 12904, pp. 129–138. Springer, Cham (2021). https://doi.org/10.1007/978-3-030-87202-1_13
31. Zhang, Z., Yu, L., Liang, X., Zhao, W., Xing, L.: TransCT: dual-path transformer for low dose computed tomography. arXiv preprint arXiv:2103.00634 (2021)

32. Zhou, B., Chen, X., Zhou, S.K., Duncan, J.S., Liu, C.: DuDoDR-Net: dual-domain data consistent recurrent network for simultaneous sparse view and metal artifact reduction in computed tomography. Med. Image Anal. **75**, 102289 (2021)

33. Zhou, B., Zhou, S.K.: DuDorNet: learning a dual-domain recurrent network for fast mri reconstruction with deep t1 prior. In: Proceedings of the IEEE/CVF Conference on Computer Vision and Pattern Recognition, pp. 4273–4282 (2020)

34. Zhou, H.Y., Guo, J., Zhang, Y., Yu, L., Wang, L., Yu, Y.: NNFormer: interleaved transformer for volumetric segmentation. arXiv preprint arXiv:2109.03201 (2021)

35. Zhou, S.K., et al.: A review of deep learning in medical imaging: imaging traits, technology trends, case studies with progress highlights, and future promises. In: Proceedings of the IEEE (2021)

36. Zhou, S.K., Le, H.N., Luu, K., Nguyen, H.V., Ayache, N.: Deep reinforcement learning in medical imaging: a literature review. Med. Image Anal. **72**, 102193 (2021)

Deep Denoising Network for X-Ray Fluoroscopic Image Sequences of Moving Objects

Wonjin Kim[1], Wonkyeong Lee[1], Sun-Young Jeon[1], Nayeon Kang[1], Geonhui Jo[2], and Jang-Hwan Choi[1,3(✉)]

[1] Division of Mechanical and Biomedical Engineering, Graduate Program in System Health Science and Engineering, Ewha Womans University, 52, Ewhayeodae-gil, Seodaemun-gu, Seoul 03760, South Korea
choij@ewha.ac.kr

[2] Department of Computer Science and Engineering, Ewha Womans University, 52, Ewhayeodae-gil, Seodaemun-gu, Seoul 03760, South Korea

[3] Department of Artificial Intelligence, Ewha Womans University, 52, Ewhayeodae-gil, Seodaemun-gu, Seoul 03760, South Korea

Abstract. Prolonged fluoroscopy procedures may involve high patient radiation doses, and a low-dose fluoroscopy protocol has been proven to be effective in reducing doses in an interventional suite. However, the low-dose protocol-caused noise degrades fluoroscopic image quality and then impacts clinical diagnosis accuracy. Here, we propose a novel deep denoising network for low-dose fluoroscopic image sequences of moving objects. The existing deep learning-based denoising approaches showed promising performance in denoising static fluoroscopic images, but their dynamic image denoising performance is relatively poor because they are not able to accurately track moving objects, losing detailed textures of the dynamic objects. To overcome the limitations of current methods, we introduce a self-attention-based network with the incorporation of flow-guided feature parallel warping. Parallel warping is able to jointly extract, align, and propagate features of dynamic objects in adjacent fluoroscopic frames, and self-attention effectively learns long-range spatiotemporal features between the adjacent frames. Our extensive experiments on real datasets of clinically relevant dynamic phantoms reveals that the performance of the proposed method achieves superior performance, both quantitatively and qualitatively, over state-of-the-art methods on a denoising task.

Keywords: X-ray fluoroscopy · Multi-frame images · Image denoising · Moving objects · Deep neural network

1 Introduction

Fluoroscopy is a fundamental and non-invasive medical imaging modality that provides real-time X-ray images for a wide variety of examinations and procedures to diagnose or treat patients. Thus, it is widely used such as barium X-rays

© The Author(s), under exclusive license to Springer Nature Switzerland AG 2022
N. Haq et al. (Eds.): MLMIR 2022, LNCS 13587, pp. 95–104, 2022.
https://doi.org/10.1007/978-3-031-17247-2_10

and enemas, catheter insertion and manipulation, placement of devices within the body like stents, angiograms, and orthopedic surgery [1,16,22,24,25]. One concern in using X-ray fluoroscopy imaging is that it induces a non-negligible threat to patients and healthcare staff due to continuous radiation exposures [20]. Therefore, low-dose X-ray fluoroscopy is commonly adopted to prevent X-ray radiation hazards. Low-dose fluoroscopy images are associated with decreased risk of radiation exposure for users, but they contain more noise and artifacts, and excessive noise and artifacts make accurate medical diagnosis more difficult. Therefore, denoising algorithms that reduce noise effectively in X-ray images are sought for clinical purposes.

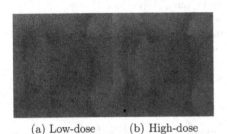

(a) Low-dose   (b) High-dose   (a) SF-RDN   (b) MF-RDN

Fig. 1. Blue arrows indicate that noise covers detail texture in low-dose X-ray image, that can be seen in high-dose X-ray image. (Color figure online)

Fig. 2. SF-RDN and MF-RDN are single-frame and multi-frame residual dense networks. Five frames are used for multi-frame input. Their corresponding PSNRs are 39.45 and 38.87, respectively.

The easiest and most common way to reduce noise is by averaging or by implementing, in the temporal domain, a recursive filter on X-ray images. This method is extremely effective for generating clear and edge-preserved X-ray images when the imaged object is static; however, for non-static objects, this method tends to generate motion blur in denoised X-ray images, and the texture of the detail can easily be lost. Thus, more efficient denoising algorithms are required for general low-dose X-ray fluoroscopy images. Some traditional denoising algorithms use filter-based denoising, which is applied in both the spatial and temporal domains [2,21,22]. In recent years, with the advent of deep learning technologies, X-ray fluoroscopy denoising has also adopted convolutional neural network (CNN)-based algorithms [13–15]. Furthermore, deep learning based denoising algorithms have shown outperforming results compared to those of traditional denoising algorithms. However, these deep learning-based studies use only spatial information and do not use temporal information. Thus, the networks used have only a one-to-one pairing between low- and high-dose X-ray images for training. However, because textures in X-ray images are quite subtle and minute, noise may cover the details and corrupt the textures. In this case, it is impossible to recover the original textures from a single low-dose X-ray image. For example, in Fig. 1(a), textures in spinal bone are hidden by noise; thus, even good denoising algorithms cannot fully recover, in low-dose X-ray images, the details, which can be seen as very silky lines in the corresponding clear, averaged X-ray images (see Fig. 1(b)).

This indicates that multi-frame denoising algorithms need to be developed to recover all the features in X-ray images. However, even though we use the same architecture as for deep learning-based denoising algorithms, simply switching from single-frame to multi-frame input does not guarantee the denoising performance, as is shown by using a single-frame input network. We tested the residual dense network (RDN) [26] with single-frame and multi-frame inputs. In this simple experiment, the RDN with one-to-one pairs of low- and high-dose X-ray images showed prominent performance among state-of-the-art denoising algorithms, but the performance of the RDN with multi-frame input was degraded, and the denoised X-ray images showed unwanted artifacts. This observation is illustrated in Fig. 2. These experimental results suggest that we need to deliberately design denoising neural networks when we want to fully utilize multi-frame inputs and reduce noise.

In this paper, we propose a new algorithm for multi-frame fluoroscopy denoising, especially, when the objects in the images are in motion. Our base network is the U-Net [19] because it can capture features at several scales through the downsampling and upsampling layers in the network. However, the network is enhanced by the addition of two features: parallel warping and self-attention. We implemented flow-guided parallel warping [12], which uses deformable convolution [5] to propagate features from adjacent frames to other frames and fuses features into them. For further performance enhancement, self-attention [23] was adopted because it can learn spatial and temporal correlation in X-ray fluoroscopy images.

Our contributions in this paper can be summarized as follows:

- We propose a new framework for multi-frame low-dose X-ray fluoroscopy images to reduce noise without much loss of the texture detail of dynamic objects.
- With the incorporation of temporal bidirectional warping (i.e., parallel warping), our proposed self-attention-based network is able to jointly extract, align, and fuse the features of moving objects in multi-frame images.
- We conduct rigorous experiments on real datasets of clinically relevant dynamic phantoms to demonstrate the performance of the proposed method. The experimental results reveal that our method achieves superior performance, both quantitatively and qualitatively, over state-of-the-art methods on a denoising task.

2 Methods

2.1 Overall Architecture

In this paper, we propose a low-dose fluoroscopy denoising algorithm based on parallel warping and self-attention. Our overall proposed methods are depicted

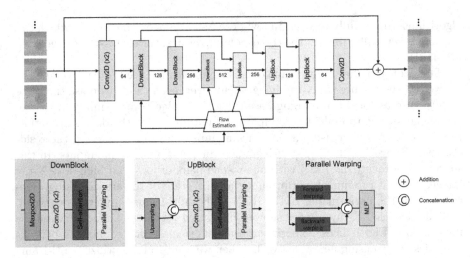

Fig. 3. Overall architecture of proposed method. The number label on the output/input arrow after each operational layer indicates the number of feature channels. Detail illustrations of parallel warping and self-attention are depicted in Fig. 4.

in Fig. 3. Our network is based on U-Net [19]; however, we modified it by adding parallel warping and self-attention in each block. We chose U-Net as our base network because it can train features of various scales in each layer; thus, it helps in training spatial and temporal relationships. To utilize information from multiple neighboring frames during the training of each frame, we adopted parallel warping for the features in each layer block. Parallel warping can also learn propagation, alignment, and aggregation, which should be considered essential elements of video restoration [3]. Finally, to boost the learning of spatial and temporal relations, we adopted self-attention, which was introduced as a non-local block [23].

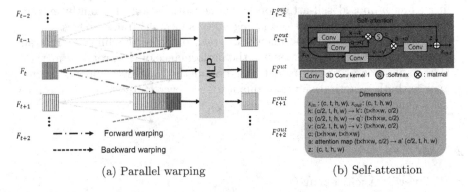

(a) Parallel warping   (b) Self-attention

Fig. 4. Illustration of parallel warping and self-attention

2.2 Parallel Warping

We used feature warping at the end of each network stage to fuse, align, and propagate the features in each layer of the network. Figure 4(a) shows the implementation details of parallel warping. For the flow estimation between frame feature F_t and its neighbouring frame features F_{t-1} and F_{t+1}, optical flows are calculated. For the frame feature F_t, F_{t_1} and F_{t+1} are warped into frame t (forward and backward warping). These features are concatenated with the original feature, and the feature dimensions are reduced by the multi-layer perceptron (MLP). To learn the residual, we added a skip connection between the input and the output of parallel warping.

For the flow estimation, we used SpyNet [18], pretrained with ImageNet [6], and we used deformable convolution [5] for the deformable alignment.

2.3 Self-attention

The self-attention module [23] is applied to each block of our proposed network. Figure 4(b) shows the details of the self-attention implementation. For the input feature vector of the self-attention layer, we define $x_{in} \in \mathbb{R}^{(c \times t \times h \times w)}$, where $\langle t \rangle$ is the number of temporal frames, $\langle c \rangle$ is the number of channels of the input feature vector, and $\langle h, w \rangle$ is the height and width of the input feature vector. Then, we formulate the key, query, and value (denoted as q, k, v) from X_{in} with the weight matrix as follows:

$$q = W_q x_{in}$$
$$k = W_k x_{in}$$
$$v = W_v x_{in} \tag{1}$$

where $q, k, v \in \mathbb{R}^{(\frac{c}{2} \times t \times h \times w)}$. After reshaping q, k, v to q', k', v' with dimensions of $(N \times \frac{c}{2})$, where $N = t \times h \times w$, we calculate the correlation matrix between queries and keys, and we obtain the attention map as follows:

$$c = Softmax(q'^T k')$$
$$a = cv' \tag{2}$$

where the dimensionality of the attention map is $(N \times \frac{c}{2})$. We reshape a to a' with dimensions of $(\frac{c}{2} \times d \times h \times w)$, apply the final weight matrix X_z, and add a residual connection "$+x_{in}$" in the self-attention layer as defined in the non-local block [23] as follows:

$$x_{out} = W_z a' + x_{in} \tag{3}$$

2.4 Optimization of the Network

We used five frames of the X-ray fluoroscopy images as the input to the network, and the output of the network consisted of five frames as well. If we denote input x as five frames $[x_1, x_2, x_3, x_4, x_5]$, y as the clean target frames $[y_1, y_2, y_3, y_4, y_5]$,

$\hat{y}$ as the output of the network, and H as the network operations, we can then formulate it as follows:

$$\hat{y} = H(x) \tag{4}$$

Then, we optimize the following L_1 loss function to train the network:

$$L_1 = ||\hat{y} - y||_1 \tag{5}$$

3   Experimental Results

3.1   Dataset Acquisition

To train and test our proposed model, we acquired X-ray fluoroscopy images of two different dynamic phantoms using tube voltage of 60 kV and tube current-exposure time product of 0.002 mAs and 0.02 mAs for the low- and high-dose fluoroscopic images, respectively. One was a real-bone X-ray hand phantom, and the other was a phantom made up of a needle and spherical objects to simulate the needle biopsy of a solitary nodule. A Model 008A Dynamic Thorax Phantom (CIRS, Norfolk, VA, USA) with CIRS motion control software was used to generate the combined translational and rotational motion of the two phantoms. The dynamic phantoms were set to translate at up to ± 2 cm. We acquired matching pairs of low- and high-dose fluoroscopic images for both of the phantoms. Although the high-dose images did not contain as much noise as the low-dose images, the high-dose target images also contained some residual noise. Noisier2Noise [17] and Noise2Noise [11] theoretically proved that setting noisy images as the target can train the denoising network, thus we did not perform image enhancement preprocessing on the original data to secure clearer target fluoroscopic images. Because we have only two limited phantom dataset, we made training and test sets by different movements and positions. Training datasets consists total twelve different motions and positions sets, and test datasets consists other six different motions and positions sets. Validation sets is randomly chosen from training set with ratio of 0.05.

3.2   Experimental Setup

We used the same setting to train our proposed and benchmark algorithms to compare their performance. We used the Adam solver [10] and set the learning rate to 0.0002. We scheduled the learning rate to halve when the minimum loss did not change after five iterations. All images were normalized to between 0 and 1. We performed augmentation on the training images, including random rotations by 90, 180, and 270° and horizontal flipping. We extracted a random patch of size 40×40 for the input to the algorithms in the training step.

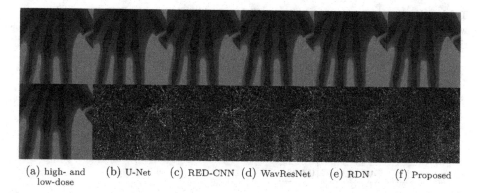

(a) high- and   (b) U-Net   (c) RED-CNN (d) WavResNet   (e) RDN   (f) Proposed
low-dose

Fig. 5. Visual performance comparison with state-of-the-art denoising algorithms on X-ray fluoroscopy images: (a) high- (top) and low-dose (bottom); (b)–(f) denoised outputs from the algorithms (top) and their corresponding difference images relative to high-dose images (bottom).

3.3   Performance Comparison with State-of-the-Art Methods

We compared the performance of our proposed method with the other representative denoising methods. Existing fluoroscopy image denoising algorithms are based on simple CNN-based architectures, so they are not suitable as a comparison target. Therefore, models with effective denoising performance on low-dose computed tomography or natural images were selected as comparison algorithms, including U-Net [19], RED-CNN [4], WavResNet [9], and RDN [26]. We used the peak signal-to-noise ratio (PSNR) and the structural similarity index measure (SSIM) as the quantitative metrics. The comparison results are summarized in Table 1, and our proposed method achieves the best denoising performance by a large margin (up to 1.2 dB) compared with the other denoising algorithms.

We also qualitatively evaluated the visual quality of the results of our proposed method with those of the other denoising algorithms. Figure 5 shows the denoised outputs of various algorithms, which show a moving hand in an X-ray image. As shown by the difference images relative to the high-dose images in columns (b)–(f), our proposed generally shows only noise, and the least hand-shaped edges. This means that our proposed method effectively reduced noise without the loss of detail and edges in the X-ray images.

3.4   Ablation Study

We evaluated how the parallel warping and self-attention components of the network affect performance. The objective quality performance, in terms of PSNR and SSIM, according to the configuration of various modules of the proposed network for the multi-frame U-Net is summarized in Table 2. As shown in Table 2, our proposed modules, parallel warping, and self-attention, gradually improve the denoising performance, as we expected.

Table 1. Performance comparison with state-of-the-art denoising algorithms on X-ray fluoroscopy images.

Algorithms	PSNR (dB)	SSIM
Noise (baseline)	36.0950	0.9794
U-Net	43.9552	0.9932
RED-CNN	44.0084	0.9932
WavResNet	44.0636	0.9933
RDN	44.4778	0.9934
Proposed	**45.1431**	**0.9938**

Table 2. Ablation study. PW is parallel warping, and SA is self-attention. Each feature is added from a multi-frame U-Net (MF U-Net), which we regard as the baseline.

Features	PSNR (dB)	SSIM
MF U-Net	43.2122	0.9929
+SA	43.7380	0.9933
+PW	45.0534	0.9937
+PW +SA	**45.1431**	**0.9938**

4   Discussion and Conclusion

In this study, we proposed a novel fluoroscopy denoising algorithm that specifically targets moving objects. Our proposed method is based on U-Net [19], but we changed the design of the architecture by adding parallel warping and self-attention. These two modules helped the network to utilize multi-frames and learn the spatial and temporal relationships between and within frames.

With our experimental settings, our proposed methods showed promising denoising results compared with the other state-of-the-art denoising algorithms. However, fluoroscopy denoising algorithms can be further enhanced from various perspectives: 1) collecting more data for various objects and settings in medical practices; 2) developing an unsupervised denoising algorithm that does not require high-dose images would be more practical than using a supervised denoising algorithm because of the difficulty in collecting and synchronizing pairs of low- and high-dose X-ray images; 3) reducing computational cost in layers of the proposed network can be more practical in the medical industry as many real applications require real-time denoising; 4) improving perceptual quality by adding VGG loss [8] or a generative adversarial network (GAN) [7] during denoising could further enhance perceptual quality performance.

In conclusion, we have presented a novel fluoroscopy denoising algorithm for moving objects. Our experiments demonstrated that our method convincingly reduced noise and outperformed state-of-the-art denoising algorithms. Even though our fluoroscopy denoising algorithms showed competitive performance, we believe that future research will further develop the fluoroscopy denoising algorithm so that it can be applied in medical practice.

Acknowledgements. This work was partly supported by the Technology development Program of MSS [S3146559], by the National Research Foundation of Korea (NRF-2022M3A9I2017587 and NRF-2022R1A2C1092072), and by the Korea Medical Device Development Fund grant funded by the Korea government (the Ministry of Science and ICT, the Ministry of Trade, Industry and Energy, the Ministry of Health & Welfare, the Ministry of Food and Drug Safety) (Project Number: KMDF_PR_20200901_0016, 9991006689).

References

1. Bifulco, P., Cesarelli, M., Cerciello, T., Romano, M.: A continuous description of intervertebral motion by means of spline interpolation of kinematic data extracted by videofluoroscopy. J. Biomech. **45**(4), 634–641 (2012)
2. Cesarelli, M., Bifulco, P., Cerciello, T., Romano, M., Paura, L.: X-ray fluoroscopy noise modeling for filter design. Int. J. Comput. Assist. Radiol. Surg. **8**(2), 269–278 (2013)
3. Chan, K.C., Wang, X., Yu, K., Dong, C., Loy, C.C.: Basicvsr: the search for essential components in video super-resolution and beyond. In: Proceedings of the IEEE/CVF Conference on Computer Vision and Pattern Recognition, pp. 4947–4956 (2021)
4. Chen, H., et al.: Low-dose CT with a residual encoder-decoder convolutional neural network. IEEE Trans. Med. Imaging **36**(12), 2524–2535 (2017)
5. Dai, J., et al.: Deformable convolutional networks. In: Proceedings of the IEEE International Conference on Computer Vision, pp. 764–773 (2017)
6. Deng, J., Dong, W., Socher, R., Li, L.J., Li, K., Fei-Fei, L.: ImageNet: a large-scale hierarchical image database. In: 2009 IEEE Conference on Computer Vision and Pattern Recognition, pp. 248–255 (2009). https://doi.org/10.1109/CVPR.2009.5206848
7. Goodfellow, I., et al.: Generative adversarial nets. In: Ghahramani, Z., Welling, M., Cortes, C., Lawrence, N.D., Weinberger, K.Q. (eds.) Advances in Neural Information Processing Systems 27, pp. 2672–2680. Curran Associates, Inc. (2014)
8. Johnson, J., Alahi, A., Fei-Fei, L.: Perceptual losses for real-time style transfer and super-resolution. In: Leibe, B., Matas, J., Sebe, N., Welling, M. (eds.) ECCV 2016. LNCS, vol. 9906, pp. 694–711. Springer, Cham (2016). https://doi.org/10.1007/978-3-319-46475-6_43
9. Kang, E., Chang, W., Yoo, J., Ye, J.C.: Deep convolutional framelet denosing for low-dose CT via wavelet residual network. IEEE Trans. Med. Imaging **37**(6), 1358–1369 (2018)
10. Kingma, D.P., Ba, J.: Adam: a method for stochastic optimization. arXiv preprint arXiv:1412.6980 (2014)
11. Lehtinen, J., et al.: Noise2Noise: learning image restoration without clean data. In: Proceedings of the 35th International Conference on Machine Learning, vol. 80, pp. 2965–2974. PMLR (2018)
12. Liang, J., et al.: VRT: a video restoration transformer. arXiv preprint arXiv:2201.12288 (2022)
13. Luo, Y., et al.: Edge-enhancement densenet for x-ray fluoroscopy image denoising in cardiac electrophysiology procedures. Med. Phys. **49**(2), 1262–1275 (2022). https://doi.org/10.1002/mp.15426. https://aapm.onlinelibrary.wiley.com/doi/full/10.1002/mp.15426
14. Luo, Y., Majoe, S., Kui, J., Qi, H., Pushparajah, K., Rhode, K.: Ultra-dense denoising network: application to cardiac catheter-based x-ray procedures. IEEE Trans. Biomed. Eng. **68**(9), 2626–2636 (2021). https://doi.org/10.1109/TBME.2020.3041571
15. Matviychuk, Y., et al.: Learning a multiscale patch-based representation for image denoising in x-ray fluoroscopy. In: 2016 IEEE International Conference on Image Processing (ICIP), pp. 2330–2334. IEEE (2016)
16. Moradi, M., et al.: Seed localization in ultrasound and registration to C-arm fluoroscopy using matched needle tracks for prostate brachytherapy. IEEE Trans. Biomed. Eng. **59**(9), 2558–2567 (2012)

17. Moran, N., Schmidt, D., Zhong, Y., Coady, P.: Noisier2Noise: learning to denoise from unpaired noisy data. In: Proceedings of the IEEE/CVF Conference on Computer Vision and Pattern Recognition, pp. 12064–12072 (2020)
18. Ranjan, A., Black, M.J.: Optical flow estimation using a spatial pyramid network. In: Proceedings of the IEEE Conference on Computer Vision and Pattern Recognition, pp. 4161–4170 (2017)
19. Ronneberger, O., Fischer, P., Brox, T.: U-Net: convolutional networks for biomedical image segmentation. In: Navab, N., Hornegger, J., Wells, W.M., Frangi, A.F. (eds.) MICCAI 2015. LNCS, vol. 9351, pp. 234–241. Springer, Cham (2015). https://doi.org/10.1007/978-3-319-24574-4_28
20. Shope, T.B.: Radiation-induced skin injuries from fluoroscopy. Radiographics 16(5), 1195–1199 (1996)
21. Tomic, M., Loncaric, S., Sersic, D.: Adaptive spatio-temporal denoising of fluoroscopic x-ray sequences. Biomed. Signal Process. Control 7(2), 173–179 (2012)
22. Wang, J., Zhu, L., Xing, L.: Noise reduction in low-dose x-ray fluoroscopy for image-guided radiation therapy. Int. J. Radiat. Oncol. Biol. Phys. 74(2), 637–643 (2009)
23. Wang, X., Girshick, R., Gupta, A., He, K.: Non-local neural networks. In: 2018 IEEE/CVF Conference on Computer Vision and Pattern Recognition, pp. 7794–7803 (2018). https://doi.org/10.1109/CVPR.2018.00813
24. Weese, J., Penney, G.P., Desmedt, P., Buzug, T.M., Hill, D.L., Hawkes, D.J.: Voxel-based 2-D/3-D registration of fluoroscopy images and CT scans for image-guided surgery. IEEE Trans. Inf. Technol. Biomed. 1(4), 284–293 (1997)
25. Yamazaki, T., et al.: Improvement of depth position in 2-D/3-D registration of knee implants using single-plane fluoroscopy. IEEE Trans. Med. Imaging 23(5), 602–612 (2004)
26. Zhang, Y., Tian, Y., Kong, Y., Zhong, B., Fu, Y.: Residual dense network for image restoration. IEEE Trans. Pattern Anal. Mach. Intell. 43(7), 2480–2495 (2020)

PP-MPI: A Deep Plug-and-Play Prior for Magnetic Particle Imaging Reconstruction

Baris Askin[1]([✉]), Alper Güngör[1,2], Damla Alptekin Soydan[2], Emine Ulku Saritas[1], Can Barış Top[2], and Tolga Cukur[1]

[1] Department of Electrical and Electronics Engineering, Bilkent University, Ankara, Turkey
`barisaskin99@gmail.com`, `{alperg,saritas,cukur}@ee.bilkent.edu.tr`
[2] Aselsan Research Center, Ankara, Turkey
`{alpergungor,dasoydan,cbtop}@aselsan.com.tr`

Abstract. Magnetic particle imaging (MPI) is a recent modality that enables high contrast and frame-rate imaging of the magnetic nanoparticle (MNP) distribution. Based on a measured system matrix, MPI reconstruction can be cast as an inverse problem that is commonly solved via regularized iterative optimization. Yet, hand-crafted regularization terms can elicit suboptimal performance. Here, we propose a novel MPI reconstruction "PP-MPI" based on a deep plug-and-play (PP) prior embedded in a model-based iterative optimization. We propose to pre-train the PP prior based on a residual dense convolutional neural network (CNN) on an MPI-friendly dataset derived from magnetic resonance angiograms. The PP prior is then embedded into an alternating direction method of multiplier (ADMM) optimizer for reconstruction. A fast implementation is devised for 3D image reconstruction by fusing the predictions from 2D priors in separate rectilinear orientations. Our demonstrations show that PP-MPI outperforms state-of-the-art iterative techniques with hand-crafted regularizers on both simulated and experimental data. In particular, PP-MPI achieves on average 3.10 dB higher peak signal-to-noise ratio than the top-performing baseline under variable noise levels, and can process 12 frames/sec to permit real-time 3D imaging.

Keywords: Magnetic particle imaging · Reconstruction · Plug and play · Deep learning

1 Introduction

Magnetic Particle Imaging (MPI) is a recent imaging modality that allows high contrast imaging of magnetic nanoparticles (MNP) with high frame rate. Important applications include cancer imaging, stem cell tracking, angiography and

© The Author(s), under exclusive license to Springer Nature Switzerland AG 2022
N. Haq et al. (Eds.): MLMIR 2022, LNCS 13587, pp. 105–114, 2022.
https://doi.org/10.1007/978-3-031-17247-2_11

targeted drug delivery [14,15,17]. In MPI, a field free region (FFR) is generated to later measure a signal that reflects the total MNP concentration within the targeted region. Since the signal response is influenced by properties of the imaging system and MNP characteristics, a common procedure is to measure a system matrix (SM) that characterizes the forward signal model. Image formation from measured MPI signals can then be cast as an inverse problem based on the SM. As the inverse problem is ill-posed, reconstructions characteristically embody regularization terms that reflect prior information on the characteristics of MNP distribution.

A common reconstruction method is based on ℓ_2-norm regularization during algebraic reconstruction technique (ART) optimization [10]. Compressed sensing methods were also proposed for image regularization via ℓ_1-norm and/or total variation (TV) terms during an alternating direction method of multipliers (ADMM) optimization [8]. While prominent results have been reported, hand-crafted regularization terms can induce well-known blurring, or blocking artifacts in the reconstructed image. As an alternative, several recent studies have proposed purely learning-based approaches. A deep image prior (DIP) method has been considered in [5] that performs reconstruction based on an untrained network via inference optimization, which may limit real-time applicability. End-to-end methods trained to map MPI signals to images have also been introduced [3,7,12]. Yet, end-to-end methods require retraining under changes to the SM, and their success relies on training datasets that match the characteristics of MPI images. Given the absence of a dedicated database of MPI images, previous studies have primarily used training sets containing simulated vessel phantoms or numerical digit images [4]. This may restrict generalization performance for experimental data and 3D imaging scenarios.

Here, we introduce a novel deep plug-and-play (PP) image prior for model-based MPI reconstruction. Inspired by the success of task-agnostic PP priors in medical imaging [1,13], we propose to train a denoising PP prior for MPI based on a training set derived from time-of-flight cerebral magnetic resonance angiograms (MRA) to closely mimic the vascular structures targeted in MPI scans. We build the prior on a residual dense convolutional neural network (CNN) [16]. During inference, we embed trained prior into a model-based ADMM optimization that includes measured SM. The PP prior enhances the quality of reconstructed images while ADMM offers a fast implementation suitable for real-time imaging. To utilize 2D dataset in 3D reconstruction and improve computational efficiency, we propose to fuse the predictions from denoised cross-sections of separate rectilinear orientations. Our main contributions are: (1) We introduce the first PP method for MPI reconstruction, (2) We propose an efficient algorithm based on ADMM and fused 2D priors for 3D reconstruction, (3) We validate the proposed method on simulated and experimental datasets [11].

2   Background

2.1   MPI Signal Model

During an MPI scan, drive field oscillations occurring at a fundamental frequency excite the MNPs, while a spatially encoded selection field creates an FFR. MNPs in FFR respond to the drive field, and responses are recorded as voltage waveforms induced on a receive coil. The MNP response is apparent in frequency bands centered on the harmonics of the fundamental frequency. The received signal can be compressed by filtering out low intensity bands in the frequency domain. The filtered signal is complex valued, and commonly represented by concatenating real and imaginary parts of the signal in separate rows of the measurement vector. The forward imaging model is:

$$\mathbf{Ax} + \mathbf{n} = \mathbf{r}, \tag{1}$$

where $\mathbf{A} \in \mathbb{R}^{M \times N}$ is the SM (M denotes twice the number of frequency components and N is the number of points on the imaging grid), $\mathbf{x} \in \mathbb{R}^N$ is the underlying MNP distribution, $\mathbf{n} \in \mathbb{R}^M$ is the measurement noise, and $\mathbf{r} \in \mathbb{R}^M$ denotes the measured MNP responses. Given the SM A, the forward model expressed in Eq. (1) can be inverted to estimate the MPI image $\mathbf{x}$ given the measurement $\mathbf{r}$. However, non-idealities regarding the imaging system and MNP characteristics prohibit accurate analytical calculation of the SM. Thus, it is common practice to experimentally measure A via calibration measurements [6]. Calibration is performed while a voxel-sized MNP sample is located at each grid point across the imaging Field of View (FOV), separately for each frequency component.

2.2   MPI Image Reconstruction

MPI reconstruction involves solution of the inverse problem characterized with the forward model in Eq. (1). Yet, since the problem is ill-conditioned, regularization terms are typically enforced to guide the reconstruction:

$$\arg\min_{\mathbf{x} \geq 0} \sum_i \alpha_i f_i(\mathbf{x}) \quad s.t \quad \|\mathbf{Ax} - \mathbf{r}\|_2 < \epsilon, \tag{2}$$

where α_i is the regularization weight for the ith regularization function $f_i(\cdot)$, and ϵ is the upper bound on noise level reflecting measurement and SM errors. Note that there is a non-negativity constraint on $\mathbf{x}$ as MNP distribution cannot assume negative values. The most common approach to solve the model-based reconstruction problem in Eq. (2) is via iterative optimization methods. Kluth et al. proposed the ART method with ℓ_2-norm regularization ($f_1(\mathbf{x}) = \|\mathbf{x}\|_2^2$), which assumes that the underlying MNP distribution is spatially smooth [9]. Ilbey et al. proposed the ADMM method with mixed ℓ_1-norm and TV regularization ($f_1(\mathbf{x}) = \|\mathbf{x}\|_1$ and $f_2(\mathbf{x}) = TV(\mathbf{x})$), which assumes that the MNP distribution is sparse in image and finite-differences domains [8]. Despite their pervasive use,

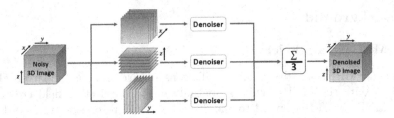

Fig. 1. Multi-orientation 2D PP priors to achieve efficient processing of 3D MPI data. Volumetric data are split into cross-sections across x, y and $z-$axes. The same denoiser processes the cross-sections in each orientation. Resultant volumes are averaged across orientations to produce the denoised 3D data.

Algorithm 1. An ADMM algorithm for PP-MPI

Initialize $z_0^{(i)}$ and $d_0^{(i)}$ for $i = 0, 1$, choose μ, set $n \leftarrow 0$
while Stopping criterion is not satisfied **do**

$\quad \mathbf{x}_{n+1} \leftarrow (mI + A^H A)^{-1}(A^H(\mathbf{z}_n^{(0)} + \mathbf{d}_n^{(0)}) + \mathbf{z}_n^{(1)} + \mathbf{d}_n^{(1)})$

$\quad \mathbf{z}_{n+1}^{(1)} \leftarrow f_{PP}(\mathbf{x}_{n+1} - \mathbf{d}_n^{(1)}; \alpha_1, \mu)$ $\triangleright$ Variable update for PP subproblem

$\quad \mathbf{d}_{n+1}^{(1)} \leftarrow \mathbf{d}_n^{(1)} + \mathbf{z}_{n+1}^{(1)} - \mathbf{x}_{n+1}$ $\triangleright$ Lagrange multiplier update for PP subproblem

$\quad \mathbf{z}_{n+1}^{(0)} \leftarrow \Psi_{l_{E(\epsilon,I,\mathbf{b})}}(A\mathbf{x}_{n+1} - \mathbf{d}_n^{(0)})$ $\triangleright$ Projection for DF subproblem

$\quad \mathbf{d}_{n+1}^{(0)} \leftarrow \mathbf{d}_n^{(0)} + \mathbf{z}_{n+1}^{(0)} - A\mathbf{x}_{n+1}$ $\triangleright$ Lagrange multiplier update for DF subproblem

$\quad n \leftarrow n + 1$
end while

---

methods that rely on hand-constructed regularizers can yield suboptimal performance when underlying assumptions are not satisfied on experimental data. Several recent studies have adopted purely learning-based reconstruction methods. In a DIP approach, an untrained neural network was optimized for reconstruction at test time based on a data-fidelity objective [5]. Because DIP requires prolonged inference, it is not ideally suited for real-time MPI. Multi-layer perceptron (MLP) architectures were proposed for MPI reconstruction [3,7]. The MLP model was trained and tested on simulated phantoms, so experimental utility remains to be demonstrated. A CNN was proposed that was similarly trained and validated on simulated vessel phantoms and numerical digit images [4,12]. While data-driven priors promise to mitigate the limitations of hand-constructed regularizers, end-to-end networks capture a prior conditioned on the SM. Therefore, they have to be retrained for notable changes in the MPI system such as scan trajectories or MNP properties.

3   Methods

3.1   Plug-and-Play MPI Reconstruction (PP-MPI)

Here, we propose a novel plug-and-play method, PP-MPI, for reconstruction of
MPI images. To improve reliability against changes in the system properties, PP-
MPI decouples the forward imaging model characterized by the SM from training
of the deep prior for data-driven regularization. As such, a task-agnostic deep
prior is first trained for image denoising on an MPI-friendly dataset. During
inference, the trained prior is then adapted to perform MPI reconstruction by
incorporating the forward imaging model in Eq. (1). For fast inference, we devised
an ADMM-based algorithm comprising two subproblems: a first problem for
data-driven regularization based on the PP prior, and a second problem for
data-fidelity projection based on the SM. Taken together, these design elements
enable PP-MPI to offer reliable and rapid reconstruction of MPI data.

MPI-Friendly Dataset: In many MPI studies, a limited number of simulated
vessel phantoms are used for demonstration of reconstruction methods as vascular imaging is a key application. However, it is difficult to generate a broad
diversity of manually designed phantoms for training deep networks. We instead
propose to generate MPI-like training images from abundant time-of-flight MRA
images in the public "ITKTubeTK - Bullitt - Healthy MR Database" by CASI-
Lab at the University of North Carolina-CH. Data from 95 healthy subjects
are split into non-overlapping training (77 subjects), validation (9) and test (9)
sets. Multiple 3D patches of size $10 \times 64 \times 64$ are randomly cropped, a thin-slab
maximum-intensity projection is performed across the first dimension, and the
resulting projection is downsampled to 32×32 MPI-like images. To avoid of

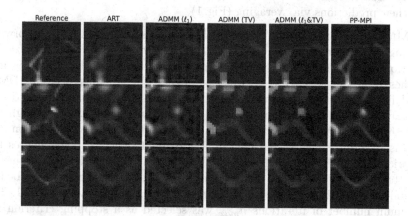

Fig. 2. 2D reconstructions for simulated vessel phantoms under 40 dB measurement
SNR. Images from competing methods are shown along with reference phantom images
for three separate phantoms (each phantom depicted on a separate row).

Table 1. Average PSNR (dB) for reconstructed simulated phantom images with varying measurement SNRs (20/30/40 dB SNRs).

Method	20 dB SNR	30 dB SNR	40 dB SNR
ART	24.57	26.79	27.87
ADMM (ℓ_1)	15.53	18.83	24.48
ADMM (TV)	25.99	27.04	27.64
ADMM (ℓ_1&TV)	25.89	27.13	28.26
PP-MPI	**29.01**	**30.49**	**31.18**

empty patches, patches with higher ℓ_2-norm of pixel intensities were retained. Resultant 2D images are normalized to a maximum intensity of 1.

Training the PP Prior: We leverage a Residual Dense Network (RDN) as backbone architecture for the PP prior given its success in image restoration tasks in computer vision studies [16]. As MPI images are substantially smaller than natural images, we devise a specialized RDN architecture with a compact set of parameters in order to match the characteristics of MPI data. We also employ rectified linear unit at the output layer to enforce non-negativity of MPI image intensities. The resulting model is trained for image denoising on the MPI-friendly dataset. Here, we consider both 2D and 3D reconstruction. For computational efficiency, we propose to employ 2D priors for both reconstruction scenarios. Because denoising cross-sections of one rectilinear orientation will offer suboptimal capture of context along the through-plane dimension, we introduce a volumetrization strategy for 3D reconstruction. During reconstruction, we first denoise cross-sections of three orientations using the same 2D prior. Then, we fuse their predictions via averaging (Fig. 1).

ADMM-Based Inference: The trained PP prior is integrated with the forward imaging model during inference on actual MPI data. An inference optimization is performed to find a reconstruction that is consistent with the PP prior and satisfies data-fidelity (DF) to MPI measurements. For fast inference, an ADMM based implementation is developed [8], where classical proximal operators in Eq. (2) for regularization functions are replaced with projections through the PP prior. The proposed algorithm splits the overall inference optimization into two easier subproblems as outlined in Algorithm 1, where $f_{PP}(\cdot)$ denotes the PP prior trained for image denoising, $\Psi_{l_{E(\epsilon,I,\mathbf{b})}}(\cdot)$ is the proximal mapping for indicator function $l_{E(\epsilon,I,\mathbf{b})}$ of being the element of set $E(\epsilon,I,\mathbf{b})$ as described in [8], and μ indicates the step size of the algorithm. μ and α_1 were set to 1. The maximum number of iterations n_{max} was selected as a stopping criterion via cross-validation. Note that large training datasets containing 3D imaging data may not be broadly available, and inference optimization with a 3D prior might elevate computational burden. Thus, here, we instead adopted a volumetrization strategy based on multi-orientation 2D priors.

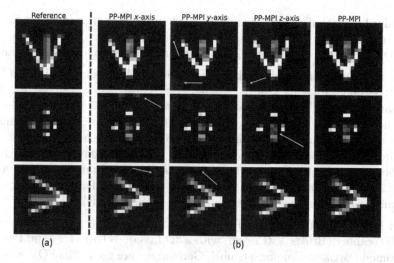

Fig. 3. 3D reconstructions of the OpenMPI resolution phantom with PP-MPI are shown along with the phantom's CAD model as visual reference. Central cross-sections along x, y, z axes are shown in separate rows. Arrows indicate notable artifacts.

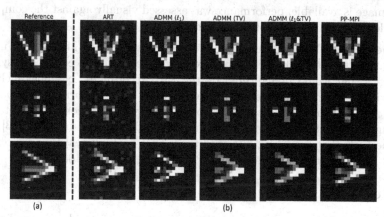

Fig. 4. 3D reconstructions of the OpenMPI resolution phantom are shown along with the CAD model of the phantom as visual reference. Central cross-sections along x, y, z axes are shown in separate rows.

3.2 Analyses

We demonstrated PP-MPI for reconstructing images from a 2D simulated dataset and a 3D experimental dataset (Open MPI) [11]. First, 2D PP priors were trained for denoising on the MPI-friendly dataset. Hyperparameters of the RDN architecture were tuned based on denoising performance on the validation set. Accordingly, RDN had 3 residual blocks, with 5 convolutional layers and 8 channels each. Original MPI-friendly images were taken as clean references, and noisy versions were then generated by adding white Gaussian noise with a standard deviation of 0.05. The RDN model was then trained to predict the clean images provided as input noise variants. Model training was performed via the ADAM optimizer and with ℓ_1-loss between predicted and reference images.

Simulated Dataset: Field-free-line (FFL) based SM was simulated for an FOV of 32×32 mm^2, imaging grid of 64×64. For reconstruction, the SM was then downsampled to 32×32 to avoid inverse crime [2]. MNP saturation, selection field and drive field were $0.55/\mu_0$, 2.5 T/m, 40 mT. The 2nd to 20th harmonics of the received signal were retained. White Gaussian noise was added to the measurement vector simulated for a numerical vessel phantom. To improve SNR, singular value truncation was performed on the SM and the measurement vector ($c = 220$ singular values out of $N = 1024$). Reconstruction performance was examined visually and via peak signal-to-noise ratio (PSNR).

Open MPI: Field-free point (FFP) data for the resolution phantom measured on a 3D scanner (Bruker, Ettlingen) with a 3D Lissajous trajectory and Perimag (Micromod Partikeltechnologie GmbH, Germany) were used. The FOV was $38 \times 38 \times 19$ mm^3, and the grid size was $19 \times 19 \times 19$. The MNP saturation, selection field and drive field were 50 mmol/L, $-0.5/-0.5/1$ T/m, 12 mT. Singular value truncation was used ($c = 2200$ singular values out of $N = 6859$). As no ground truth image is available, performance was assessed visually against the computer aided design (CAD) model of the phantom.

Competing Methods: We comparatively demonstrated PP-MPI against methods that use task-agnostic priors for flexible generalization to changes in system properties that would be captured by the SM. Accordingly, baselines included ART with ℓ_2-norm regularization [9], and ADMM with ℓ_1-norm, TV-norm and mixed ℓ_1&TV norm regularization [8]. Note that we did not consider end-to-end learning-based methods that require retraining under changes to the SM [3], and DIP methods that have long inference times that prohibit real-time processing [5]. All methods were implemented in PyTorch on a Tesla V100 GPU.

4   Results

PP-MPI was first demonstrated for 2D reconstruction of simulated vessel phantoms. PSNR metrics from competing methods are listed in Table 1. On average, PP-MPI outperforms the closest competitor by 3.10 dB PSNR across the test set. Representative reconstructions are displayed in Fig. 2. ART suffers from smoothing and ADMM variants have relatively poor vessel localization with occasional block artifacts. In contrast, PP-MPI alleviates reconstruction artifacts and maintains sharp vessel localization.

We then demonstrated PP-MPI for 3D reconstruction of experimental data. In this case, we first compared results from the multi-orientation 2D priors against 2D priors along singular axes. Representative results are displayed in Fig. 3. While priors in singular directions can suffer from reconstruction artifacts in other orientations containing the through-plane axis, PP-MPI with multi-orientation priors achieves uniformly high quality across all orientations. Afterwards, PP-MPI with multi-orientation priors was compared against competing baselines as illustrated in Fig. 4. ART has prominent background artifacts and vessel smoothing, whereas ADMM variants produce block artifacts particularly in the vicinity of areas with high MNP concentration. In contrast, PP-MPI achieves the highest visual quality with sharp vessel depiction and low artifacts.

Lastly, we examined 3D reconstruction times to assess suitability for real-time imaging. All methods were executed until convergence for fair comparison. ART with 5 iterations yielded a run time of 1.380 s due to its sequential nature of processing. ADMM variants with 200 iterations had run times of 0.076 (ℓ_1-norm), 0.633 (TV-norm) and 0.648 (ℓ_1-TV-norm). In comparison, PP-MPI achieves run times of 0.078 (single-orientation 2D priors), 0.082 (multi-orientation 2D priors) sec. These run times indicate that PP-MPI can be adopted for real-time reconstruction of a $19 \times 19 \times 19$ volume at 12 frames/sec. In contrast, a variant based on 3D priors could only run at 6 frames/sec.

5 Discussion

In this study, we introduced the first PP approach for MPI reconstruction for improved flexibility in coping with variations in system properties that inevitably alter the forward imaging model as captured by the system matrix. PP-MPI leverages a task-agnostic prior trained on an MPI-friendly dataset for denoising. This deep denoiser is then embedded into a fast model-based reconstruction implemented via an ADMM algorithm. Demonstrations were performed against state-of-the-art MPI reconstruction methods based on hand-crafted regularizers. Quantitative and qualitative improvements were achieved with PP-MPI on both simulated and experimental data. The performance and computational efficiency of PP-MPI render it a promising candidate for real-world MPI applications.

References

1. Ahmad, R., et al.: Plug-and-play methods for magnetic resonance imaging: Using denoisers for image recovery. IEEE Signal Process. Mag. **37**(1), 105–116 (2020). https://doi.org/10.1109/MSP.2019.2949470
2. Bathke, C., Kluth, T., Brandt, C., Maass, P.: Improved image reconstruction in magnetic particle imaging using structural a priori information. Int. J. Magn. Part. Imaging. **3**, 1703015 (2017). https://journal.iwmpi.org/index.php/iwmpi/article/view/64
3. Chae, B.G.: Neural network image reconstruction for magnetic particle imaging (2017). https://doi.org/10.48550/ARXIV.1709.07560, https://arxiv.org/abs/1709.0756
4. Deng, L.: The MNIST database of handwritten digit images for machine learning research. IEEE Signal Process. Mag. **29**(6), 141–142 (2012)
5. Dittmer, S., Kluth, T., Baguer, D.O., Maass, P.: A deep prior approach to magnetic particle imaging. In: Deeba, F., Johnson, P., Würfl, T., Ye, J.C. (eds.) MLMIR 2020. LNCS, vol. 12450, pp. 113–122. Springer, Cham (2020). https://doi.org/10.1007/978-3-030-61598-7_11

6. Güngör, A., et al.: TranSMS: Transformers for super-resolution calibration in magnetic particle imaging. IEEE Trans. Med. Imaging. 1 (2022). https://doi.org/10.1109/TMI.2022.3189693

7. Hatsuda, T., Shimizu, S., Tsuchiya, H., Takagi, T., Noguchi, T., Ishihara, Y.: A basic study of an image reconstruction method using neural networks for magnetic particle imaging. In: 2015 5th International Workshop on Magnetic Particle Imaging (IWMPI), p. 1 (2015). https://doi.org/10.1109/IWMPI.2015.7107046

8. Ilbey, S., et al.: Comparison of system-matrix-based and projection-based reconstructions for field free line magnetic particle imaging. Int. J. Magn. Part. Imaging. **3**, 1703022 (2017). https://doi.org/10.18416/IJMPI.2017.1703022, https://journal.iwmpi.org/index.php/iwmpi/article/view/81

9. Kluth, T., Jin, B.: Enhanced reconstruction in magnetic particle imaging by whitening and randomized SVD approximation. Phys. Med. Biol. **64**(12), 125026 (2019). https://doi.org/10.1088/1361-6560/ab1a4f

10. Knopp, T., et al.: Weighted iterative reconstruction for magnetic particle imaging. Phys. Med. Biol. **55**(6), 1577–1589 (2010). https://doi.org/10.1088/0031-9155/55/6/003

11. Knopp, T., Szwargulski, P., Griese, F., Graser, M.: OpenMPIData: An initiative for freely accessible magnetic particle imaging data. Data Brief **28**, 104971 (2020). https://doi.org/10.1016/j.dib.2019.104971, https://www.sciencedirect.com/science/article/pii/S2352340919313265

12. Koch, P., et al.: Neural network for reconstruction of MPI images. In: 9th International Workshop on Magnetic Particle Imaging, pp. 39–40 (2019)

13. Li, J., Li, J., Xie, Z., Zou, J.: Plug-and-play ADMM for MRI reconstruction with convex nonconvex sparse regularization. IEEE Access **9**, 148315–148324 (2021). https://doi.org/10.1109/ACCESS.2021.3124600

14. McCarthy, J.R., Weissleder, R.: Multifunctional magnetic nanoparticles for targeted imaging and therapy. Adv. Drug Deliv. Rev. **60**(11), 1241–1251 (2008)

15. Zhang, X., Le, T.A., Yoon, J.: Development of a real time imaging-based guidance system of magnetic nanoparticles for targeted drug delivery. J. Magn. Magn. Mater. **427**, 345–351 (2017)

16. Zhang, Y., Tian, Y., Kong, Y., Zhong, B., Fu, Y.: Residual dense network for image restoration. IEEE Trans. Pattern Anal. Mach. Intell. **43**(7), 2480–2495 (2021). https://doi.org/10.1109/tpami.2020.2968521

17. Zheng, B., et al.: Magnetic particle imaging tracks the long-term fate of in vivo neural cell implants with high image contrast. Sci. Rep. **5**(1), 1–9 (2015)

Learning While Acquisition: Towards Active Learning Framework for Beamforming in Ultrasound Imaging

Mayank Katare, Mahesh Raveendranatha Panicker$^{(\boxtimes)}$, A. N. Madhavanunni, and Gayathri Malamal

Department of Electrical Engineering and Center for Computational Imaging, Indian Institute of Technology Palakkad, Palakkad, India
mahesh@iitpkd.ac.in

Abstract. In the recent past, there have been many efforts to accelerate adaptive beamforming for ultrasound (US) imaging using neural networks (NNs). However, most of these efforts are based on static models, i.e., they are trained to learn a single adaptive beamforming approach (e.g., minimum variance distortionless response (MVDR)) assuming that they result in the best image quality. Moreover, the training of such NNs is initiated only after acquiring a large set of data that consumes several gigabytes (GBs) of storage space. In this study, an active learning framework for beamforming is described for the first time in the context of NNs. The best quality image chosen by the user serves as the ground truth for the proposed technique, which trains the NN concurrently with data acqustion. On average, the active learning approach takes 0.5 s to complete a single iteration of training.

Keywords: Active learning · Beamforming · Ultrasound

1 Introduction

Medical ultrasound (US) has been a popular non-invasive diagnostic imaging tool with widespread applications in cardiac, abdominal, fetal, musculoskeletal, and breast imaging [1]. Typically US imaging employs a pulse-echo technique where a piezoelectric transducer array transmits acoustic pulses into the tissue and receives the reflections, which are beamformed to produce an output image. During beamforming, the raw data acquired from the piezoelectric transducer array is space mapped and converted to form an image as shown in the upper pipeline (red dotted rectangle) of Fig. 1. Commercial US systems use low-complex, delay-and-sum (DAS) [2] beamforming to enable real-time reconstruction. DAS applies

The authors would like to acknowledge the funding from the Department of Science and Technology - Science and Engineering Research Board (DST-SERB (ECR/2018/001746)) and the support from NVIDIA Corporation for the donation of CLARA AGX Developer Kit through the Academic Hardware Grant program.

N. Haq et al. (Eds.): MLMIR 2022, LNCS 13587, pp. 115–122, 2022.
https://doi.org/10.1007/978-3-031-17247-2_12

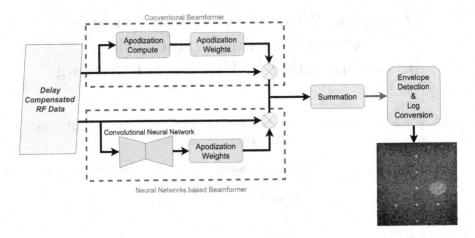

Fig. 1. Workflow from delay compensated RF data to Brightness (B)-mode image in conventional (upper pipeline (red)) and convolutional neural network (CNN) based (Bottom pipeline (green)) beamformers. In the CNN based approach, the main objective is to replace and accelerate the computationally intensive estimation of apodization weights. The process involves, the delay compensated RF data as input (of size $2400 \times 128 \times 128$), multiplication of the estimated apodization weights (of size $2400 \times 128 \times 128$) with the delay compensated data and channel wise sum to get the beamformed data (of size 2400×128). This is further envelope detected and Log compressed to the desired dynamic range. (Color figure online)

pre-determined delays and geometry-driven weights to the individual transducer (channel) signals, and sums up the individual contributions to yield the final beamformed signal. Advanced beamforming algorithms like filtered delay multiply and sum (F-DMAS) [3], minimum variance distortionless response (MVDR) [4] and generalized coherence factor (GCF) [5] based beamformers that provide considerable improvement in the image quality over DAS have also been proposed. However, these beamforming schemes are computationally intensive [6] which limits the real-time implementation and consequently the adaptability for clinical usage.

Accelerating computationally complex beamforming algorithms with deep neural networks has been gaining acceptance in the recent past [6–9]. A fully connected neural network [6] and a fully connected convolutional network with an identical number of samples along the depth and lateral directions throughout the network [9] have been developed. Recently, in [8], a self-supervised learning based approach has also been proposed. A general framework for beamforming acceleration with convolutional neural networks is shown in the bottom pipeline (green dotted rectangle) of Fig. 1. However, the NN based approaches in the literature have two concerns: 1) the bias in the assumption that the best image is always from a specific beamforming scheme (e.g. MVDR), and 2) the training is initiated post acquiring a significant amount of radio-frequency (RF) data.

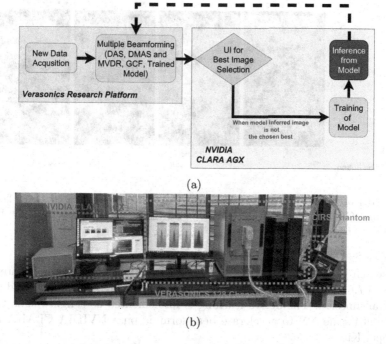

(a)

(b)

Fig. 2. (a) Proposed active learning framework for beamforming. The important steps are generation of images based on DAS, DMAS, MVDR, GCF and proposed model based beamforming which will be shown to the user for selection of the best image, followed by the training of the model in case the user has not chosen the model based beamforming as the best image. (b) Data acquisition setup for the proposed active learning frame work. The data acquisition will be done using the Verasonics 128 channel research platform and the UI and the training of the model will be done on the NVIDIA CLARA AGX Developer Kit. The CIRS flow mimicking phantom which was employed for one of the acquisition is also shown.

In this work, a novel active learning framework is proposed for US beamforming. To the best of our knowledge, this is a first of its kind in the literature. The proposed framework aims at:

1. Beamforming-agnostic learning by training the NN based on the ground truth selected by the user and not specific to any beamforming.
2. Reduced data storage compared to the conventional training methods.
3. Integration of data acquisition and the NN training into a single workflow.

2   Active Learning for US Beamforming

The proposed framework is as shown in Fig. 2a and the experimental setup is illustrated in Fig. 2b. The training data is acquired employing the Verasonics Vantage

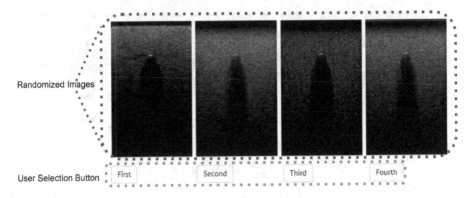

Fig. 3. GUI of Active Learning Framework. The images generated by DAS, DMAS, MVDR and GCF are randomized and provided to the user. In this case, the image generated by the model is not shown.

128 research US platform using 128 channel L11-5v transducer with a center frequency of 7.6 MHz and a sampling frequency of 31.25 MHz for non-steered plane wave transmission. The active learning is implemented as a lightweight U-Net based multi-scale NN to accelerate beamforming on a NVIDIA CLARA AGX Developer Kit.

The workflow starts with data acquisition using the Verasonics research US platform. Simultaneously, the acquired data along with the DAS, F-DMAS, MVDR, GCF images and the trained model image (except for the initial few cases) are shared with the NVIDIA CLARA AGX Developer Kit. In the NVIDIA CLARA AGX Developer kit, a python list of datasets are generated and the user is provided with the anonymized beamformed images through a streamlit [11] graphical user interface (GUI) as in Fig. 3 to avoid bias in image selection. Once the user selects the best image according to his/her perception, the same is used to train the NN. The process is repeated for every new batch of data and on successful completion, the model is saved as the final trained model. The flow of the implementation of work is presented in Fig. 4.

The choice of the best image in ultrasound imaging is always challenging due to operational and system variability. In order to have a uniformity across users, a criteria as given below is employed for the best image selection:

1. Determine regions of high intensity and compare for axial/lateral resolution.
2. Determine regions of homogeneous speckle and compare for speckle resolution.
3. Determine regions of contrast difference (e.g. cyst) and compare for contrast resolution.

Neural Network Architecture. A U-Net [10] based architecture is selected for the proposed approach due to its capability for global and local feature learning. The proposed U-Net architecture consists of a double convolution

Fig. 4. The flow of Active Learning implementation. The data acquired using the Verasonics platform is shared with the NVIDIA CLARA AGX Kit. The data is converted to a python list and subsequently displayed to the user as in Fig. 4. Based on the user selected best image as ground truth, the U-Net model is trained and saved.

layer followed by three hidden layers of downsampling, three hidden layers of upsampling, and the final convolution layer. The input to the model is the delay compensated RF data of size $m \times n \times N_{ch}$ where m and n are the number of pixels in depth and lateral directions respectively (2400×128) while N_{ch} is the number of channels. The double convolution layer changes the number of channels from 128 to 64 while keeping the data size in depth and lateral direction unchanged. The layer consists of a convolution layer followed by batch normalization and an activation function. The batch normalization is used after every convolution to increase the stability during training. The anti-rectifier activation function avoids 'dying' nodes when dealing with the RF data unlike ReLU [6]. The final convolution layer changes the number of channels from 64 back to 128 (the same size as the input delay compensated RF data). The output of the model are the apodization weights of size same as the input. The delay compensated RF data are weighted by the apodization weights generated by the model, summed over the channels, envelope extracted and log compressed to generate the final B-mode image (as shown in Fig. 1).

Training Details: The training data is collected from scans of the longitudinal and cross section scans of carotid artery, forearm muscles including brachioradialis and wrist of healthy volunteers following the principles outlined in the Helsinki Declaration of 1975, as revised in 2000. The reason for selection of these scans is to restrict to peripheral imaging (<5 cm depth) due to the planewave excitation. The models are implemented in Pytorch and trained on the 24 GB RTX6000 GPU available with the NVIDIA CLARA AGX developer kit. The input for the model is the delay compensated RF data and the ground truth for the loss function is the user-selected beamformed image (one out of DAS, F-DMAS, MVDR, GCF, and the trained model (except for the initial few cases)). The mean squared error (MSE) between the U-Net and the user-selected beamformed images is the employed loss function. Considering the active learning scenario, the current batch size is set to 1. The Adam optimizer is used with a learning rate of 1e-3 as in concurrence with [9]. The trained models are tested on an *in-silico* dataset with point targets and *in-vitro* datasets provided by the plane-wave imaging challenge for medical ultrasound (PICMUS) [12] and the challenge on ultrasound beamforming with deep learning (CUBDL) [13–15] of 2016 and 2020 IEEE International

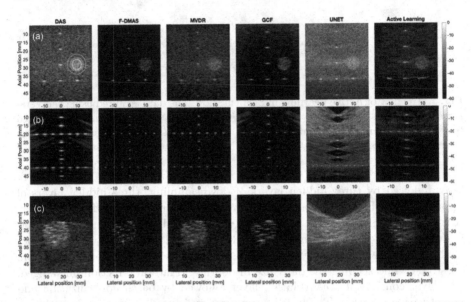

Fig. 5. Results from the *in-silico* and *in-vitro* experimental datasets (a) for a CIRS Multi-Purpose US Phantom (Model 040GSE). The region used for contrast measurement is indicated in the DAS image (b) PICMUS simulation dataset having point targets (c) An *in-vitro* experimental dataset having inclusion targets (INS009 dataset of CUBDL and more details on the same is available in [14,15]. The yellow circle and the green circle regions indicate the regions employed for CNR/CR calculations in Table 1. (Color figure online)

Ultrasonics Symposium, respectively. The training and test data have no overlap (i.e., the source of the data generated for the training and test are different).

3   Results

The section discusses the key results of the proposed approach in comparison with standard adaptive and classical beamforming approaches. The raw beamformed images without post-processing like speckle reduction or histogram corrections (thresholding, non-linear gamma correction, and other similar techniques for image enhancement) are presented to highlight the intrinsic differences between the beamformers. The qualitative and quantitative comparison of the results are shown in Fig. 5 and Tables 1, 2 respectively. The quantitative comparisons are presented for contrast ratio (CR), contrast to noise ratio (CNR), axial and lateral full width half maximum (FWHM) metrics. The beamformed images with the conventional U-Net trained model with DAS as ground truth (i.e. non-user selected and typical NN approach) and with the active learning model are visually comparable to the images created with conventional beamforming algorithms. The results of active learning are certainly encouraging and are expected to improve with further training.

Table 1. Contrast and resolution metrics for DAS, F-DMAS, MVDR, GCF, U-NET (DAS), and the proposed active learning framework for Fig. 5(a).

	CR	CNR (dB)	Axial FWHM (mm)	Lateral FWHM (mm)
DAS [2]	0.665	4.851	0.485	1.327
F-DMAS [3]	0.677	4.614	0.458	0.646
MVDR [4]	0.669	1.736	0.481	0.586
GCF [5]	0.623	6.677	0.433	0.832
UNET (DAS) [9], [10]	0.714	2.947	0.488	0.769
Proposed UNET (Active Learning)	0.785	3.269	0.305	0.650

Table 2. Resolution metrics for DAS, F-DMAS, MVDR, GCF, UNET (DAS), and the proposed Active Learning framework for Fig. 5(b).

	Axial FWHM (mm)	Lateral FWHM (mm)
DAS [2]	0.406	1.131
F-DMAS [3]	0.352	0.485
MVDR [4]	0.506	0.519
GCF [5]	0.325	0.377
UNET (DAS) [9], [10]	0.383	0.399
Proposed UNET (Active Learning)	0.297	0.456

4   Discussion and Conclusions

In the recent past, accelerating computationally intensive adaptive beamforming with NNs has been gaining popularity. However, such models are static as they are trained against a particular algorithm (e.g. MVDR) and acquiring and storing large datasets (nearly 1000 diverse images) for training is time and memory consuming. These concerns are overcome by the proposed active learning framework. The results from conventionally trained NN and the NN trained in the active learning framework are certainly encouraging. The results of the active learning framework could be improved with more training and tuning of the framework. From the statistics reported, it is estimated that the DAS beamforming has been selected in 22%, the F-DMAS in 20%, the MVDR and GCF in 29% of the total number of datasets used for training. Using the same framework, the model can be shared between different institutes for training with the dataset acquired using different machines to make the model more robust under the federated learning framework. Also the estimation of the image quality can be automated to accelerate the learning process independent of the user in a true active learning sense.

References

1. Travis, C.R.A.C: Ultrasonic Bioinstrumentation, 1st edn. Wiley, Hoboken (1988)
2. Perrot, V., Polichetti, M., Varray, F., Garcia, D.: So you think you can DAS? A viewpoint on delay-and-sum beamforming. Ultrasonics **111**, 106309 (2021)
3. Matrone, G., Savoia, A.S., Caliano, G., Magenes, G.: The delay multiply and sum beamforming algorithm in ultrasound B-mode medical imaging. IEEE Trans. Med. Imaging **34**(4), 940–949 (2015)
4. Holfort, I.K., Gran, F., Jensen, J.A.: Broadband minimum variance beamforming for ultrasound imaging. IEEE Trans. Ultrason. Ferroelectr. Freq. Control **56**(2), 314–325 (2009)
5. Li, P.-C., Li, M.-L.: Adaptive imaging using the generalized coherence factor. IEEE Trans. Ultrason. Ferroelectr. Freq. Control **50**(2), 128–141 (2003)
6. Luijten, B., et al.: Adaptive ultrasound beamforming using deep learning. IEEE Trans. Med. Imaging **39**(12), 3967–3978 (2020)
7. Sloun, R., Cohen, R., Eldar, Y.: Deep learning in ultrasound imaging. Proc. IEEE **108**, 11–29 (2020)
8. Zhang, J., He, Q., Xiao, Y., Zheng, H., Wang, C., Luo, J.: Ultrasound image reconstruction from plane wave radio-frequency data by self-supervised deep neural network. Med. Image Anal. **70**, 102018 (2021)
9. Mathews, R.P., Panicker, M.R.: Towards fast region adaptive ultrasound beamformer for plane wave imaging using convolutional neural networks. In: 43rd Annual International Conference of the IEEE Engineering in Medicine & Biology Society (EMBC), Virtual, pp. 2910–2913. IEEE (2021)
10. Ronneberger, O., Fischer, P., Brox, T.: U-Net: convolutional networks for biomedical image segmentation. In: Navab, N., Hornegger, J., Wells, W.M., Frangi, A.F. (eds.) MICCAI 2015. LNCS, vol. 9351, pp. 234–241. Springer, Cham (2015). https://doi.org/10.1007/978-3-319-24574-4_28
11. Streamlit. https://streamlit.io/. Accessed 22 June 2022
12. Liebgott, H., Rodriguez-Molares, A., Cervenansky, F., Jensen, J.A., Bernard, O.: U-net: plane-wave imaging challenge in medical ultrasound. In: 2016 IEEE International Ultrasonics Symposium (IUS), pp. 1–4. IEEE (2016)
13. Bell, M.A.L., Huang, J., Hyun, D., Eldar, Y.C., Van Sloun, R., Mischi, M.: Challenge on ultrasound beamforming with deep learning (CUBDL). In: 2020 IEEE International Ultrasonics Symposium (IUS), pp. 1–5. IEEE (2020)
14. Hyun, D., et al.: Deep learning for ultrasound image formation: CUBDL evaluation framework and open datasets. IEEE Trans. Ultrason. Ferroelectr. Freq. Control **68**(12), 3466–3483 (2021)
15. Bell, M., et al.: Challenge on Ultrasound Beamforming with Deep Learning (CUBDL) Datasets. IEEE Dataport. https://dx.doi.org/10.21227/f0hn-8f92.s. Accessed 22 June 2022

DPDudoNet: Deep-Prior Based Dual-Domain Network for Low-Dose Computed Tomography Reconstruction

Temitope Emmanuel Komolafe[1], Yuhang Sun[1], Nizhuan Wang[1], Kaicong Sun[1], Guohua Cao[1], and Dinggang Shen[1,2,3]([✉])

[1] School of Biomedical Engineering, ShanghaiTech University, Shanghai 201210, China
{tekomolafe,sunkc,caogh,dgshen}@shanghaitech.edu.cn
[2] Shanghai United Imaging Intelligence Co., Ltd., Shanghai 201210, China
[3] Shanghai Clinical Research and Trial Center, Shanghai 201210, China

Abstract. Low-dose computed tomography (LDCT) reconstruction has been an active research field for years. Although deep learning (DL)-based methods have achieved incredible success in this field, most of the existing DL-based reconstruction models lack interpretability and generalizability. In this paper, we propose a novel deep prior-based dual-domain network (DPDudoNet) by unrolling the model-based algorithm using iteratively-cascaded DenseNet and deconvolutional network. The proposed model embeds the intrinsic imaging model constraints, inherited from the foundational model-based algorithm, to tackle the issue of lacking interpretability. Besides, it contains fewer learnable parameters, compared to many representative networks, thus leading to simpler decision boundary and better generalizability. Moreover, a random initialization of the network based on Gaussian distribution is introduced as a deep prior for the LDCT reconstruction. The proposed model integrates the deep prior into both the image and sinogram domains via a dual-domain update scheme. Experimental results on the public AAPM LDCT dataset show that our proposed method has significant improvement over both the state-of-the-art (SOTA) DL-based methods and the traditional model-based algorithms with less model parameters and less computational load.

Keyword: Low-dose computed tomography · DenseNet · Dual-domain · Generalizability · Interpretability · Data consistency

1 Introduction

Computed Tomography (CT) is a non-invasive imaging modality that adopts X-rays to monitor anatomic structures of humans. However, ionizing radiation exposure increases the risk of cancer which is one major limitation of using this technique [1]. Therefore, reduction of ionizing radiation exposure without compromising image quality has been an active research area [2]. Low-dose CT (LDCT) can be acquired via a fewer number of projections (sparse view or limited angle CT acquisition) [3] or using a low tube current during CT acquisition. Conventional methods such as back projection (BP) or filtered back projection (FBP) have been adopted for CT reconstruction in the early times, but these methods require full-view projections or high tube current

N. Haq et al. (Eds.): MLMIR 2022, LNCS 13587, pp. 123–132, 2022.
https://doi.org/10.1007/978-3-031-17247-2_13

to obtain reasonable reconstruction results thereby exposing patients to high radiation. To overcome the shortcomings of the aforementioned algorithms, various model-based reconstruction algorithms have been proposed by employing handcrafted image priors [4]. More recently, due to the success of deep learning (DL), it has been popularly used for image reconstruction, denoising, super-resolution, and metal artifact reduction [5–7]. The DL-based LDCT reconstruction methods can be classified into three sub-categories: 1) the sinogram-domain-based models that apply convolutional neural network (CNN) to restore the missing part in the sinogram [8]; 2) the image-domain-based methods that adopt residual CNN [9] or generative adversarial network (GAN) [10] to conduct denoising in the image domain; 3) the dual-domain-based methods that take full advantage of dual domain information and can often achieve better performance than two subcategories of aforementioned methods [11, 12].

Although these DL-based methods [8–12] have shown promising results for LDCT reconstruction, most of them lack interpretability and generalizability [13]. In order to tackle these challenges, Yan *et al.* [14] unroll the model-based algorithm, which is formulated in the alternating direction method of multipliers (ADMM) framework, using iteratively cascaded CNN for the reconstruction of fast magnetic resonance imaging (MRI). Joas and Ozan [15] unroll the primal-dual hybrid gradient (PDHG) algorithm for LDCT reconstruction. Xia *et al.* [16] explore the manifold and graph integration convolutional networks (MAGIC) to unroll the iterative optimization in both the image and manifold spaces. Zhang *et al.* [17] propose the LEARN ++ model which unfolds the gradient descent update algorithm by CNN blocks to perform image restoration and sinogram inpainting in the image and projection domains, respectively. However, it requires a large amount of iterations for the unrolled network to achieve reasonable results, which makes it computationally intensive. Using the principle of unrolling, in this paper, we propose a novel deep prior-based dual-domain network (DPDuDoNet) for LDCT reconstruction with better interpretability and generalizability The proposed method unrolls the ADMM framework efficiently in both the image and sinogram domains. Besides, a deep prior is integrated into the proposed network by randomly initializing the weights of the CNNs based on Gaussian distribution.

2   Method

In this section, we first give a detailed description of the proposed DPDudo algorithm, and then present the proposed DPDudoNet which is an unrolled representation of the DPDudo algorithm via the framework of CNN.

2.1   The DPDudo Algorithm

To reconstruct a high-quality image from the LDCT acquisition through a neural network, the inputs are the LDCT image $X_L \in \mathbb{R}^{n \times m}$ and the low-dose sinogram $Y_L \in \mathbb{R}^{N_b \times N_p}$, where n and m denote the height and width of the LDCT image and N_b and N_p are the numbers of detector bins and projection views, respectively. The LDCT reconstruction is formulated as an optimization problem in both the image and sinogram domains according to the following Eq. 1:

$$\min_{Y_H, X_H} f(X_H, Y_H, X_L, Y_L) + \|\lambda_1 W_1 X_H\|_{1,2} + \|\lambda_2 W_2 Y_H\|_{1,2} \quad (1)$$

By formulating the data fidelity term f with three data consistency constraints, we have

$$\frac{1}{2}\|R_{\Gamma^c}(Y_H - Y_L)\|_2^2 + \frac{\alpha}{2}\|R_{\Gamma}(\mathcal{P}X_H - Y_H)\|_2^2 + \frac{\gamma}{2}\|R_{\Gamma^c}(\mathcal{P}X_H - Y_L)\|_2^2 \quad (2)$$
$$+\|\lambda_1 W_1 X_H\|_{1,2} + \|\lambda_2 W_2 Y_H\|_{1,2}$$

where $\mathcal{P}$ is the forward projection matrix. R_{Γ} and R_{Γ^c} are the sampling operators for the missing and available data, respectively. α and γ are the weighting parameters for data consistency in the sinogram and image domains, respectively. W_i $(i = 1, 2)$ are the sparsity transform and λ_i $(i = 1, 2)$ are the regularization parameters for image and sinogram domains, respectively [18]. To solve the optimization problem in Eq. 2, the ADMM algorithm with multi-block is introduced. By adopting the Langragian function, multiple variables $\mathbf{b}$, $\mathbf{d}$, and $\boldsymbol{\mu}$ are given by $\mathbf{d} = \begin{pmatrix} d_1 \\ d_2 \end{pmatrix}$, $\boldsymbol{\mu} = \begin{pmatrix} \mu_1 \\ \mu_2 \end{pmatrix}$, $\mathbf{W} = \begin{pmatrix} W_1 \\ W_2 \end{pmatrix}$, $\mathbf{b} = \begin{pmatrix} b_1 \\ b_2 \end{pmatrix}$ according to Yang et al. [14]. Specially, μ_1 and μ_2 are positive regularization parameters for the update of X_H and Y_H, b_1 and b_2 are dual variables, and d_1 and d_2 denote the regularization terms for the image and sinogram, respectively. The solution to Eq. 2 involves the following process. First, the dual variables are initialized as zero $(b_1 = b_2 = 0)$, and then X_H is updated via solving the quadratic approximation of Eq. 2 w.r.t. X_H as follows:

$$X_H^{k+1} = \mathcal{A}^{-1}[\alpha \mathcal{P}^T R_{\Gamma} Y_H^k + \gamma \mathcal{P}^T R_{\Gamma^c} Y_L + \mu_1 W_1^T (d_1^k - b_1^k)] \quad (3)$$

$$d_1^{k+1} = \mathcal{T}_{\lambda_1/\mu_1}(W_1 X_H^{k+1} + b_1^k) \quad (4)$$

$$b_1^{k+1} = b_1^k + (W_1 X_H^{k+1} - d_1^{k+1}) \quad (5)$$

where $\mathcal{T}_{\lambda_1/\mu_1}$ is a thresholding operator in the image domain. Finally, we update Y_H as follows:

$$Y_H^{k+1} = \mathcal{B}^{-1}[\alpha R_{\Gamma} \mathcal{P} X_H^k + R_{\Gamma^c} Y_L + \mu_2 W_2^T (d_2^k - b_2^k)] \quad (6)$$

$$d_2^{k+1} = \mathcal{T}_{\lambda_2/\mu_2}(W_2 Y_H^{k+1} + b_2^k) \quad (7)$$

$$b_2^{k+1} = b_2^k + (W_2 Y_H^{k+1} - d_2^{k+1}) \quad (8)$$

where $\mathcal{A}$ and $\mathcal{B}$ in Eqs. 3 and 6 are updated as $\mathcal{A} = \mathcal{P}^T(\alpha R_{\Gamma} + \gamma R_{\Gamma^c})\mathcal{P} + \mu_1$ and $\mathcal{B} = \alpha R_{\Gamma} + \gamma R_{\Gamma^c} + \mu_2$, respectively. $\mathcal{T}_{\lambda_2/\mu_2}$ is a thresholding operator in the sinogram domain. When X_H and Y_H perform iterative update for a certain amount of iterations, the LDCT reconstruction is complete.

2.2 The DPDudoNet

The goal of DPDudoNet is to unroll the aforementioned DPDudo algorithm and approximate some of the operators using CNN. According to Sect. 2.1, the solution to Eq. 2 has been given in Eqs. 3–8. The inverse operators $\mathcal{A}^{-1}$, $\mathcal{B}^{-1}$ and the thresholding operators $\mathcal{T}_{\lambda_1/\mu_1}$, $\mathcal{T}_{\lambda_2/\mu_2}$ are approximated using CNNs. Deep prior is imposed by initializing the weights of the network (convolutional and deconvolutional networks) with random variables z which obey the Gaussian distribution $z \sim \aleph(0, 1)$ [19] as shown in Fig. 1. The forward and backward projections are approximated by the transform layer and reconstruction layer as shown in Fig. 1.

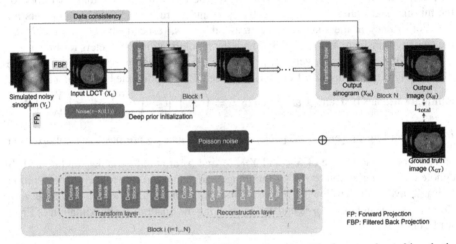

Fig. 1. The framework of DPDudoNet for LDCT reconstruction. The framework combines both projection and image priors with imaging physics in a semi-supervised manner. A series of blocks which represent the unrolled iterative update are updated in each epoch based on the defined loss function via an end-to-end training. The sinogram raw data is employed in each block to preserve data consistency. N is the number of iterations corresponding to the number of blocks in DPDuDoNet. $z \sim \aleph(0, 1)$ is the random variable for initialization of the network which obeys Gaussian distribution to enforce deep prior.

2.3 Interpretability of the DPDudoNet

The DPDudoNet can be explained in four stages, namely the transform layer, the denoising layer, the reconstruction step, and the update step. The transform layer converts the input noisy image to projection data, which is solved by the data-consistency update in Eq. 6. The denoising layer is composed of a stack of convolutional layers and non-linear transform as shown in Eqs. 4 and 7 for the image and sinogram domains, respectively. The proximal operator is approximated by a 4-layer CNN, where each layer consists of BN + ReLU + Conv in each dense block of the transform layer. The denoised images are fed into the deconvolutional network for image reconstruction based on Eq. 3. Finally, the update step updates the learned weights from both image and sinogram with Eqs. 5

and 8, respectively. After N-blocks, the unrolled DPDudoNet completes the reconstruction of the CT image X_H. Thanks to the dense connections between different layers of DenseNet [20], transferring low-level and high-level features is enabled for better convergence, and thus mitigates the issues of varnishing and exploding gradients [3]. In the proposed method, the number of iterations is set as $N = 4$.

2.4 Training Loss

We adopt a joint loss function which contains a l_2-norm with a structural similarity index (SSIM) loss [21] to preserve the perceptual quality of the reconstructed images, as purely using l_2-norm is often prone to over smoothness. The loss function is given below:

$$L_{\text{Total}} = \alpha_1 l_2(X_H, X_{GT}) + \alpha_2(1 - SSIM(X_H, X_{GT})) \qquad (9)$$

where X_{GT} is the ground-truth standard dose computed tomography image and X_H is the output of DPDudoNet. α_1 and α_2 are parameters used to balance the weights of l_2-norm and $SSIM$, which are empirically set as 0.8 and 0.2 in the following experiments, respectively.

3 Experimental Results

3.1 Clinical Data

To validate the performance of the proposed DPDudoNet, a clinical CT dataset from the 2016 NIH-AAPM-Mayo Clinic Low Dose CT Grand Challenge [20, 22] was used. The dataset contained 5,777 CT slices with a resolution of 512×512 and a thickness of 1 mm from 10 patients. In our experiment, we randomly extracted 1000 slices for training and 250 slices for testing. From these standard-dose slices, we generated the corresponding low-dose projections. Specifically, the projections of the LDCT images were generated using Siddon's ray-driven method [23]. The source to rotation-center distance was set as 40 cm, and the detector to rotation-center was 40 cm with an image region of 20 cm × 20 cm. The detector elements were set as 512, and 1024 views were uniformly placed in the full scan range. According to Chen *et al.* [9], Poisson noise is added to the projections as follows:

$$n_i \approx Poisson\{b_i e^{-l_i} + r_i\}, i = 1, ..., I, \qquad (10)$$

where n_i represents the measurement of the i-th ray path, l_i denotes the integral of the attenuation coefficients along the i-th ray, r_i is the read-out noise, and b_i is the blank scan factor $b_i = b_0 = 1 \times 10^5$. The low-dose CT images were reconstructed by the FBP algorithm as the input to the network. For the other competitive DL-based methods, i.e., RED-CNN [9] and WGAN-VGG [10], 4326 and 250 paired slices were randomly extracted for training and testing, respectively.

3.2 Evaluation Metrics

For performance evaluation, three image quality assessment indices, i.e., peak signal-to-noise ratio (PSNR) [24], structural similarity index measure (SSIM) [25], and root mean squared error (RMSE), are used in this study.

3.3 Training Details

The network was trained on the NVIDIA GeForce RTX 3060 installed on Window OS of i7-10700k CPU@3.80 GHZ with 32.0 GB RAM. The network was trained using the TensorFlow framework [26]. Adam was used as the optimizer with $\beta_1 = 0.9$ and $\beta_2 = 0.999$, and the initial learning rate was set as 1×10^{-5} and decreased by a half every 50 epochs. The total number of epoch is 100,000 with a mini-batch size of 5. The weights and bias of both the convolution and deconvolution filters were initialized with Gaussian distributions of zero mean and a standard deviation of 0.01 and 0.1, respectively, for the weights and bias for the convolutional layers, and also 0.05 and 0.5, respectively, for the deconvolutional layers. The hyperparameters of the DPDudoNet was initialized according to the work [14].

3.4 Performance Evaluation

We compare the DPDudoNet with some state-of-the-art (SOTA) LDCT reconstruction algorithms, including the model-based reconstruction method for sparse sampling BM3D [27], and the DL-based methods such as RED-CNN [9] and WGAN-VGG [10]. Table 1 depicts quantitative results for different SOTA methods and the proposed DPDudoNet.

Table 1. Comparison of the proposed DPDudoNet with other methods in PSNR, SSIM, and RMSE.

	PSNR ± SEM	SSIM ± SEM	RMSE ± SEM
LDCT (FBP)	36.8064 ± 0.0901	0.9049 ± 0.0016	0.0097 ± 0.00005
BM3D [27]	39.5140 ± 0.1123	0.9476 ± 0.0005	0.0079 ± 0.00009
WGAN-VGG [10]	40.0085 ± 0.0710	0.9555 ± 0.0007	0.0068 ±0.00005
RED-CNN [9]	40.8545 ± 0.0690	0.9683 ± 0.0008	0.0065 ±0.00004
DPDudoNet(Ours)	**44.9260 ± 0.0450**	**0.9898 ± 0.0002**	**0.0064 ± 0.00003**

It is observed that the DL-based algorithms, WGAN-VGG and RED-CNN, outperform the model-based iterative algorithm BM3D as expected. Through visual comparison, we can observe that WGAN-VGG shows more details and the results are more similar to the ground-truth images as shown in Figs. 2 and 3, although there is a slight decrease in quantitative comparison with the RED-CNN. This might be attributed to the adopted Wasserstein distance and perceptual loss which give better perceptual details of the reconstructed images as shown in the absolute difference image in Fig. 3. RED-CNN compromises some fine details due to oversmoothing, which might hamper the detection of other vital lesions. The BM3D shows visible artifacts as can be seen in the absolute difference image demonstrated in Fig. 3. These artifacts might be caused by the total variation regularization which tends to make the image piecewise smooth. The proposed DPDuduNet has 10%–12% (4–5 dB) increase in average PSNR, 2%–4% (0.022–0.0343) increase in SSIM, and 2%–6% (0.0001–0.0004) decrease in RMSE, compared to the other DL-based methods. We can see that the proposed DPDudoNet outperforms both the model-based BM3D and the DL-based algorithms (RED-CNN and WGAN-VGG) quantitatively and qualitatively (by visual inspection). Besides, the proposed method has less trainable parameters (4.19×10^5) compared to RED-CNN (4.66×10^5) and WGAN-VGG (3.41×10^7). This implies that it has simpler decision boundary and thus has better generalizability according to the law of parsimony [28].

3.5 Ablation Study

To evaluate the effectiveness of the deep-prior initialization on the proposed network, we empirically varied the weights and bias of the convolutional layers of the network and found no significant improvement in the performance. Then, we varied the initialization of weights and bias in the deconvolutional layer, and observed substantial performance changes. In addition, increasing the number of network parameters led to a decrease in the performance of generalizability and an increase of the training time as shown in Table 2. The weight of $w = 0.005$ and bias of $b = 0.5$ gave the best performance in DPDudoNet. The filter size of 7×7 had the best performance since it had a larger receptive field and extracted finer details compared to the filter sizes of 3×3 and 5×5. Therefore, our filter size was set as 7×7 in the experiments.

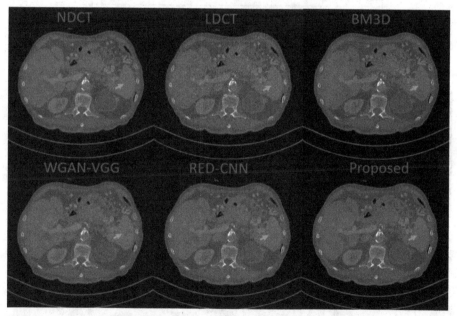

Fig. 2. Comparison of reconstruction results from abdominal CT scans for different methods, displayed at [−800 1000]HU. The green arrows indicate tiny vessels of the spleen, while the red ones show noticeable artifacts in the BM3D images. (Color figure online)

Similarly, we evaluated the effect of the number of filters in use, and we experimented with $n = 8, 16,$ and 24, respectively. The result with $n = 24$ shows a slight improvement in image quality over the result by $n = 16$ but with much more training time (approximately

2 times). The number of filters increases the width of the network which slows down the network convergence. Therefore, we set $n = 16$ for balancing the overall performance.

Table 2. Ablation study to show the effectiveness of the deep-prior random initialization, the filter size, and the number of filters on the performance of DPDudoNet.

Deep-prior initialization	PSNR	SSIM	RMSE	Training time
$w = 0.05, b = 0.5$	45.3818	0.9919	0.0054	25 h 36 min
$w = 0.1, b = 0.9$	44.9301	0.9914	0.0057	28 h 30 min
$w = 0.5, b = 0.5$	39.3927	0.9695	0.0107	29 h 00 min
$w = 0.9, b = 0.5$	36.0113	0.9495	0.0158	29 h 18 min
Filter size				
3×3	41.8600	0.9815	0.0081	19 h 36 min
5×5	45.0325	0.9915	0.0056	23 h 24 min
7×7	45.3818	0.9919	0.0054	25 h 36 min
Number of filters				
8	44.03330	0.9892	0.0063	18 h 48 min
16	45.3818	0.9919	0.0054	25 h 36 min
24	45.5623	0.9925	0.0053	47 h 12 min

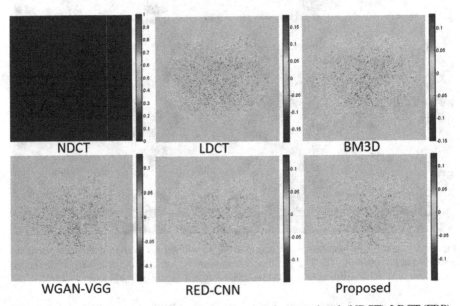

Fig. 3. The normalized absolute difference map between the ground truth (NDCT), LDCT (FBP), and other SOTA methods.

4 Conclusion

In this paper, we have proposed a novel deep-prior based dual-domain reconstruction algorithm DPDudoNet for low-dose CT reconstruction. We unroll the model-based algorithm into a CNN-based iterative framework. An initialization of the network parameters based on Gaussian distribution is considered as a deep prior for the LDCT reconstruction, and the proposed network integrates the prior into both the spatial and sinogram domains via a dual-domain update scheme. Furthermore, the proposed method shows good interpretability through the unrolled model-based architecture and also good generalizability by the lightweight network structure. Experimental results have validated the effectiveness of our proposed DPDudoNet for LDCT reconstruction with an improved performance over the SOTA methods in both quantitative measure and visual inspection. In the future, we will compare our method with other unrolled models such as LEARN++, MAGIC, and the learned primal-dual algorithms.

Acknowledgments. This work was supported in part by the National Natural Science Foundation of China (62131015), the Key R&D Program of Guangdong Province (2021B0101420006), Science and Technology Commission of Shanghai Municipality (STCSM) (21010502600).

References

1. Journy, N., et al.: Are the studies on cancer risk from CT scans biased by indication? Elements of answer from a large-scale cohort study in France. Br. J. Cancer **112**(1), 185–193 (2015)
2. Brink, J.A., Miller D.L.: U.S. national diagnostic reference levels: closing the gap. Radiology **277**(1), 3–6 (2015)
3. Zhang, Z., Liang, X., Dong, X., Xie, Y., Cao, G.: A sparse-view CT reconstruction method based on combination of DenseNet and Deconvolution. IEEE Trans. Med. Imaging. **37**(6), 1407–1417 (2018)
4. Mileto, A., Guimaraes, L.S., McCollough, C.H., Fletcher, J.G., Yu, L.: State of the art in abdominal CT: the limits of iterative reconstruction algorithms. Radiology **293**(3), 491–503 (2019)
5. Tian, C., et al.: Deep learning on image denoising: an overview. Neural Netw **131**, 251–275 (2020)
6. Zhang, Z., et al.: Self-supervised CT super-resolution with hybrid model. Compt. Biol. Med. **138**, 104775 (2021)
7. Wang, H., et al.: InDuDoNet: an interpretable dual domain network for CT metal artifact reduction. In: de Bruijne, M., et al. (eds.) MICCAI 2021. LNCS, vol. 12906, pp. 107–118. Springer, Cham (2021). https://doi.org/10.1007/978-3-030-87231-1_11
8. Ghani, M.U., Karl, W.C.: Deep learning-based sinogram completion for low-dose CT. In: 2018 IEEE 13th Image, Video, and Multidimensional Signal Processing Workshop (IVMSP), pp. 1–5 (2018)
9. Chen, H., et al.: Low-dose CT with a residual encoder-decoder convolutional neural network. IEEE Trans. Med. Imaging **36**(12), 2524–2535 (2017)
10. Yang, Q., et al.: Low-dose CT image denoising using a generative adversarial network with Wasserstein distance and perceptual loss. IEEE Trans. Med. Imaging **37**(6), 1348–1357 (2018)
11. Jiao, F., et al.: A dual-domain CNN-based network for CT reconstruction. IEEE Access **9**, 71091–71103 (2021)

12. Wu, W., et al.: DRONE: dual-domain residual-based optimization NEtwork for sparse-view CT reconstruction. IEEE Trans. Med. Imaging. **40**(11), 3002–3014 (2021)
13. Monga, V., Li, Y., Eldar, Y.C.: Algorithm unrolling: interpretable, efficient deep learning for signal and image processing. IEEE Signal Process **38**(2), 18–44 (2021)
14. Yang, Y., Sun, J., Li, H., Xu, Z.: ADMM-CSNet: a deep learning approach for image compressive sensing. IEEE Trans. Pattern Anal. **42**(3), 521–538 (2020)
15. Adler, J., Öktem, O.: Learned primal-dual reconstruction. IEEE Trans. Med. Imaging **37**(6), 1322–1332 (2018)
16. Xia, W., et al.: MAGIC: manifold and graph integrative convolutional network for low-dose CT reconstruction. IEEE Trans. Med. Imaging **40**(12), 2459–3472 (2021)
17. Zhang, Y., et al.: LEARN++: Recurrent Dual-Domain Reconstruction Network for Compressed Sensing CT. arXiv preprint arXiv:2012.06983 (2020)
18. Zhang, H., Dong, B., Liu, B.: JSR-Net: A deep network for joint spatial-radon domain CT reconstruction from incomplete data ICASSP 2019. In: 2019 IEEE International Conference on Acoustics, Speech and Signal Processing (ICASSP), pp. 3657–3661 (2019)
19. Ulyanov, D., Vedaldi, A., Lempitsky, V.: Deep image prior. Int. J. Comput. Vision **128**(7), 1867–1888 (2020). https://doi.org/10.1007/s11263-020-01303-4
20. Huang, G., Liu, Z., Van Der Maaten, L., Weinberger, K.Q.: Densely connected convolutional networks. In: Proceedings of the IEEE Conference on Computer Vision and Pattern Recognition, pp. 4700–4708 (2017)
21. Zhao, H., Gallo, O., Frosio, I., Kautz, J.: Loss functions for image restoration with neural networks. IEEE Trans Comput Imaging **3**(1), 47–57 (2017)
22. AAPM. (2015). Low Dose CT Grand Challenge. [Online]. Available: https://www.aapm.org/GrandChallange/LowDoseCT/#
23. Siddon, R.L.: Fast calculation of the exact radiological path for a three-dimensional CT array. Med. Phys. **12**(2), 252–255 (1985)
24. Damera-Venkata, N., Kite, T.D., Geisler, W.S., Evans, B.L., Bovik, A.C.: Image quality assessment based on a degradation model. IEEE Trans. Image Process **9**, 636–650 (2000)
25. Wang, Z., Bovik, A.C., Sheikh, H.R., Simoncelli, E.P.: Image quality assessment: from error visibility to structural similarity. IEEE Trans. Image Process **13**, 600–612 (2004)
26. Abadi, M., et al.: Tensorflow: a system for large-scale machine learning. In: 12th {USENIX} symposium on operating systems design and implementation {OSDI 16}, pp. 265–283 (2016)
27. Dabov, K., Foi, A., Katkovnik, V., Egiazarian, K.: Image denoising by sparse 3-D transform-domain collaborative filtering. IEEE Trans. Image Process **16**(8), 2080–2095 (2007)
28. Guan, S., Loew, M.: Analysis of generalizability of deep neural networks based on the complexity of decision boundary. In: 19th IEEE International Conference on Machine Learning and Applications (ICMLA), pp.101–106 (2020)

MTD-GAN: Multi-task Discriminator Based Generative Adversarial Networks for Low-Dose CT Denoising

Sunggu Kyung[1], JongJun Won[2], Seongyong Pak[1], Gil-sun Hong[3], and Namkug Kim[2,3(✉)]

[1] Department of Bioengineering, Asan Medical Center, Asan Medical Institute of Convergence Science and Technology, Seoul, South Korea
[2] Department of Convergence Medicine, Asan Medical Center, University of Ulsan College of Medicine, Seoul, South Korea
namkugkim@gmail.com
[3] Department of Radiology, Asan Medical Center, University of Ulsan College of Medicine, Seoul, South Korea

Abstract. Radiation dose reduction of computed tomography (CT) is an important research topic due to the potential risk of X-rays. However, low-dose CT (LDCT) images inevitably have a noise that can compromise diagnoses. Recently, although various deep learning algorithms were applied for LDCT denoising, there are still some issues including over-smoothness and visually awkwardness for radiologists. In this paper, we propose a multi-task discriminator based generative adversarial network (MTD-GAN) simultaneously conducting three vision tasks (classification, segmentation, and reconstruction) in a discriminator. To stabilize GAN training, we introduce two novel loss functions termed non-difference suppression (NDS) loss and reconstruction consistency (RC) loss. Furthermore, we take a fast Fourier transform with convolution block (FFT-Conv Block) in the generator to make use of both high- and low-frequency features. Our model has been evaluated by pixel-space and feature-space based metrics in the head and neck LDCT denoising task, and results show outperformance quantitatively and qualitatively than the state-of-the-art denoising methods.

Keywords: Multi-task learning · Generative adversarial network · Low-dose CT denoising · Head and neck CT

1 Introduction

Computed tomography (CT) is one of the most essential diagnostic modalities utilized in contemporary medical centers. However, X-rays could cause genetic damage and cancer with a chance proportional to the radiation dose [1, 2]. ALARA (As Low As Reasonably Achievable) principles are widely applied in CT imaging in an effort to limit unwanted

Supplementary Information The online version contains supplementary material available at https://doi.org/10.1007/978-3-031-17247-2_14.

N. Haq et al. (Eds.): MLMIR 2022, LNCS 13587, pp. 133–144, 2022.
https://doi.org/10.1007/978-3-031-17247-2_14

consequences [3]. Reducing the radiation dose raises noise and artifacts in generated images, which might have a negative impact on the radiologists' confidence. Therefore, considerable effort has been expended to develop improved image reconstruction or image processing techniques for low-dose CT (LDCT).

1.1 Deep Denoiser

As deep learning technology has advanced, several algorithms have been proposed to use deep neural networks for the LDCT denoising task, with promising results. Convolution neural network (CNN), transformer network, and generative adversarial network (GAN) are the three major approaches for designing a deep denoiser.

CNNs. Many CNNs have been used for LDCT image processing since CNN is excellent at capturing the high-frequency components of images [4]. Chen *et al.* was a pioneer work that employed convolution, deconvolution, and skip connections into the residual encoder-decoder structure [5]. Although the network improved the performance by a large margin than traditional image processing methods, the important structural details of CT images were often ignored and over-smoothed [6, 7]. To strengthen the sharpness, Liang *et al.* designed an edge enhancement module consisting of the trainable Sobel convolution to merge the edge information [8]. However, the sharpness of the noise also has been enhanced.

Transformers. With the recent necessity for acquiring long-range contextual information in images, an attention-based transformer has been applied to vision tasks. Zamir *et al.* devised several critical blocks, including multi depth-wise convolution transposed attention and a gated depth-wise convolution feed-forward network, that can capture long-range pixel interactions while remaining applicable to high-resolution images [9]. Wang *et al.* developed a convolution-free token to token dilated vision transformer to avoid the vanilla transformer's tendency to disregard the dependence between adjacent tokens [10]. The network dilates and shifts features to optimize contextual information and leverage spatial relations across a greater region. However, the computational complexity of the transformer increases quadratically with the spatial resolution, therefore a solution for high-resolution images is still required.

GANs. By dynamically assessing the similarity between the denoised and normal dose CT (NDCT) during the GAN training, the generator can preserve more texture information from NDCT and generates a real texture pattern. Yang *et al.* utilized the Wasserstein GAN with gradient penalty and perceptual loss [11]. Shan *et al.* designed a modularized adaptive processing neural network using a cascaded structure for LDCT imaging [12]. Huang *et al.* used U-Net based discriminators [13] in GANs to distinguish global and local distinctions between normal-dose and denoised images to regularize LDCT denoising [14]. To strengthen edge features, they added a second U-Net based discriminator in the image gradient domain. However, due to dynamic changes in GAN training, generated images with inconsistent structural patterns sometimes emerge [15, 16]. Thus, there is still an opportunity for stabilization and improvement in GAN training for LDCT denoising tasks.

1.2 Multi-task Learning

MTL targets learning multiple different tasks simultaneously by leveraging comprehensive information for the generalization performance of all tasks. This strategy has resulted in an average performance improvement and is beneficial for tasks with similar features [17]. As a method of applying multi-task learning to GAN, there are multi-task generators, multi-task discriminators, and multiple discriminators. Multi-task generators are used to alleviate the lack of data concerns or boost super-resolution task quality [18, 19]. In a multi-task discriminator, a discriminator is designed to not only guide the generator to produce a more realistic image but also extract the discriminative task features through multi-tasks [20–22]. In multiple discriminators, they usually used two discriminators in charge of individual tasks for more detailed control characteristics [14, 23].

In this study, we propose the multi-task discriminator GAN (MTD-GAN) to mitigate these problems with three novel accretions:

- Develop a multi-task discriminator to enhance the LDCT denoising, which leverages three multi-tasks (classification, segmentation, reconstruction) on discriminators in the GANs framework to identify both global and local differences between the de normal-dose and noised images.
- Introduce two novel losses for avoiding the confusion of discriminator training in the CT denoising. Non-difference suppression (NDS) loss is a refined least-square GAN (LSGAN) loss in the segmentation task. Reconstruction consistency (RC) loss regulates the sensitivity of the discriminator to perturbations using reconstruction images.
- Design a novel generator, FFT-Generator to improve LDCT denoising. The proposed generator can learn the fine structural details using both image and Fourier domains through Fast Fourier Transform with Convolution Block (FFT-Conv Block).

2 Methods

Here, we provide the details of MTD-GAN (See Fig. 1). Our architecture includes a discriminator and a generator. To better distinguish between the denoiser's output and the NDCT image target, the discriminator conducts three types of vision multi-tasks: reconstruction, segmentation, and classification. In addition, we added two losses for improved representation and the regulation of the discriminator's sensitivity. Considering the Fourier domain's merits, we added FFT-Conv Block in our generator for improving performance. Through an adversarial strategy, our MTD-GAN is optimized.

2.1 Multi-task Discriminator

A typical discriminator is susceptible to forgetting prior samples since the distribution of synthetic samples shifts as the generator constantly varies during training, failure to maintain a powerful representation to identify the global and local image difference [13]. To solve the challenges, we introduce multi-task discriminators using classification, segmentation (*cf.* In this paper, segmentation means not segmenting different anatomical structures but a pixel-wise classification of true and false), and reconstruction (*cf.* In this

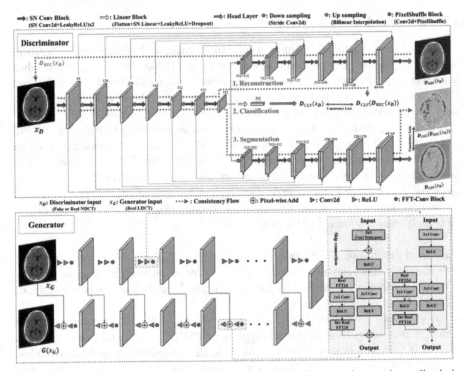

Fig. 1. Schematic overview of the MTD-GAN framework. Our framework comprises a discriminator and generator: A discriminator is trained for distinguishing the real normal-dose and denoised images by three multi-tasks (classification, segmentation, reconstruction) with consistency loss using reconstruction output. In the generator, we adopted the RED-CNN as a base denoiser and added the FFT-Conv block at every layer for better denoising performance. Note: SN; spectral normalization [25]. The number above each feature map represents the channel. (Color figure online)

paper, the reconstruction means not converting sinogram to image but restoring the input image). To conduct effective multi-task learning for capturing the semantic denoised and normal-dose image features, we adopted a hard parameter sharing architecture, which has a shared encoder and three types of task-specific layers for proposed vision tasks. Our multi-task discriminator learns a powerful representation that can characterize both global and local differences between the normal-dose and denoised images (See Fig. 1 discriminator part).

Reconstruction (REC). The first target-specific layer for REC guides the discriminator to realize a reconstruction task, which helps improve the discrimination and generalization abilities of the classifier module. This REC task is performed unsupervised manner to reconstruct the fake or real NDCT image through the encoding-decoding process, which enables the network to better learn the semantic contextual representation by capturing the image characteristics [24]. The REC loss was defined as the mean absolute error loss.

$$L_{REC} = \mathbb{E}_{x_D}[|\boldsymbol{D}_{REC}(x_D) - x_D|], \tag{1}$$

Classification (CLS). The second task-specific layer for CLS is performed to determine whether the image is fake or real like conventional discriminators with a scalar value, which enables the network to learn the most discriminate difference by focusing on the global structure between the fake and real images, which regularizes the generator accordingly. The CLS loss is defined as the LSGAN [26].

$$L_{CLS} = \mathbb{E}_{x_{D\_real}}[D_{CLS}(x_{D\_real}) - 1]^2 + \mathbb{E}_{x_{D\_fake}}[D_{CLS}(x_{D\_fake})]^2, \tag{2}$$

where x_{D_real} is the real normal-dose input and x_{D_fake} is the denoised input to discriminator.

Segmentation (SEG). The third task-specific layer for SEG is performed to decide if the image is fake or real with a per-pixel confidence map, which makes the network recognize the variation of local details between the normal-dose and denoised images. The SEG loss is also defined as the LSGAN.

$$L_{SEG} = \mathbb{E}_{x_{D\_real}}[D_{SEG}(x_{D\_real}) - 1]^2 + \mathbb{E}_{x_{D\_fake}}[D_{SEG}(x_{D\_fake})]^2, \tag{3}$$

2.2 Non-difference Suppression Loss and Consistency Loss

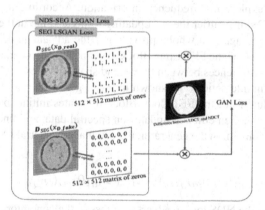

Fig. 2. A concept of our NDS loss to LSGAN loss in segmentation task.

Non-difference Suppression (NDS) Loss. Due to the nature of the medical image, the regions of background and bone with the same LDCT and NDCT occupy a large portion of the CT image, which causes serious confusion when the discriminator makes a decision. In other words, according to the previous Eq. (4) process [14], the background parts of NDCT and LDCT are the same, but different label values are calculated, and incorrect information can be passed to the generator. To improve the stable GAN training, we apply the NDS loss where the regions without difference were excluded from the loss calculation (See Fig. 2). The NDS-SEG loss is defined as follows:

$$L_{NDS-SEG} = L_{SEG} \times boolean(|I_{LDCT} - I_{NDCT}|), \tag{4}$$

Reconstruction Consistency (RC) Loss. As shown in Fig. 1 green flows, we proposed the novel consistency regularization using reconstruction output for stabilizing GAN training. The consistency regularization penalizes the sensitivity of the discriminator [27]. In this paper, we considered with emphasis the difference between the input and the reconstructed images. The RC loss is defined as follows:

$$L_{Consist.} = \mathbb{E}_{x_D}[\|D_{CLS}(x_D) - D_{CLS}(D_{REC}(x_D))\| + \|D_{SEG}(x_D) - D_{SEG}(D_{REC}(x_D))\|], \tag{5}$$

In discriminator, the total loss function for the multi-tasks is defined by:

$$L_D = \lambda_1 L_{CLS} + \lambda_2 L_{NDS-SEG} + \lambda_3 L_{REC} + \lambda_4 L_{Consist.}, \tag{6}$$

where λ controls the between different loss factors.

2.3   FFT-Generator

We selected the RED-CNN [5] stacked 10 (de)convolutional layers at both encoder and decoder as the base denoiser to demonstrate the effect of the multi-task based discriminators. A convolutional operator is good at extracting high-frequency details, but it may lack the ability to explore low-frequency information. According to the spectral convolution theorem [28] in Fourier theory, updating a single value in the spectral domain globally affects the image as a whole, providing it the advantage of a wide receptive field [29]. Thus, we added the FFT-Conv Block to get benefits from modeling both high- and low-frequency differences between blurry and sharp features, while capturing both long- and short-term interactions. As shown in Fig. 1 generator part, besides a conventional spatial residual flow, the FFT-Conv Block translates initial spatial features into some spectral domain, then efficient updates on spectral data, and finally converts data back to the spatial domain. In the generator, the original adversarial LSGAN loss for the generator is Eq. (7).

$$L_{adv} = \mathbb{E}_{x_G}[D_{CLS}(x_{D\_fake}) - 1]^2 + \mathbb{E}_{x_G}[D_{SEG}(x_{D\_fake}) - 1]^2, \tag{7}$$

We also applied the NDS loss to adversarial loss in the generator.

$$L_{NDS-adv} = \mathbb{E}_{x_G}[D_{CLS}(x_{D\_fake}) - 1]^2 + \mathbb{E}_{x_G}[D_{SEG}(x_{D\_fake}) - 1]^2 \times boolean(|I_{LDCT} - I_{NDCT}|), \tag{8}$$

Inspired by [30], we used the Charbonnier loss to achieve better performance on the denoising task.

$$L_{pixel} = \mathbb{E}_{x_G}\left[\sqrt{\|I_{NDCT} - G(x_G)\|^2 + \varepsilon^2}\right], \tag{9}$$

where I_{NDCT} and x_G are the normal-dose image and low-dose input (I_{LDCT}) to generator, and ε is 10^{-6}. To further improve the fidelity of high-frequency details, we used the additional edge loss to control the high-frequency components between the NDCT image and the denoised image.

$$L_{edge} = \mathbb{E}_{x_G}\left[\sqrt{\|\Delta(I_{NDCT}) - \Delta(G(x_G))\|^2 + \varepsilon^2}\right], \tag{10}$$

where Δ denotes the Laplacian operator. The total generator loss is defined as follows:

$$L_G = \lambda_5 L_{NDS-adv} + \lambda_6 L_{pixel} + \lambda_7 L_{edge}, \tag{11}$$

where λ controls the between different loss weights.

3   Experiments and Results

3.1   Experiments Settings

Dataset. The head and neck CT denoising dataset was acquired by retrospectively searching the Asan Medical Center in Korea database for patients who had consecutive CT scans from July 2020 through August 2020. In 130 patient CT data, 6,054 pairs of images (100 patients) were randomly sampled as a train set, 845 pairs of images (15 patients) were sampled as a validation set, and 859 pairs of images (15 patients) were sampled as a test set. The model is trained using quarter-dose LDCT images with Poisson random noise inserted by a reconstruction program [31] and normal-dose CT (NDCT) images. All CT scans are B30 kernel and 3 mm thick.

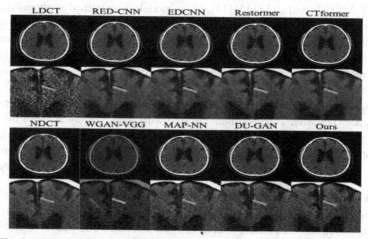

Fig. 3. The denoising results of previous methods on the test set. The display window is [0, 80] HU. We zoomed ROI marked by the red square where have clinically meaningful area. Red and yellow arrows indicate sulcus and falx cerebri, respectively. (Color figure online)

Preprocessing. We used a brain window that clips [0, 80] Hounsfield units (HU) and scales to [0, 1] for network input. We cropped the CT image's foreground and then randomly extracted 8 patches of 64×64 sizes from each 512×512 original image. Data augmentation is used to extend the dataset by keeping a duplicate of the original image and randomly rotating and flipping it.

Training Setting. For fair comparison within limited resources, the batch size of all experiments was set to the maximum for the single GPU memory, respectively. We used an AdamW optimizer with a learning rate of $1e^{-4}$ using a warmup of 10 epochs, and weight decay of $5e^{-4}$. The learning rate was reduced during the training of the polynomial learning rate schedule. The total number of epochs was up to 500.

Weight Setting. We empirically set λ identically to intensively compare the role of MTL ($\lambda_{1-4} = 1$). The multi-task weights λ in Eq. (11) were first adjusted manually to improve performances ($\lambda_5 = 1$ and $\lambda_{6-7} = 50$). The weights λ could be optimized by a grid search but with our restricted resources, it would be a quite expensive process. To reduce detrimental gradient interference between multi-tasks, we used a projecting conflicting gradients (PCGrad) algorithm [32], which projects the gradient of one task onto the normal plane of the gradient of any other task with a conflicting gradient.

3.2 Comparison Results

Comparison of Previous Works. Our model is compared with state-of-the-art baseline algorithms: RED-CNN [5], EDCNN [8], Restormer [9], CTformer [10], WGAN-VGG [11], MAP-NN [12], and DU-GAN [14]. These models were trained as official codes but the training settings including optimizer, patch size, epochs, and learning rate scheduler were united equally for a fair comparison. For the quantitative evaluation of denoising image quality, we used peak signal-to-noise ratio (PSNR), structural similarity (SSIM), and root mean square error (RMSE). However, because those metrics are vulnerable to over-smoothed images [8, 14], we additionally adopted perceptual loss (PL) [11], texture matching loss (TML) [33], and Fréchet inception distance (FID) [34] to measure feature space similarity. The quantitative results from Table 1 show that our model has the best FID, PL, TML, and SSIM performances than other models and competitive performance on RMSE and PSNR. As illustrated in Fig. 3, our MTD-GAN preserves clinically significant anatomical structures, resulting in radiologist-friendly images.

Ablation Study. We conducted excessive ablation studies to investigate the effect of the individual elements of the MTD-GAN. The training settings were fixed equally for a fair comparison and the number of epochs in the ablation study was up to 200 and the batch size was 20. From the results reported in Table 2 and Fig. 4 and 5, it is evident that when individual elements of MTD-GAN were added gradually, both quantitative and qualitative performances improved.

Table 1. Quantitative results for a comparative analysis with previous methods on the test set.

Previous works	FID↓	PL↓	TML↓	RMSE↓	PSNR↑	SSIM↑	Params
RED-CNN [5]	34.7098	0.1493	15.5072	0.0330	33.3131	0.9012	1.8M
EDCNN [8]	38.0299	0.1487	14.9475	0.0343	32.9481	0.8988	23.6M
Restormer [9]	32.7898	0.1469	15.2586	**0.0323**	**33.5237**	0.9026	26.1M
CTformer [10]	33.5319	0.1496	14.2172	0.0344	32.1764	0.8979	1.4M
WGAN-VGG [11]	53.9002	0.2629	29.7508	0.0589	26.3789	0.8454	7.8M
MAP-NN [12]	19.5778	0.1373	11.4723	0.0383	32.0321	0.8995	18.0M
DU-GAN [14]	18.8156	0.1285	10.5245	0.0364	32.5533	0.9035	114.6M
MTD-GAN (Ours)	**17.4655**	**0.1239**	**9.9462**	0.0359	32.6926	**0.9052**	68.9M
GT (NDCT)	9.8371	0.0	0.0	0.0	100.0	1.0	–
Input (LDCT)	39.7624	0.1821	20.4434	0.0575	28.9550	0.8743	–

Note: Params, the number of parameters; p-values were calculated between MTD-GAN vs. others and MTD-GAN showed a significant difference (P < 0.0001) between all previous works in all metrics except FID.

Table 2. Quantitative results for a comparative analysis in ablation study on the test set.

Ablation Study	FID↓	PL↓	TML↓	RMSE↓	PSNR↑	SSIM↑
(a) G: RED-CNN / D: CLS-Discriminator	20.0615	0.1332	11.1556	0.0366	32.5082	0.9032
(b) + D: CLS&SEG-Discriminator	19.1339	0.1329	10.9765	0.0375	32.3491	0.9027
(c) + D: CLS&SEG&REC-Discriminator	18.3820	0.1324	10.9761	0.0372	32.4050	0.9025
(d) + D: L_{NDS}	18.2724	0.1329	11.0543	0.0369	32.4347	0.9028
(e) + D: $L_{Consist.}$	18.2577	0.1329	11.0562	0.0370	32.4502	0.9026
(f) + G: FFT-Generator	17.9308	0.1275	10.2946	0.0371	31.2766	0.9035
(g) + PCGrad (Ours)	17.6212	0.1276	10.3559	0.0369	31.2932	0.9037
High	9.8355	0.0	0.0	0.0	100.0	1.0
Low	39.7582	0.1821	20.4448	0.0575	28.9550	0.8743

Note: The red color represents the best performance, and the blue color represents the second-highest performance.

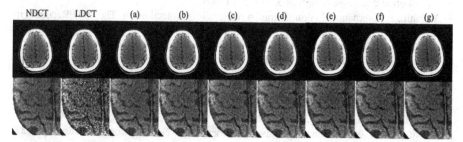

Fig. 4. The denoising results in the ablation study on the test set. The display window is [0, 80] HU. (a)–(g) are from the same as the label shown in Table 2.

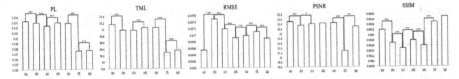

Fig. 5. The statistical analysis in the ablation study on the test set. (a)–(g) are from the same as the label shown in Table 2. We conducted paired t-tests only at each inter-stage. p-values were calculated: *, P < 0.01; **, P < 0.001; ***, P < 0.0001.

4   Conclusion

In this paper, a novel GAN algorithm using a multi-task based discriminator for LDCT denoising is developed for clinical applications. To the best of our knowledge, this is the first study to apply three vision multi-tasks to the discriminator in the LDCT denoising task. Primarily, we contribute in three ways: (1) An architecture based on multi-tasks makes the discriminator stronger, which guides the generator to synthesize images maintaining global and local realism. (2) To avoid the confusion of GAN training, the NDS loss makes the discriminator robust by excluding confusing parts in the segmentation task, and the RC loss using the generated reconstruction allows the network to obtain more contextual information. (3) The introduction of the FFT-Conv Block to the LDCT denoising task enables the generator to utilize both high- and low-frequency components and to expand the receptive field, resulting in images with a higher level of detail. In experimental results, the proposed MTD-GAN achieves better denoising performance than other methods and has potential for clinical use.

References

1. Brenner, D.J., Hall, E.J.: Computed tomography—an increasing source of radiation exposure. N. Engl. J. Med. **357**, 2277–2284 (2007)
2. de Gonzalez, A.B., Darby, S.: Risk of cancer from diagnostic X-rays: estimates for the UK and 14 other countries. Lancet **363**, 345–351 (2004)
3. Valentin, J.: International commission on radiological protection. In: The 2007 Recommendations of the International Commission on Radiological Protection, vol. 103, pp. 2–4. Annals of the ICRP, ICRP Publication (2007)
4. Wang, H., Wu, X., Huang, Z., Xing, E.P.: High-frequency component helps explain the generalization of convolutional neural networks. In: Proceedings of the IEEE/CVF Conference on Computer Vision and Pattern Recognition, pp. 8684–8694 (2020)
5. Chen, H., et al.: Low-dose CT with a residual encoder-decoder convolutional neural network. IEEE Trans. Med. Imaging **36**, 2524–2535 (2017)
6. Goodfellow, I., et al.: Generative adversarial nets. Adv. Neural Inform. Process. Syst. **27**, (2014)
7. Wang, Z., Bovik, A.C., Sheikh, H.R., Simoncelli, E.P.: Image quality assessment: from error visibility to structural similarity. IEEE Trans. Image Process. **13**, 600–612 (2004)
8. Liang, T., Jin, Y., Li, Y., Wang, T.: EDCNN: Edge enhancement-based densely connected network with compound loss for low-dose CT denoising. In: 2020 15th IEEE International Conference on Signal Processing (ICSP), pp. 193–198. IEEE (2020)

9. Zamir, S.W., Arora, A., Khan, S., Hayat, M., Khan, F.S., Yang, M.-H.: Restormer: efficient transformer for high-resolution image restoration. In: Proceedings of the IEEE/CVF Conference on Computer Vision and Pattern Recognition, pp. 5728–5739 (20220)

10. Wang, D., Fan, F., Wu, Z., Liu, R., Wang, F., Yu, H.: CTformer: Convolution-free Token2Token Dilated Vision Transformer for Low-dose CT Denoising. arXiv preprint arXiv:2202.13517 (2022)

11. Yang, Q., et al.: Low-dose CT image denoising using a generative adversarial network with Wasserstein distance and perceptual loss. IEEE Trans. Med. Imaging **37**, 1348–1357 (2018)

12. Shan, H., et al.: Competitive performance of a modularized deep neural network compared to commercial algorithms for low-dose CT image reconstruction. Nat. Mach. Intell. **1**, 269–276 (2019)

13. Schonfeld, E., Schiele, B., Khoreva, A.: A u-net based discriminator for generative adversarial networks. In: Proceedings of the IEEE/CVF Conference on Computer Vision and Pattern Recognition, pp. 8207–8216 (2020)

14. Huang, Z., Zhang, J., Zhang, Y., Shan, H.: DU-GAN: generative adversarial networks with dual-domain U-Net-based discriminators for low-dose CT denoising. IEEE Trans. Instrum. Meas. **71**, 1–12 (2021)

15. Lin, C.H., Chang, C.-C., Chen, Y.-S., Juan, D.-C., Wei, W., Chen, H.-T.: COCO-GAN: generation by parts via conditional coordinating. In: Proceedings of the IEEE/CVF International Conference on Computer Vision, pp. 4512–4521 (2020)

16. Zhang, H., Goodfellow, I., Metaxas, D., Odena, A.: Self-attention generative adversarial networks. In: International Conference on Machine Learning, pp. 7354–7363. PMLR (2019)

17. Vandenhende, S., Georgoulis, S., Van Gansbeke, W., Proesmans, M., Dai, D., Van Gool, L.: Multi-task learning for dense prediction tasks: a survey. IEEE Trans. Pattern Anal. Mach. Intell. **44** (2021)

18. Hang, R., Zhou, F., Liu, Q., Ghamisi, P.: Classification of hyperspectral images via multitask generative adversarial networks. IEEE Trans. Geosci. Remote Sens. **59**, 1424–1436 (2020)

19. Rad, M.S., et al.: Benefiting from multitask learning to improve single image super-resolution. Neurocomputing **398**, 304–313 (2020)

20. Liu, M.-Y., et al.: Few-shot unsupervised image-to-image translation. In: Proceedings of the IEEE/CVF International Conference on Computer Vision, pp. 10551–10560 (2019)

21. Cha, J., Chun, S., Lee, G., Lee, B., Kim, S., Lee, H.: Few-shot compositional font generation with dual memory. In: Vedaldi, A., Bischof, H., Brox, T., Frahm, JM. (eds.) European Conference on Computer Vision. LNIP, vol. 12364, pp. 735–751. Springer, Cham (2020). https://doi.org/10.1007/978-3-030-58529-7_43

22. Wan, W., Lee, H.J.: Generative adversarial multi-task learning for face sketch synthesis and recognition. In: 2019 IEEE International Conference on Image Processing (ICIP), pp. 4065–4069. IEEE (2019)

23. Liu, Y., Wang, Z., Jin, H., Wassell, I.: Multi-task adversarial network for disentangled feature learning. In: Proceedings of the IEEE Conference on Computer Vision and Pattern Recognition, pp. 3743–3751 (2018)

24. Kyung, S., et al.: Improved performance and robustness of multi-task representation learning with consistency loss between pretexts for intracranial hemorrhage identification in head CT. Med. Image Anal. **81**, 102489 (2022)

25. Miyato, T., Kataoka, T., Koyama, M., Yoshida, Y.: Spectral normalization for generative adversarial networks. arXiv preprint arXiv:1802.05957 (2018)

26. Mao, X., Li, Q., Xie, H., Lau, R.Y., Wang, Z., Paul Smolley, S.: Least squares generative adversarial networks. In: Proceedings of the IEEE International Conference on Computer Vision, pp. 2794–2802 (2016)

27. Zhang, H., Zhang, Z., Odena, A., Lee, H.: Consistency regularization for generative adversarial networks. arXiv preprint arXiv:1910.12027 (2019)

28. Katznelson, Y.: An introduction to Harmonic Analysis. Cambridge University Press (2004)
29. Chi, L., Jiang, B., Mu, Y.: Fast fourier convolution. Adv. Neural. Inf. Process. Syst. **33**, 4479–4488 (2020)
30. Zamir, S.W., et al.: Multi-stage progressive image restoration. In: Proceedings of the IEEE/CVF Conference on Computer Vision and Pattern Recognition, pp. 14821–14831 (2021)
31. Kramer, M., et al.: Computed tomography angiography of carotid arteries and vertebrobasilar system: a simulation study for radiation dose reduction. Medicine **94** (2015)
32. Yu, T., Kumar, S., Gupta, A., Levine, S., Hausman, K., Finn, C.: Gradient surgery for multi-task learning. Adv. Neural. Inf. Process. Syst. **33**, 5824–5836 (2020)
33. Sajjadi, M.S., Scholkopf, B., Hirsch, M.: Enhancenet: single image super-resolution through automated texture synthesis. In: Proceedings of the IEEE International Conference on Computer Vision, pp. 4491–4500 (2017)
34. Heusel, M., Ramsauer, H., Unterthiner, T., Nessler, B., Hochreiter, S.: Gans trained by a two time-scale update rule converge to a local nash equilibrium. Adv. Neural Inform. Process. Syst. **30** (2017)

Uncertainty-Informed Bayesian PET Image Reconstruction Using a Deep Image Prior

Viswanath P. Sudarshan[1], K. Pavan Kumar Reddy[1(✉)], Mohana Singh[1],
Jayavardhana Gubbi[1], and Arpan Pal[2]

[1] Embedded Devices and Intelligent Systems, TCS Research, Bangalore, India
pavank.reddy@tcs.com
[2] Embedded Devices and Intelligent Systems, TCS Research, Kolkata, India

Abstract. Model-based image reconstruction (MBIR) methods using
convolutional neural networks (CNNs) as priors have demonstrated superior image quality and robustness compared to conventional methods.
Studies have explored MBIR combined with supervised and unsupervised
denoising techniques for image reconstruction in magnetic resonance
imaging (MRI) and positron emission tomography (PET). Unsupervised
methods like the deep image prior (DIP) have shown promising results
and are less prone to hallucinations. However, since the noisy image is
used as a reference, strategies to prevent overfitting are unclear. Recently,
Bayesian DIP (BDIP) networks that model uncertainty tend to prevent
overfitting without requiring early stopping. However, BDIP has not been
studied with data-fidelity term for image reconstruction. In this work, we
propose an MBIR framework with a modified BDIP. Specifically, a novel
uncertainty-based penalty is included to the BDIP to improve reconstruction across iterations. Results on simulated and *in vivo* data show that
our method yields improved reconstruction compared to methods with
conventional priors and typical DIP without uncertainty. Notably, the
uncertainty maps across iterations provide insights on improving image
quality and can aid in risk management.

Keywords: Reconstruction · Bayesian · PET-MRI · Uncertainty

1 Introduction and Related Work

Positron emission tomography (PET) is a molecular imaging technique that
maps the uptake of an injected radiotracer. Clinicians infer functional and
metabolic information from the spatial distribution of the radiotracers, e.g., fluo-
rodeoxyglucose (FDG). Despite high specificity, PET suffers from challenges such

---

V. P. Sudarshan and K. P. K. Reddy—Equal contribution.

Supplementary Information The online version contains supplementary material
available at https://doi.org/10.1007/978-3-031-17247-2_15.

as poor spatial resolution (detector geometry) and low signal-to-noise ratio (limited number of photons). Thus, typically, PET image reconstruction is guided by structural information from an anatomical modality such as magnetic resonance imaging (MRI). This work focuses on PET image reconstruction aided by structural information from corresponding coregistered MRI image.

After the seminal work that proposed the maximum-likelihood-based expectation maximization (MLEM) algorithm for PET image reconstruction [16], subsequent works exploited image gradient-based priors within the EM framework [9], and later works included anatomical information from MRI [2,12,13]. With the advent of multimodal imaging systems, works focused on segmentation-free approaches that modeled joint priors enforcing similarities of (i) image gradients and their orientations across MRI and PET images at local neighborhoods [6,7,11] or (ii) at a patch-level [18,20]. The work in [23] proposed an asymmetrical version of the Bowsher prior [2], demonstrating improved partial volume correction for PET images. Recent PET image enhancement approaches include denoising in the image domain using a learned convolutional neural network (CNN) [5]. The work in [19] used an uncertainty-aware loss function to train a CNN to predict standard-dose PET from low-dose PET. However, their work focused on mapping a given low-dose PET image to a standard-dose PET image using a training set (supervised method). Alternatively, the PET data is denoised in the sinogram domain and subsequently reconstructed using MLEM or other variants [15]. More recently, for PET reconstruction, work in [8] employed a Plug-and-Play (PnP) approach [3,17] which uses the alternating direction method of multipliers (ADMM) based optimization scheme to alternate between the data-fidelity term and the image-denoising term.

The PnP framework for image reconstruction poses a constrained optimization problem [1,3,8] that decouples the data-fidelity term and the image-denoiser term. This enables the use of well-known denoisers as regularizers/priors coupled with a suitable data-fidelity term for image enhancement. E.g., [8], uses a CNN that is based on the deep image prior (DIP) [22] as the regularizer for PET reconstruction. While DIP has the advantage of not requiring training data, it easily overfits to the noisy reference image and hence, strategies to prevent overfitting are not clear. The work in [21] proposed a Bayesian DIP (BDIP) extending the work by [10], for image denoising. Importantly, BDIP showed that early stopping was not necessary and that the predicted images showed non-decreasing peak signal-to-noise ratio (PSNR) with respect to the noiseless image, across epochs. However, BDIP does not focus on a data-fidelity term that is critical for severely *ill-posed* problems such as low-dose (or noisy) PET image reconstruction. On the other hand, the PnP framework do not focus on quantifying uncertainty and utilizing the uncertainty information for improving image quality across iterations. This work addresses the said issues by proposing a modified BDIP within the PnP framework for PET image reconstruction. This is the first work to incorporate Bayesian uncertainty information within a PnP framework for image reconstruction.

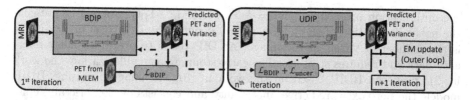

Fig. 1. The UDIP-MBIR Framework. The thresholded uncertainty maps (risk maps) are used for providing additional penalty for subsequent iterations. The CNN-predicted PET followed by the EM update acts as the reference image for the next iteration. For the first iteration, as there is no $\mathcal{L}_{\text{uncer}}(\cdot)$, the network reduces to BDIP.

In this work, we propose a modified version of the BDIP, that includes an uncertainty-weighted loss, which in turn is used as the unsupervised CNN-based regularizer within the PnP framework for image reconstruction. We propose an uncertainty-weighted loss term to train the BDIP so that the regions with higher uncertainty are penalized more compared to regions with lower uncertainty. Our BDIP predicts at each iteration (i) denoised PET image and (ii) per-voxel predictive uncertainty through estimation of aleatoric and epistemic uncertainty. At each iteration, we generate a risk map using the two uncertainty components that indicates regions with high uncertainty values and use the same in subsequent iterations (via the uncertainty-weighted loss) to improve the reconstruction quality. Empirical results on simulated and *in vivo* data show that the proposed framework provides improved PET quantification in addition to risk maps for improved risk management.

2   Methods

We describe the PET forward model, followed by the CNN prior with novel uncertainty-weighted loss used across iterations. Later, we show how the iterative PET reconstruction with the novel prior is solved within the PnP framework.

Model-Based Image Reconstruction (MBIR) for PET. Let U and V represent the coregistered pair of PET and MRI images, respectively, each containing N voxels. Let operator $\mathcal{A}$ model the PET forward process to generate the measurements M (sinogram) from D detector pairs. We model $\mathcal{A}$ as strip integrals[1]. Assuming M follows a Poisson distribution (independent and identically distributed), the log-likelihood function for PET can be written as $\log(P(M|U)) = \sum_{d=1}^{D} M_d \log W_d - W_d - \log M_d!$, where $W = (\mathcal{A}U)$.

Unsupervised CNN-Based Image Denoising. The initially proposed DIP [22], uses random noise, say E, as input to a deep CNN, say $\Phi_{\Theta}(\cdot)$, parameterized by Θ. Typically, a mean squared error (MSE) between the predicted image and the noisy reference image is used as the loss function resulting in

---

[1] https://web.eecs.umich.edu/~fessler/code/.

the optimization problem: $\arg\min_\Theta \frac{1}{N}\sum_i \|\Phi_\Theta(E)_i - Y_i\|_2^2$, where Y represents the noisy observation of the image, and Y_i denotes the i-th voxel in Y, and N is the number of voxels in the image. As DIP tends to overfit to noisy reference data and requires strategies like early-stopping as regularization, the work in [21] proposed BDIP based on the work in [10], for image denoising. BDIP models the per-voxel predictive uncertainty and consists of aleatoric and epistemic uncertainty. As mentioned earlier, BDIP showed that early stopping was not necessary the predicted images showed non-decreasing PSNR for the predicted image. In this work we build on BDIP coupled with a data-fidelity term that is critical for severely *ill-posed* problems such as image reconstruction. Similarly, we show how Bayesian uncertainty can be quantified within the PnP framework for improving image quality across iterations. Specifically, we propose an improved PnP with uncertainty quantification which includes a modified BDIP with the uncertainty-weighted loss term. Our modified BDIP is called uncertainty-weighted DIP (UDIP), which acts as the unsupervised CNN-based regularizer within the PnP framework for image reconstruction.

Let $\widehat{Y}$ and $\widehat{C}$ represent the two outputs of the CNN representing the predicted image and the per-voxel variance, respectively. We split the final layer of the CNN to predict these two variables. Now, for computing the aleatoric uncertainty, we consider the MSE loss with the variance term defined as $\mathcal{L}_{\text{BDIP}} = \frac{1}{N}\sum_{i=1}^{N}\left(\frac{\|\widehat{Y}_i - Y_i\|_2^2}{\widehat{C}_i} + \log\widehat{C}_i\right)$. Here, $\widehat{C}$ is used to compute the aleatoric uncertainty. For numerical stability, (i) we predict $\log\widehat{C}$ and then exponentiate to retrieve the variance term and (ii) add a small scalar to the denominator in Equation above. We employ variational dropout to quantify epistemic uncertainty as in [10,19,21]. The CNN is trained with dropouts activated, i.e., randomly masked weight parameters. The final predicted image $\widehat{Y}$ and the variance image $\widehat{C}$ is then obtained by performing K forward passes also with dropouts. Thus, the predicted image is obtained as $\widehat{Y} = \frac{1}{K}\sum_{k=1}^{K}\widehat{Y}^k$. Similar to [10], the aleatoric uncertainty is given as the mean variance image from the K samples, i.e., $C_A := \frac{1}{K}\sum_{k=1}^{K}\widehat{C}^k$ and the epistemic uncertainty is computed as the variance of the set of predicted PET images, $\{\widehat{Y}^k\}_{k=1}^{K}$, as $C_E := \frac{\sum_{k=1}^{K}\left(\widehat{Y}^k - C_A\right)^2}{K}$.

Uncertainty-Weighted MSE Loss for UDIP. For the first iteration ($n = 1$), the CNN is trained based on the loss $\mathcal{L}_{\text{BDIP}}$. Subsequently, for the $(n+1)$-th iteration, the total uncertainty obtained in the n-th iteration, $C_{\text{total}}^n = C_A^n + C_E^n$, is used to provide an additional penalty. Particularly, we define a global scalar threshold τ_U denoting the permissible uncertainty value. Next, we generate a binary risk map R^n (for the n−th iteration)by thresholding the total uncertainty (C_{total}) i.e., assigning 1 to voxels where $C_{\text{total}_i}^n \geq \tau_U$ and 0 otherwise. For the $(n+1)$-th iteration, we add an additional loss term, called $\mathcal{L}_{\text{uncer}}$ defined as

$\mathcal{L}_{\text{uncer}} = \frac{1}{N} \sum_{i=1}^{N} \|R_i^n(Y_i^n - \widehat{Y}_i^n)\|_2^2$. Thus, the overall loss function becomes

$$\mathcal{L}_{\text{UDIP}} = \underbrace{\frac{1}{N} \sum_{i=1}^{N} \left(\frac{\|\widehat{Y}_i - Y_i\|_2^2}{\widehat{C}_i} + \log \widehat{C}_i \right)}_{\text{MSE with variance term included}} + \underbrace{\frac{\eta}{N} \sum_{i=1}^{N} \|R_i^n(Y_i^n - \widehat{Y}_i^n)\|_2^2}_{\text{Uncertainty-weighted term}} \quad (1)$$

where η is a hyperparameter. The proposed framework is summarized in Fig. 1. We call the above mentioned CNN trained with the loss $\mathcal{L}_{\text{UDIP}}$ as $\Phi_\Theta^{\text{UDIP}}(\cdot)$.

PnP with UDIP Prior for PET Reconstruction. Similar to previous works employing PnP framework [3], we adopt the ADMM optimization scheme to reconstruct the PET images, by combining the PET data-fidelity term and the UDIP prior mentioned above. We obtain our reconstructed PET image as the solution to the optimization problem $\arg\max_U \log(P(M|U)) + \alpha \log(P(U|V))$, where α denotes the regularization constant and $\log(P(U|V))$ denotes the prior term conditioned on the MRI image V. To decouple the data-fidelity and the regularizer terms, we employ variable splitting and obtain the following constrained optimization problem: $\arg\max_U \log(P(M|U)) + \alpha \log(P(Z|V))$ such that $U = Z$. Using the ADMM scheme to solve the said problem, results in the following update equations with the auxiliary variable Z and the penalty variable ρ

$$U^{n+1} = \arg\max_U \log(P(M|U)) - \frac{\rho}{2}\|U^n - Z^n + \Gamma^n\|_2^2 \quad (2)$$

$$Z^{n+1} = \Phi_{\Theta^{n+1}}^{\text{UDIP}}(U^{n+1}|V) \quad (3)$$

$$\Gamma^{n+1} = \Gamma^n + U^{n+1} - Z^{n+1} \quad (4)$$

Equation 2 has a fixed-point update obtained by formulating a surrogate function involving the MLEM update and the solution to the quadratic term as shown in [8]. Equation 3 is obtained by replacing the proximal map with the update from the denoiser $\Phi_\Theta^{\text{UDIP}}(\cdot)$, which is trained with the loss $\mathcal{L}_{\text{UDIP}}$ for a fixed number of iterations. Equation 4 is the update for the dual variable Γ.

Implementation Details. We use a U-net [14] architecture for the UDIP network with 4 cascaded layers of 2D convolutions, batch normalization, leaky ReLU activation function, and dropouts with a heuristically chosen probability of 0.2. Parameters ρ and η both were set to $= 1$. Analysis on the effect of hyperparameters (ρ, η) has not been performed in this work. We used Adam optimizer with an initial learning rate of 10^{-4} followed by weight decay. For Eq. 3, we train the network for 500 epochs, chosen heuristically. Note that the regularization constant α is absorbed within the denoiser in Eq. 3.

3   Data and Experiments

We evaluate the proposed framework on *three* different datasets. First, we use the simulated PET and MRI phantom data used in [7]. Second, we simulate a PET image based on the brain segmentation map from the BrainWeb database [4], such that the uptake in the grey matter is 4× greater than that of the white matter. For both the datasets, we smooth the PET image using a Gaussian filter to represent smooth metabolic variations in the brain. Third, we use the *in vivo* multimodal data from the Alzheimer's Database Neuroimaging Initiative (ADNI) across three classes: cognitively normal (ADNI-CN), mild cognitive impairment (ADNI-MCI), and Alzheimer's Dementia (ADNI-AD). The FDG-PET image resolution was 2 mm and that of MRI was 1.5 mm isotropic and were aligned using rigid registration. The PET data was retrospectively obtained as in the case of BrainWeb data. We compare our proposed algorithm with *five* other PET reconstruction methods: (i) MLEM with post-reconstruction smoothing, (ii) PLS prior, representing the quadratic PLS prior proposed in [7] and penalizes the location and orientation of the joint image gradients in PET and MRI, (iii) Asym-Bowsher prior, as in [23], which employs a weighted Huber-loss where the weights are computed using the MRI image, (iv) joint dictionary prior (JD), where a joint dictionary of MRI and PET images are learned based on sparsity constraints on the learned coefficients, and (v) ADMM-CDIP, which is the iterative PET reconstruction scheme used in [5] with a DIP-based CNN. We use PSNR as the image-quality metric for quantitative comparison across methods.

Hyperparameter Tuning. For the phantom data, we tune the hyperparameters for all the methods to obtain maximum PSNR between the reconstructed and the true PET image. For the BrainWeb data, hyperparameters were tuned based on validation data. For the phantom and the BrainWeb data, τ_U was found to be 10^{-5} and 10^{-4}, respectively. Hyperparameters for the *in vivo* data were retained from the experiments on BrainWeb data.

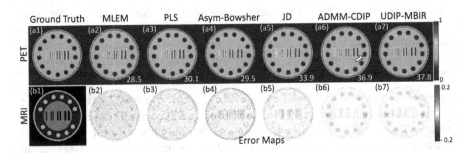

Fig. 2. Reconstructed Images from phantom data. Top (a1–a7): Ground truth and reconstructed PET images from all the methods. **Bottom (b1–b7):** MRI image and error maps with respect to (a1). The PSNR value is provided within each panel. (Color figure online)

4 Results and Discussion

Results on Simulated Data. Figure 2 shows the reconstructed images from all the methods and the corresponding error maps. The MLEM method, which does *not* include any prior, retains a large amount of noise. The PLS and Asym-Bowsher (Fig. 2(a3), (a4)) achieve a sharper PET image (red bars) leveraging the anatomical information from the MRI image. However, these methods suffer from artifacts (distorted central blue blob) arising from joint/multimodal priors. The JD method restores the regularity in structure for the red bars and the circular blobs, both. However, the separation between the closely-placed red bars is quite blurred compared to the other methods. While the ADMM-CDIP removes the noise to a great extent, it shows behavior akin to PLS and Asym-Bowsher priors. Our method improves over the ADMM-CDIP method by restoring the circular blob (arrow) with greater resistance to cross-modality artifacts leveraging uncertainty information discussed in detail later. For both the simulated data, our method yields quantitative improvement, in terms of PSNR, over other comparison methods.

Figure 3 shows the results on the BrainWeb data. Similar to the phantom data, the PLS, Asym-Bowsher, and the ADMM-CDIP restore the structure and contrast with the help of MRI information while showing some cross-modal information (arrow in Fig. 3(a6)). The proposed UDIP-MBIR method restores the regularity as found in the ground truth PET image while removing the noise to a large extent. The error maps show that both ADMM-CDIP and UDIP-MBIR lower residual values with our method showing minimal structure.

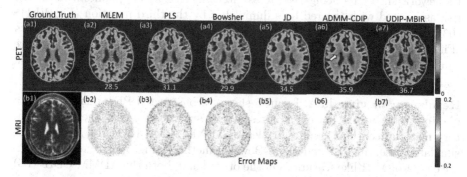

Fig. 3. Reconstructed Images from BrainWeb data. Top: Ground truth PET and reconstructed PET images from all the methods. **Bottom:** MRI image and error maps with respect to (a1). The PSNR value is provided within each panel.

Evolution of Uncertainty Maps Across Iterations. Figure 4 shows the reconstructed PET images, associated risk maps, and the error maps for both the simulated datasets. The risk maps are obtained for each iteration by applying a global threshold, determined based on validation data. Our UDIP-MBIR

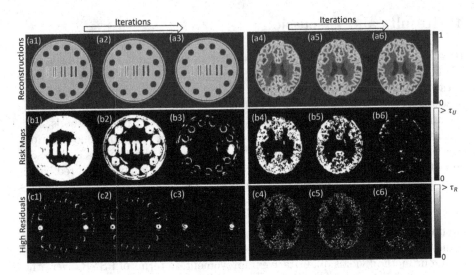

Fig. 4. Evolving PET images and warning maps across iterations. The risk maps (row 2) are obtained by thresholding using τ_U and high residual maps (row 3) using τ_R. For the phantom: $\tau_U = 10^{-5}$ and $\tau_R = 10\%$ and for the BrainWeb data: $\tau_U = 10^{-4}$ and $\tau_R = 5\%$. The risk maps provide additional penalties during subsequent iterations. Areas with high residual correspond to areas with high uncertainty values demonstrating the usefulness of the risk maps in the absence of ground truth. (Color figure online)

framework shows reducing risk across iterations, e.g., for phantom data, the risk associated with the red bars diminishes by the third iteration (Fig. 4(b1)–(b3)). Similar observation can be made for the ventricles in the BrainWeb data (Fig. 4(b4)–(b6)). The high residual maps (Fig. 4 row c) represent the absolute values of the error maps with values greater than 10%. Importantly, high residual regions do coincide with regions with high uncertainty.

Results on *in vivo* data. Figure 5 shows reconstructed PET images for data obtained retrospectively from a representative subject with AD. The Supplementary material contains results for classes ADNI-MCI and ADNI-CN. As in the simulated case, the PLS and Asym-Bowsher methods (Fig. 5(a4) and (b1)) introduce a lot of MRI-like features. On the other hand, both the ADMM-CDIP (b3) and the proposed UDIP-MBIR (b4) methods produce images that retain similar activity distribution as the scanner-provided image. In addition, our method provides additional risk maps shown in the right panel of the figure. While in the first iteration (c2), the overall scale of the image is slightly reduced compared to the scanner image (c1), in the second iteration (c3), there is an overestimation indicated by the green arrow, and these in turn are in agreement with the high intensities in the risk map. The final image shows activity distribution similar to the scanner-provided image along with improvements in finer details aided

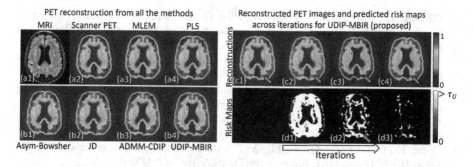

Fig. 5. Results on *in vivo* data. Representative subject with AD condition. *Left:* Qualitative comparison of reconstructed images from noisy PET data obtained retrospectively using the scanner-provided PET image (a2). *Right:* The reconstructed images (row c) and associated risk maps (row d) from the proposed UDIP-MBIR. (Color figure online)

by the MRI image (cortical foldings). The risk maps inform about the potential risk involved in clinically interpreting the reconstructed images and can act as a proxy for the error maps in the absence of ground truth.

5   Conclusion

We have developed a method to quantify uncertainty within the PnP framework for model-based iterative image reconstruction. Furthermore, we leverage the uncertainty information to penalize regions with higher uncertainty resulting in improved image quality in the subsequent iterations. Results on simulated and *in vivo* data both show that as the iterations progress, we observe a (i) reduction in number of voxels prone to risk and (ii) an increase in PSNR. In the absence of ground truth, the thresholded uncertainty maps serve as a proxy for error maps and can potentially enable the clinician to make an informed diagnosis or prescribe a rescan. Future work can focus on reconstruction from measurement data, detailed analysis on hyperparametersand other factors such as computational speed and complexity.

References

1. Ahmad, R., et al.: Plug-and-play methods for magnetic resonance imaging: using denoisers for image recovery. IEEE Signal Process. Mag. **37**(1), 105–116 (2020)
2. Bowsher, J., Johnson, V., Turkington, T., Jaszczak, R., Floyd, C., Coleman, R.: Bayesian reconstruction and use of anatomical a priori information for emission tomography. IEEE Trans. Med. Imaging **15**, 673 (1996)
3. Chan, S., Wang, X., Elgendy, O.: Plug-and-play ADMM for image restoration: fixed-point convergence and applications. IEEE Trans. Comput. Imaging **3**(1), 84–98 (2016)

4. Cocosco, C., Kollokian, V., Kwan, R., Pike, G., Evans, A.: Brainweb: online interface to a 3D MRI simulated brain database. In: NeuroImage. Citeseer (1997)
5. Cui, J., et al.: PET image denoising using unsupervised deep learning. Eur. J. Nucl. Med. Mol. Imaging **46**(13), 2780–2789 (2019). https://doi.org/10.1007/s00259-019-04468-4
6. Ehrhardt, M., et al.: PET reconstruction with an anatomical MRI prior using parallel level sets. IEEE Trans. Med. Imaging **35**, 2189 (2016)
7. Ehrhardt, M., et al.: Joint reconstruction of PET-MRI by exploiting structural similarity. Inverse Prob. **31**, 015001 (2014)
8. Gong, K., Catana, C., Qi, J., Li, Q.: Pet image reconstruction using deep image prior. IEEE Trans. Med. Imaging **38**(7), 1655–1665 (2018)
9. Green, P.: Bayesian reconstructions from emission tomography data using a modified EM algorithm. IEEE Trans. Med. Imaging **9**, 84 (1990)
10. Kendall, A., Gal, Y.: What uncertainties do we need in Bayesian deep learning for computer vision? In: Advances in Neural Information Processing Systems, p. 5574 (2017)
11. Knoll, F., Holler, M., Koesters, T., Otazo, R., Bredies, K., Sodickson, D.: Joint MR-PET reconstruction using a multi-channel image regularizer. IEEE Trans. Med. Imaging **36**, 1 (2017)
12. Leahy, R., Yan, X.: Incorporation of anatomical MR data for improved functional imaging with PET. In: Colchester, A.C.F., Hawkes, D.J. (eds.) IPMI 1991. LNCS, vol. 511, pp. 105–120. Springer, Heidelberg (1991). https://doi.org/10.1007/BFb0033746
13. Nuyts, J., Fessler, J.: A penalized-likelihood image reconstruction method for emission tomography, compared to post-smoothed maximum-likelihood with matched spatial resolution. IEEE Trans. Med. Imaging **22**, 1042 (2003)
14. Ronneberger, O., Fischer, P., Brox, T.: U-Net: convolutional networks for biomedical image segmentation. In: Navab, N., Hornegger, J., Wells, W.M., Frangi, A.F. (eds.) MICCAI 2015. LNCS, vol. 9351, pp. 234–241. Springer, Cham (2015). https://doi.org/10.1007/978-3-319-24574-4_28
15. Sanaat, A., Arabi, H., Mainta, I., Garibotto, V., Zaidi, H.: Projection-space implementation of deep learning-guided low-dose brain PET imaging improves performance over implementation in image-space. J. Nucl. Med. 119 (2020)
16. Shepp, L., Vardi, Y.: Maximum likelihood reconstruction for emission tomography. IEEE Trans. Med. Imaging **1**, 113 (1982)
17. Sreehari, S., et al.: Plug-and-play priors for bright field electron tomography and sparse interpolation. IEEE Trans. Comput. Imaging **2**(4), 408–423 (2016)
18. Sudarshan, V.P., Chen, Z., Awate, S.P.: Joint PET+MRI patch-based dictionary for Bayesian random field PET reconstruction. In: Frangi, A.F., Schnabel, J.A., Davatzikos, C., Alberola-López, C., Fichtinger, G. (eds.) MICCAI 2018. LNCS, vol. 11070, pp. 338–346. Springer, Cham (2018). https://doi.org/10.1007/978-3-030-00928-1_39
19. Sudarshan, V., Upadhyay, U., Egan, G., Chen, Z., Awate, S.: Towards lower-dose pet using physics-based uncertainty-aware multimodal learning with robustness to out-of-distribution data. Med. Image Anal. **73**, 102187 (2021)
20. Tang, J., Wang, Y., Yao, R., Ying, L.: Sparsity-based PET image reconstruction using MRI learned dictionaries. In: IEEE International Symposium on Biomedical Imaging, p. 1087 (2014)

21. Tölle, M., Laves, M., Schlaefer, A.: A mean-field variational inference approach to deep image prior for inverse problems in medical imaging. In: Medical Imaging with Deep Learning, pp. 745–760. PMLR (2021)
22. Ulyanov, D., Vedaldi, A., Lempitsky, V.: Deep image prior. In: IEEE Conference on Computer Vision and Pattern Recognition, pp. 9446–9454 (2018)
23. Vunckx, K., Nuyts, J.: Heuristic modification of an anatomical Markov prior improves its performance. In: IEEE Nuclear Science Symposuim & Medical Imaging Conference, pp. 3262–3266. IEEE (2010)

Author Index

Printed in the United States
by Baker & Taylor Publisher Services